Dr. Deborah Gill h[illegible] powerfully as a leader, mer[illegible] professor. Dr. Barbara Cav[illegible] countries as a missionary-educator with cross-cultural sensitivity and anointing. Their gifts as ministers of the gospel have enabled them to articulate in the writing of the book, *God's Women—Then and Now*, the biblical place for women in the ministry.

— THOMAS E. TRASK, *General Superintendent*
General Council of the Assemblies of God

With superb scholarship the authors analyze and explain the meanings of words, metaphors, concepts, and cultural contexts. With no hint of protest or controversy, the authors make explicit the scriptural teachings concerning gender relationships and leadership processes. So objective and precise that it could serve as a study in biblical interpretation as well as a text on the subject of women's place in Christian ministry, this book is enriched by living and current experiences of the authors who have lived, taught, and addressed major gatherings in many countries and cultures. They speak with a unique combination of knowledge and experience of *God's Women—Then and Now*.

— BILLIE DAVIS, *Professor Emeritus, Evangel University*

It is refreshing to find a truly scholarly treatment of the role of women by two highly respected and competent women. Dr. Cavaness and Dr. Gill once served as single women making a very positive impact on the mission field. Both are now married and continue their ministry as professors and leaders in the Church. They are not crusaders, but earnest seekers after the truths that will guide women to serve the Lord in His divine plan. I highly recommend this book to those who will approach it with an open mind and an open Bible.

— RONALD A. IWASKO, *President, Global University*

Pentecostalism owes a great debt of gratitude to the pioneering contributions of women preachers. Yet the fact that the Holy Spirit has been equally poured out on men and women still surprises many Christians. Gill and Cavaness provide an insightful biblical theology of women that is faithful to the text of Scripture and relevant for women in ministry in today's church.

— GARY B. MCGEE, *Professor of Church History and Pentecostal Studies*
Assemblies of God Theological Seminary

Biblically sound and culturally relevant. A book for our time. Since the time of the prophet Joel (2:28-29), God has made it clear that He pours out His Spirit on "sons and daughters," men and women alike. It is time to embrace all whom God has called. *God's Women—Then and Now,* carries this profound message and encourages all to support women who are following the Lord in ministry.

— JOHN BUENO, *Executive Director*
Assemblies of God World Missions

The authors take their readers on a journey through Scripture, history, theology, and ministry experience that authenticates the role of women in ministry, missions, and leadership today. I believe that God will use this writing to be a defining work that brings hope and encouragement to many women who have been called into ministry.

— LILLIAN E. SPARKS, *Former Director*
National Women's Ministries Department, Assemblies of God

This book is a powerful exposition of God's use and intention for women in ministry. It clearly shows the importance God attaches to the ministry of His female prophets, preachers, and teachers through the ages. The few proof texts against women in ministry are plausibly explained and fall into logical order before the clear exposition of two experienced and academically qualified women ministers who have given us a fine handbook that ought to be read by all ministers, male and female.

— EDGAR LEE, *Senior Professor of Spiritual Formation and Pastoral Theology*
Assemblies of God Theological Seminary

I am delighted to see this important work. Gill and Cavaness represent the often-silenced feminine voices that we need to hear—not only on the issue of women's roles in ministry, but on issues of biblical interpretation, church ministry, and spiritual authority.

— JOSEPH L. CASTLEBERRY, *Academic Dean*
Assemblies of God Theological Seminary

Barbara Cavaness and Deborah Gill bring us a very readable book, deep in biblical scholarship, and rich with practical understanding from their own personal histories of effective ministry as women.

— EDMUND L. TEDESCHI, *Pastor, Summit Church*
Assistant District Superintendent, Minnesota District of the A/G.

Like legal counsel before a jury, two anointed women make the compelling case for the full release of women in unrestricted gospel ministry. The progressive building of argument, based on solid exegesis, leaves the reader with a well-substantiated verdict—it is God's will to use all of his servants, male and female, in the fulfillment of His plan to build His Church.

— RICHARD L. DRESSELHAUS, *Executive Presbyter*
General Council of the Assemblies of God

This book is destined to become an indispensable guide to readers who want to deepen their knowledge of the effective place for women in life and ministry. It is a thought-provoking volume and extremely practical in helping pastors and church leaders apply exegetical understandings of the biblical basis for women in ministry. This is one of the most important studies on the leadership of women available today.

— ROBERT E. COOLEY, *President Emeritus*
Gordon-Conwell Theological Seminary

With the spirit of sincere seekers after truth, Barbara Cavaness and Debbie Gill portray with clarity biblical teachings concerning women. Using principles of sound scholarship they walk us through difficult passages to an understanding of the freedom women have in Christ. This book will greatly benefit the Church as both men and women gain understanding of the propriety and value of releasing women for ministry.

— PEGGY MUSGROVE, *Former Director*
National Women's Ministries Department, Assemblies of God

God's Women is written the way books should be—compelling arguments made in a clear and concise manner. Its straightforward style makes it accessible to everyone. Both clergy and laypersons will profit from the reading of this book.

— DANIEL CRABTREE, *Associate Professor*
Central Bible College

A must-read for women in ministry and for men interested in God's ways, this book is chock full of helpful information. Though coming with much study of Bible texts, contexts and history, Doctors Gill and Cavaness have managed to write an easily accessible book, which will teach, encourage and inspire.

— CAROLYN TENNANT, *Professor of English*
North Central University

What an excellent resource you will find here by two outstanding biblical scholars! This will become a standard tool for anyone genuinely interested in the role of women in the Church, in the marketplace, or in the home. The authors present comprehensive biblical and theological evidence on this extremely important subject in a very readable style with superb summaries at the end of each chapter. Additionally, their practical applications in the last three chapters assist the reader in moving from theory to everyday life. I commend this book as a must read for men and women alike.

— DON MEYER, *President, Valley Forge Christian College*

In light of the full scope of Scripture, the authors approach the oft-quoted, controversially-interpreted words of Paul regarding women in ministry. This work is a gift, not only for its excellent biblical scholarship but for its positive approach to an issue that sadly divides the body of Christ. One need not agree with every point the authors make to recognize they serve the Church well by bringing readers face-to-face with God's ideals for men and women in relationship and in ministry and by encouraging us to grow toward them with integrity.

— BETH GRANT, *Chairperson*
Assemblies of God Task Force for Women in Ministry

I commend the authors for their systematic foundational appeal for the legitimacy of women in ministry both "then and now." They have built their case. It is biblically solid and historically clear. Now is the time to move ahead to proactively empower women who need a nudge toward greatness and will pay the price for the next generation to be mainstreamed. God's call and being part of eschatological destiny is empowerment at its best.

— BYRON KLAUS, *President*
Assemblies of God Theological Seminary

As a credentialed minister, I am sadly aware of the tragic loss to the Church and pain to the called caused by those who would limit the ministry of women. Thank you, Barbara and Debbie, for this well-written book. May the Holy Spirit use it to help readers consider the New Testament record of ministering women, and then rethink their position to be sure it is a biblical one.

— ARLENE ALLEN, *Director*
National Women's Ministries Department, Assemblies of God

Dr.'s Gill and Cavaness have provided the Church with a solid presentation of the biblical, theological, and historic basis for women in ministry. They have examined the tough texts and with an excellent hermeneutic and exegesis, their presentation is right!

— DON ARGUE, *President, Northwest University*

Deborah M. Gill
and Barbara L. Cavaness

GOD'S WOMEN—THEN AND NOW
published by Grace & Truth

International Standard Book Number: 0-9749539-0-3

Cover and book design by Koechel Peterson and Associates, Inc., Mpls., MN

Printed in the United States of America

For information:

Grace & Truth, 3242 W. Windward Pass, Springfield, MO 65810

Library of Congress Control Number: 2004101317

To Our Parents

Menke and Rhoda Menken

Cecil and Leona Liddle

(*"present with the Lord"*)

Table of Contents

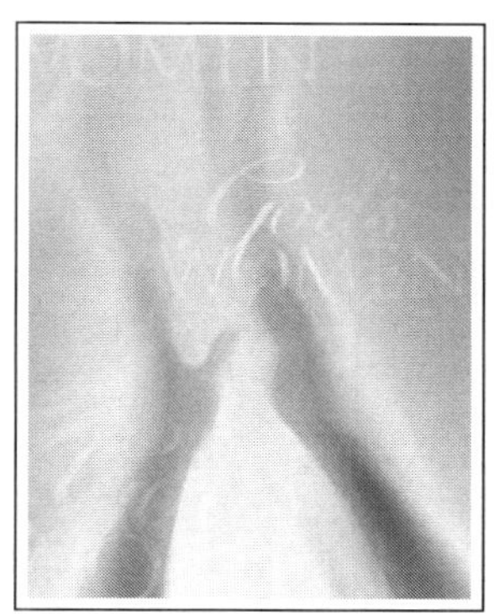

Foreword

A. ELIZABETH WEIDMAN AND HER SISTER RUTH left their home in Cleveland, Ohio, in 1924 for missionary service in Northwest China and Tibet. The Assemblies of God was then only 10 years old, but it had commissioned these women, then 26 and 28 years of age respectively, to follow the example of the first person to tell another of the Resurrection—a woman named Mary Magdalene (John 20:18). Elizabeth and Ruth were at the vanguard of a host of women sent forth or recognized by the Assemblies of God as missionaries, pastors, leaders, and ministers of the gospel.

For 55 years Elizabeth served as an ordained minister of the Assemblies of God. I know her well, for she is my mother. Growing up in my parents' home I never knew a time when it was unnatural for a woman to serve in a preaching, teaching, or leadership role. We believed in the Assemblies of God that the Lord was an equal opportunity employer—and so was His Church!

Only as an adult did I come to realize that not every Christian felt the same way. Many of my friends, who held to a more restrictive role for women in the Church, threw biblical texts my way that appeared to suggest our stance on women in ministry was erroneous and even heretical.

Now, at last, we have a work written by Assemblies of God women ordained ministers and scholars—Barbara Cavaness and Deborah Gill—that undergirds our historic stance on women in ministry by a masterful exegetical and hermeneutical approach to the Scripture.

I think this book will do for its audience what Priscilla and her husband Aquila did for Apollos. Do you remember Apollos? He was "a learned man, with a thorough knowledge of the Scriptures." Yet there were things about Jesus he did not know. He had the grace to let a woman help teach him by explaining "to him the way of God more accurately" (Acts 18:24-26). So also today, there are many in the body of Christ who are learned, know the Scriptures thoroughly, and speak with fervor; but their knowledge of God's design for women needs the more accurate and adequate knowledge of "the way of God" as revealed in His Word.

This book, *God's Women—Then and Now,* will take its place as an important support for all women in ministry. And, beyond that, it will help all within the Church to better understand and value the role God intends for women in life, family, and ministry.

GEORGE O. WOOD, General Secretary
General Council of the Assemblies of God
Springfield, Missouri
2004

Acknowledgments

I WISH TO THANK Cathie and Dick Kroeger, Alvera and the late Berkeley Mickelsen, and Kari and Bob Malcolm, who welcomed me to a community of students of Scripture concerned with these issues; who have modeled mutual submission in their marriages; and who have been precious friends for many years.

I wish to thank my husband Jan for believing that women can be ministers, and for loving this one.

Debbie

I AM GRATEFUL TO Twila Edwards for sharing her insights with me in and out of the classroom; to the late Pauline Smith, Adeline Wichman, and a host of other female evangelists and missionaries who have served as my role models and mentors; and to male mentors like the late Dick Champion and Everett Phillips who believed in me, opened doors, and encouraged me to dream big dreams with God.

I am very grateful for my husband R. B., whose patience and love helped make this book a reality.

Barbara

BOTH OF US EXPRESS APPRECIATION TO Billie Davis and Ruby Banks for their editorial assistance, to all those friends who read the manuscript and helped us make it better, and to David Koechel for using his gift to enhance our work.

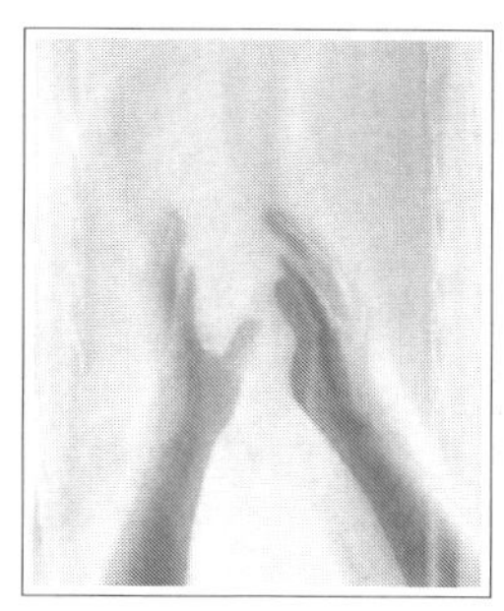

UNIT ONE

A BIBLICAL APPROACH

CHAPTER 1

THE BIBLE AND WOMEN

I, DEBORAH, WAS IN MY JUNIOR YEAR at a major secular university in the United States. The course was a study of the future. My professor's solution to women's suffering was to throw away the Bible. His pathway to a brighter future included rejecting the Church and beginning again.

"The *Bible* is the reason women are treated badly!" the teacher declared to our class. "Women's problems in the world today—especially their suppression[1] and subordination[2]—can all be traced back through the Church to Jesus."

He spoke with such passion. Many students were nodding their heads. It seemed they all agreed. He was a smart person and well respected. But was he right? Was he telling the truth?

At the time my Sunday school class had just read a book that claimed only men could be leaders. The author said the way women influence others is through sex. (It seemed she was coaching women to use manipulation.) I had also recently attended a seminar in the city's largest public auditorium where a Christian speaker had taught that God puts every woman (married or single, young or old) under the authority of a man. He claimed that God expects a woman to obey her male authority even if that man tells her to sin.

I had asked myself, "Is this really what God wants? Is this truly what the Bible says? Are these Christian leaders (the author and the speaker) telling the truth? Who can I trust on the issue of the proper roles for women? Though doors of opportunity have opened to women, is leadership to be the domain only of men? What about male-female relationships in society, the church, and the home? Does the Bible give clear answers?"

These questions had led me on my own study of the Bible—and just in time to speak up that day in my university class. Raising my hand, I said to the teacher, "Sir, I beg to differ from your opinion. May I have permission to share my view?"

"Go ahead, if you think you can convince us," he welcomed my input. "I'd like to hear what you have to say."

For most of the rest of the hour he let me speak to the class. I gave examples from the Bible to show how God values women and men equally. He chose women as leaders in religion and society. Jesus treated women with respect in settings where others showed them no respect. The New Testament describes many female church leaders made powerful by the Holy Spirit for work God called them to do. I ended by saying, "Sir, unfortunately the church has not always lived by what the Bible says. But the Bible, when properly understood—and especially Jesus himself—have been great advocates for women."

The honest openness of my teacher impressed me. He announced to the class, "I stand corrected. I will never blame the Bible or Jesus for what women suffer today."

This book will discuss an important contemporary issue affecting women and men around the world. Christians hold strong opinions and many different views on what women may or may not do, in or out of the church. One denomination will not support any church that has a woman on staff. Another will not ordain anyone who does not believe in women ministers.

William and Catherine Booth founded the Salvation Army. His famous line reflects the active leadership women give in that church group. He said, "My best men are women." The Salvation Army has more than once elected a woman as its international general.

Other church leaders limit the service of women to singing in the choir, cooking fellowship meals, or teaching children. God does not deny spiritual manifestations and ministry gifts to women. Why should the Church do any different?

I, Barbara, have worked in a number of countries where local churches treat women in surprisingly different ways. Some places train women in their Bible schools and use them as pastors and church leaders. Others accept only men in their Bible schools and do not allow women to serve as church leaders. Although this situation is slowly changing, I have asked myself whether or not their teachers have clouded the presentation of Christ's practices and words with ideas they have learned from their old culture and exported to their new one.

Klaus Fiedler has written the story of faith missions. He gives examples of teachers from different missions, working in the same African tribe. One mission allows women to preach in church; another forbids it. After much study Fiedler concluded that the reason can be found not in the African culture, but in the missionaries' cultures.[3]

I experienced a similar example of the exporting of cultural bias instead of the application of scriptural truth in another country. The first church I attended invited women to preach occasionally, but only if they wore long hair, white dresses with long sleeves, and no earrings. Their first missionary had taught them this.

God's women have made up a large part of the Church from Bible times to the present. This study will help you learn how God related to women in the Old Testament. It will also describe what roles women played in the first-century church. The book's goal is to suggest what today's church should be like, wherever people know and follow Jesus Christ. God, the Holy Spirit, empowers and equips both men and women to expand His kingdom. It was the Holy Spirit in the Upper Room (Acts 2) and in many revival movements since then who has opened doors for God's women.

If you are not a Christian, you will be delighted to discover the wonderful Person on whom the Church is founded, Jesus Christ. He came to earth as history's most loving, caring, considerate person. His example will convince every woman of her worth in God's eyes and inspire every man to nurture godly relationships with women.

If you are a Christian, this book will help you shape your life like Jesus' and help you influence your church to live by the Bible, which is the guidebook of the Church.

You may discover, through this study, that not all Christians agree. They may love Jesus and want to follow Him, but disagree with other Christians on certain points. In such situations, you must know how to decide for yourself. You must not choose to trust a person just because they are well educated and respected (like the university teacher). You cannot rely on someone's word just because they are important or have influence (like the author or seminar speaker). You must know how to study the Bible for yourself and apply its truths to your life.

It is a very exciting and life-changing journey you begin today—to learn about God's women and to discover for yourself how you can come to know truth that you can trust. Your journeys to know about God's women and to understand the Bible better are journeys that we both share with you. May you enjoy them as much as we have, for there are joys waiting for you in what you discover.

CONCEPTS CONSIDERED IN CHAPTER 1

INTRODUCTION

- It is common for people, including Christians, to differ in their views about women.
- Many of these differences are based more on people's background or teaching than on the Bible.
- This book focuses on how to study the Bible for yourself to find *God's* view.
- In the process of this study, seekers will discover Jesus, the greatest example, and Christians will be challenged to live their lives like His.
- This adventure in learning can change your life.

CHAPTER 2

BIBLE ANSWERS TO TODAY'S QUESTIONS

AN AMERICAN MISSIONARY COUPLE went to Greece for their first assignment. A local church invited the husband to preach, although he had just arrived in the country. Everything went smoothly until the translator invited him to stand at the back of the church to greet the people as they left the service. He put out his hand to shake hands with the first man leaving. Imagine the missionary's surprise and shock when instead of shaking hands, this man and every man following him reached up and kissed the missionary on the mouth.

Paul and Peter repeatedly commanded early Christians to greet each other with a holy kiss (Rom. 16:16; 1 Pet. 4:14). Though the command was never cancelled, most Western believers today do not practice this kiss. They believe the instruction applied to that specific culture and group at that time in history, then and there, not here and now.

The task of interpreting the Bible presents some complex challenges. Sincere, dedicated, born-again Christians sometimes arrive at different conclusions about the same passages. Some people use only "proof texts" they have memorized and exclude other factors. Others combine their experience or lack of experience with teaching they have received about the Scriptures.

The New Testament gives an example of how the Early Church resolved one of their first differences. In Acts 15, one group quoted a number of texts, while Peter, Paul, and Barnabas testified to what God had done in baptizing Gentiles in the Holy Spirit. Sometimes the texts have to be looked at again as understanding of God's ways increases. George Wood concludes that the first church council "brought their experience to bear on the text; they brought the text to bear on their experience. And they found a complete consistency between the written words inspired by the Spirit and the present-day leading of the Spirit."[1]

Two Questions

Two important questions can help people interpret a Bible passage. The first asks, "What was God saying through the human writer of Scripture to the first hearers or readers of the passage?" The second asks, "What does this passage say to readers today, in this place?"[2]

Servants of God wrote the Bible in Hebrew, Aramaic, and Greek between two and three thousand years ago. At times it is hard to be sure what God was saying to the people then or exactly what they understood Him to say. Some definite clues, however, make the task easier.

Context. Perhaps the most important clues come from the literary context or surroundings in which the verse occurs. The reader has to consider the message of the paragraph, the section, and the book to understand the whole situation being addressed. One must ask whether the book teaches history, laws, parables, proverbs, or psalms, or whether it comes to readers as a letter, sermon, or prophecy. Knowing the genre[3] (type of writing) is an important starting place.[4]

For example, although the prophet Joel predicted future events, his immediate reference concerns a literal locust plague his country had suffered. In letters to Timothy, Paul keeps talking about false teachers and persons who had left the faith. The individual verses must be seen against the background of the larger overall message of the section and book.

The literature, history, and even the myths of the secular culture provide more understanding of the author and readers. The customs and traditions of the people in a certain place and period often shed light on parts of the Bible written to them. The occasion or purpose of the writing also gives information about the meaning. Students of the Bible call this the historical context.

If the reader first asks what the passage meant to its first hearers, he or she will be less likely to make a foolish interpretation. The primary message of the writer was for the original readers.

Content. After understanding the context, one goes on to decide what the passage means and whether or not it applies to today. It becomes important to consider the definitions of words, how they relate to each other in a sentence, and which of several variations of meaning one will choose. These are questions of content. Scholars emphasize that "a text cannot mean what it never meant ... . The true meaning of the biblical text for us is what God originally intended it to mean."[5] The Holy Spirit, who inspired the original intent of each passage, will not contradict himself to now let it mean something entirely different.

One must then consider all other texts in the Bible that refer to the same topic. Instructions for similar situations should be compared. A person should try to fairly examine every relevant passage, not just the ones that are easily understood or that agree with his or her previous opinion. Sometimes the passage does not seem to apply, only because the situation today has changed so much that the reasons for the original teaching or information no longer exist.

Categories

Finding the meaning of a text is the reader's goal. God's Word has eternal relevance and also historical particularity.[6] Bible texts can be divided into several categories, 1) highest norms or standards (timeless truths), 2) regulations for people where they were,[7] and,

3) records of history. All the Bible is "God-breathed and is useful for teaching, rebuking, correcting and training in righteousness" (2 Tim. 3:16-17).[8] Yet, not all passages apply equally to every situation. How can today's readers tell the difference between the timeless truths and the regulations for people where they were?

Category 1. Timeless truths are the highest norms or standards taught in the Bible. They take priority in our values, our thinking, and the way we act. Sometimes Jesus, Paul, and others clearly identify these principles. The "Golden Rule"[9] is one such example. Matthew quotes it as Jesus' standard for behavior: "So in everything, do to others what you would have them do to you, for this sums up the Law and the Prophets" (7:12, see also Matt. 22:37-40 and 5:17). Paul repeats a timeless truth in Romans 13:9-10—"The commandments ... are summed up in this one command: 'Love your neighbor as yourself.' Love does no harm to its neighbor. Therefore love is the fulfillment of the law."

Other times highest norms can be found in the way Bible writers evaluate a single event, such as the Day of Pentecost (Acts 2). On that day Peter quoted Joel 2:28 to show the significance of the coming of the Holy Spirit on women and men, young and old, servants and masters. Jesus had told the disciples that they would be empowered by the Spirit to be His witnesses (Acts 1:4-8). And Luke and Paul explain the ongoing application of Jesus' words to the Gentiles (Acts 11:15-18) and all who are in Christ (Gal. 3:26-29).

Sometimes the end of a whole book explains a timeless truth. The writer of the Book of Hebrews teaches readers why Christians are not required to fulfill Old Testament sacrifices and regulations. Christ's sacrifice, "once for all," "has made perfect forever those who are being made holy." Therefore, "sacrifice for sin is no longer necessary" (Heb. 10:8-18). Readers agree that is a timeless, eternal, truth.[10]

Much of Jesus' teaching helps today's believers understand the necessity of breaking with the practices of their former life. Christians live under a new covenant (Luke 22:20; Jer. 31:31-34). Paul told the Corinthian believers that they were "ministers of a new covenant—not of the letter but of the Spirit; for the letter kills, but the Spirit gives life" (2 Cor. 3:6, 7-18). Jesus broke with the teachings and practices of Judaism and referred to this as pouring new wine into new wineskins (Luke 5:37-38). He defined true leadership as servanthood (Matt. 20:25-28). He taught women God's truth and respected them as His messengers.[11]

Jesus did reinforce commands of the Old Testament and even made them stronger in some cases. For instance, He taught, "You have heard that it was said, 'Do not commit adultery.' But I tell you that anyone who looks at a woman lustfully has already committed adultery with her in his heart" (Matt. 5:27-28).

Other times Christ's teaching, His highest ideals, replaces old laws. He warned His hearers not to set aside the commands of God in order to observe their own traditions (Mark 7:9). When people continued to emphasize old customs of washing and old food laws, Jesus called them to a higher standard. He explained that nothing a person eats can defile her or him, but the evils that come out of the heart are what defile a person (Mark 7:15-23).

Category 2. Many examples of regulations for people where they were appear in both the Old and New Testaments. Some of the meanings are not clear because so much time has passed and culture has changed. For instance, Leviticus 19:19 directed farmers not to sow two different kinds of seed in the same field and people not to wear different fibers in the same fabric. Deuteronomy 22:8 instructs home builders to "put a parapet" around the roof.

In the New Testament, Paul writes Timothy to come to him before winter and to bring his cloak and scrolls (2 Tim. 4:13, 21). Obviously these instructions concerned only the first reader. Paul also advised him to stop drinking only water and use a little wine for his digestive problems (1 Tim. 5:23). This is understood as Paul's concern for his friend who had "frequent illnesses," but not a prescription for all people for all times.

Category 3. Many verses in the Bible record history. These texts may or may not have normative relevance. Following the resurrection of Jesus Christ on the first day of the week, the Church shifted its day of worship from Saturday to Sunday. The early Christians' pattern has set the norm for us today. Yet not all events of history are meant to shape our lives today.

Any teachings that seem contrary to the high norms taught by Christ must be weighed and examined carefully. It might be that local or temporary situations related to the original audience might have caused the seeming contradiction. That's why all texts on any given subject need to be read to come to a proper interpretation of the whole counsel and purpose of God.

Mistakes to Avoid

Errors of interpretation happen when a person makes up his or her mind on a subject and then selects only certain passages to support that view. Using this method, the Bible can be misused to try to "prove" human ideas.

For example, at one time church leaders believed women should rely only on God's grace for relief of the pain in childbirth. As their "proof" they cited Eve's punishment (Gen. 3:16) and Paul's words about women being saved through childbearing (1 Tim. 2:15). The leaders burned a new mother at the stake because she had taken herbs to ease her pain while delivering twins.[12] People today who want to preach against borrowing money or using credit for any purpose select Romans 13:8 for support: "Owe no man any thing" (*King James Version*, KJV).

Other mistakes occur when verses are taken out of their context to be interpreted wrongly, twisting their original meaning. Verses which contain an opposite view are then ignored or are taken to have a symbolic meaning, not a literal one. People cannot just pick and choose the passages they like or agree with and ignore the passages that they do not like or cannot understand. Nor should a person begin with today's situations and read into a passage meanings that were not there in the situation of the original reader. The cultural, historical, and literary contexts always help explain the text.

For instance, some readers interpret 2 Timothy 2:9 as a *figurative* command and say that the wearing of "gold or pearls or expensive clothes" is permitted for women now. But they interpret verses 11-12 of the same chapter as a *literal* command against women teaching men. In a similar way, Christians who practice foot washing take Jesus' command in John 13:14 literally. Those who do not wash feet in church give the passage a more symbolic meaning.

Observing context and comparing similar passages also often keep people from reading meaning into a text that is not there. For example, consider the idea that Adam's being created first means all males should therefore have dominance over all females. The Bible neither says nor implies that. In fact, God created the animals before Adam. And in many events of the Bible, God chose younger persons for positions of leadership. They appeared later, but had authority over persons who were "created" earlier: Moses over Aaron (Exod. 4), Jacob over Esau (Rom. 9:11-12), and David over his older brothers (1 Sam. 16).

Some problems of finding the Bible's answers to today's questions come about by translators' work. The task of translation involves some degree of interpretation. Not everyone has the chance to study the original Greek and Hebrew words used by the first writers. To make up for that, however, several translations can be compared to understand various readings of the texts.

A Bible teacher had a young daughter who asked him, "Why does God love boys and not girls?"

The shocked father replied, "What makes you ask that?"

She answered, "My Bible says here, 'God ... wants all men to be saved' (1 Tim. 2:4, *New International Version,* NIV)." So he had to try to explain to his small daughter that the original Greek word in that verse refers to all human beings, not just males.

Where does bias come from and who can best correct it? Children learn it from their parents' teaching and Christians learn it from their leaders. Thus those in positions of influence can make a difference in many lives.

Conclusion

To find Bible answers to today's questions one looks at individual texts in their context and tries to determine meaning—the then-and-there meaning as well as the here-and-now meaning. An honest student of the Word will also try to let scripture interpret scripture by examining all that the Bible says on any given subject. Comparing new passages and gaining greater understanding of context may require the reader to change previously held ideas.

People want to know which meaning most adequately expresses the whole of biblical teaching. How can a person know enough about God and His will to be obedient in the twenty-first century? Insights into texts that appear obscure must be gained from texts that are plain. Comparing translations and consulting Bible study aids help one understand context and content, but reading the Bible itself is the primary task. The essential help promised to believers for this task is the Holy Spirit—the Spirit of Truth—who "will guide you into all truth" (John 16:13).

CONCEPTS CONSIDERED IN CHAPTER 2

STEPS IN INTERPRETING THE BIBLE

A. Ask two questions.

- Question 1. What did this text *mean then?*
- Question 2. How does it *apply today?*

B. Observe these clues to interpretation.

- Context: Literary (consider genre also) and Historical
- Content: Words and Grammar

C. Recognize there are categories of meaning.

- Category 1. Timeless Truths (highest norms or standards)
- Category 2. Restricted Regulations (for people where they were)
- Category 3. Historical Records (that may or may not have normative relevance)

D. Be mindful of mistakes commonly made and be careful to avoid them.

- Bias-based Proof-texting
  - Admit to presuppositions.
  - Confront and conform them to truth.
- Ignoring Context
  - Carefully observe context, both literary and historical.
  - Compare similar passages.
  - Ask whether the text is meant literally or figuratively.
  - Compare other translations.

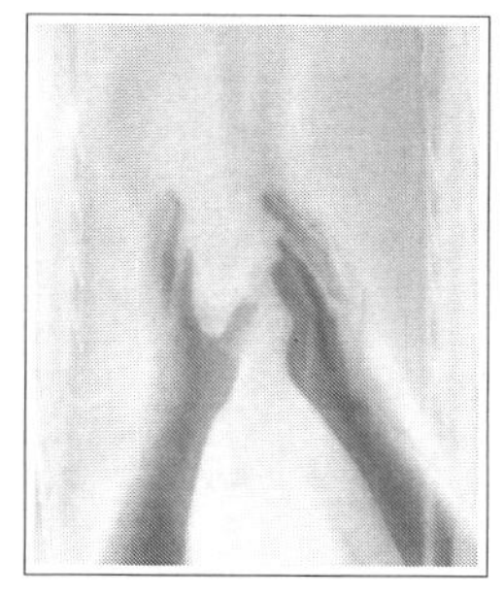

UNIT TWO

OLD TESTAMENT FOUNDATION

CHAPTER 3

CREATION AND THE FALL INTO SIN

EARNEST CHRISTIANS WITH QUESTIONS about the role of women sometimes begin with what their parents have said, with traditions they observe in their culture, or with patterns their church leaders have taught. These starting points may or may not lead to a clear understanding of the biblical truth. Clearly, in some cases such ideas—more than the Bible—have influenced views on gender. To examine the whole counsel of God, it is wise to start at the beginning, with the Old Testament (Hebrew Bible). This chapter challenges the reader to take a fresh look at the text itself and compare it to ideas passed on to them.

Children can now enjoy Old Testament narratives—exciting true stories—in illustrated Bibles or comic book form. Sometimes children even act out what happened. Often, however, the popular version of the story or drama strays from the Bible facts. The boy playing Adam in the Genesis story falls asleep or gets busy with some task, while Eve wanders away by herself. She acts startled by the snake, who tricks her into eating the apple. Then she comes back to find Adam and gets him to eat it too. Does this sound familiar?[1] Perhaps no Bible story has been more misinterpreted than this one and few characters more criticized than Eve. The text actually states that Adam was with Eve; she was not alone: "She also gave some to her husband, who was with her, and he ate it" (Gen. 3:6).[2]

Creation

To see what Scripture really teaches, one has to begin with

creation itself. The Garden of Eden was a place of innocence where God showed His ideal for male-female relationships. The first two chapters of Genesis clearly show us how He desires to relate to human beings and how they are to relate to each other. The other times God revealed this ideal were in the life of Jesus, the only sinless, innocent human, and on the Day of Pentecost. On that occasion God poured the Holy Spirit on both men and women.

These defining moments in God's dealing with humanity become key texts of theology. They give unique glimpses of divine intent—moments that reveal the nature of the triune God. He created life in the Garden, but humankind sinned and had to be judged. He then came in the flesh, to show again what God is like. Christ showed us how to live and He died for the sins of all people. After He ascended He sent the Holy Spirit to enable men and women to relate to each other in a godly way and to work together to build the Church.

When the Bible says, "God created man in his own image" (Gen. 1:27), the word translated *man* does not represent a male person in this instance.[3] The word is better understood as meaning humankind or human beings. In fact, the verse goes on to say, "in the image of God he created him; male and female he created them." These verses show that both men and women are created equally in God's image. Since God is Spirit, *image* does not refer to a physical likeness. Scholars believe that God's image may refer to humans' creativity, intelligence, leadership, or even the relationship people have with one another. In every instance, it is understood that both men and women reflect God's image. Some have taught that women are defective, not made in God's image. The Bible does not teach that.

God is neither male nor female. The commandments forbid making an idol representing Yahweh[4] as either man or woman (Deut. 4:15-19). The use of male pronouns for God is not to teach that God is a male being, but to show us that He is a personal God. Jesus was a male person, but the Greek New Testament rarely identifies Him with the Greek word for "male person" *(aner)*. The overwhelming number of references to Jesus' personhood uses the Greek word for "human being" *(anthropos)*.[5] Thus the emphasis of the Incarnation is not Christ's maleness, but His humanness. Maleness is not a factor in the image of God. All human beings—both male and female—are equally in His image.

God described clearly His purpose and instructions for humankind using the plural pronoun "them" several times. He said, "Let them rule" (1:26). "God blessed them and said to them, 'Be fruitful and increase in number; fill the earth and subdue it. Rule over ... every living creature'" (1:28). God spoke to both the man and the woman. Producing children—being fruitful—takes two acting together. Both male and female were told to rule and take dominion over the earth in a shared way. Both were called to develop their gifts to do God's work on earth. God created them equal in being and equal in function. And God saw that "it was very good" (1:31). They had equality and mutuality[6]—working as a team.

Genesis 2 further explains God's plan. He put the first man in the beautiful garden and then told him it was not good for him to be alone. The man didn't have anyone "like him." None of the animals served as a suitable partner for the man. God said, "I will make a helper suitable for him" (2:18). The Hebrew word for "helper" *('ezer)* in the Old Testament never refers to a subordinate or an inferior.[7] It actually can indicate a superior and most often refers to God himself as our helper.[8] (See Ps. 121.)

The Hebrew dictionary says that *'ezer* "is predominately used in reference to Israel's God." Thirteen times it declares God's "ability to save and deliver." Six times it is linked with "shield" referring to "divine protection afforded to Israel." In Genesis 2:18, "it need not necessarily imply divine assistance, and the context rather suggests it is used ... to denote mutual assistance in the marriage relationship by one who corresponds *(kenegdo)* to man."[9] The word for "suitable" *(kenegdo)* means "equal and corresponding to." Eve was not just to keep the man company and bear his children, but to be an equal partner in ruling and having dominion over the earth.

The woman was neither superior nor inferior to the man. They held the same rank. The fact that God created Eve after Adam says nothing about status, worth, or authority. Creation order is not significant. Adam was created after the animals, yet no one would say that he was in any way inferior to them or ruled by them. Although the Hebrews did give privileges to the first-born son, God on occasion did the opposite. God chose Jacob, instead of Esau the first-born, to be the father of the Hebrews. God called Moses, Aaron's younger brother, to lead His people out of Egypt and give them the Commandments. And He selected David, the youngest son of Jesse, to be King of Israel and ancestor of Christ.

So God created the woman from the man's side.[10] Adam recognized joyfully that her flesh and bones were like his. He speaks for the first time in the story and rejoices:[11]

> "This is now bone of my bones
> and flesh of my flesh;
> she shall be called 'woman,'
> for she was taken out of man" (Gen. 2:23).

They had equality. They had instructions to work as a team to have children and subdue the earth—that was mutuality. Then, because they were made of the same stuff and built for one another, they also had unity. God's plan was for a man to "leave" his family and "cleave" to his wife and for them to be joined as "one flesh" (Gen. 2:24, KJV). And they had intimacy. They stood naked and felt no

GOD'S IDEAL SEEN IN CREATION	
Equality	sameness celebrated
Mutuality	ruling together, working as a team
Unity	joined as one flesh
Intimacy	naked without shame

shame. There was no hierarchy,[12] just an emphasis on oneness and union—one whole person glued to another whole person.

Does Adam's naming of Eve, "the mother of all the living" (Gen. 3:20), show his dominance over her? No, the Bible does not indicate special authority to the one who gives a name. Eve named Seth, their son (Gen. 4:25). Rachel and Leah named Jacob's twelve sons (Gen. 29-30). The angel told Mary to name Jesus (Luke 1:31). Other times the father or both parents chose the child's name. Isaac and Rebekah named Jacob and Esau (Gen. 25:25-26).

The Fall into Sin

Some traditions have put all the blame for the Fall on the woman, but the Bible makes it clear that she alone was not responsible for the consequences of sin. Adam bore equal blame. The suffering caused by the Fall affected not only Eve, but Adam and all the creation as well. Yes, Eve was deceived and first to sin. Adam, however, was not deceived but knowingly broke God's command not to eat of the tree of the knowledge of good and evil (1 Tim. 2:14). The New Testament stresses the fact that Adam's sin resulted in our all being sinners (Rom. 5:12-19).

The serpent's words to Eve and her responses make it clear that he was talking to both Adam and Eve. All the "yous" in the Hebrew text are plural and the woman answers in terms of "we."[13] Adam stood by her side, but remained silent. From the time of her creation, the Scripture narrator never mentions their being apart. They were tempted together, yielded together, and ate together. The text does not say that Eve tempted Adam or that he ate reluctantly. She gave him some fruit and he ate it. Then they realized they were naked and sewed fig leaves together to cover themselves.

Results of Sin

God knew what had happened, but He still came into the Garden looking for Adam and Eve at the usual time. The humans hid in fear, so God called to them. Faced with his disobedience, the man blamed God and Eve for what he himself had done. He said, "The woman you put here with me—she gave me some fruit from the tree, and I ate it" (Gen. 3:12). When God talked to Eve, she accused the serpent but did not accuse God or Adam.

Sin damaged relationships between people and God, between people and nature, and between people and people—Adam and Eve.[14] God cursed only the serpent and the ground. The ground was cursed to produce thorns and thistles. The serpent was cursed to crawl on his belly, to eat dust, and to be crushed in the end by the seed of the woman (Gen. 3:14-15). Jesus Christ—the virgin's seed—would one day come to restore God's plan and reverse the effects of the Fall into sin. In the middle of the curses, a ray of hope shines!

The statements concerning the man and the woman are not curses, but rather a description of what lay ahead of them in the future. This was not a statement of God's purpose nor instructions for how Christian believers should act. God's created beings had departed from His ideal of equality and mutuality described in Genesis 1 and 2. Since God knows all things, He predicted or shared with them what would happen. Thus God described for them their future state under sin.[15]

The woman would have pain in childbearing (Gen. 3:16). As is common in Hebrew poetry, the same thought is repeated twice. Does this verse mean that bearing children would be woman's only role in the world and planting crops and fighting weeds the man's only role? No, in many countries women plant the crops too. And the weeds come up in their gardens just like they do in the men's. Proverbs 31 commends many roles of the "wife of noble character"—weaver, tailor, real estate buyer, trader, teacher, and vineyard keeper, among others. God, in mercy, has also allowed the discovery of pain killers and methods to lessen the pain women suffer in giving birth.

The woman's desire would be for her husband and he would

rule over her (3:16). Again, the Hebrew pattern uses two ways of saying the same thing. One of the meanings is sexual attraction, as in Solomon's desire for his wife in Song of Solomon 7:10. Eve's husband would be very attractive to her, in spite of the risk of conceiving a child whose birth would bring pain and maybe even death. Because of his sexual attraction for her and a desire to dominate, Adam would rule over her. Instead of the oneness they had before sin entered the world, they now had a power struggle. Who would fulfill whose desire, and when? This striving was not God's plan, but a result of the Fall.

Some people do everything they can to do away with the effects of the Fall. They try to lessen the pain of childbirth and the growth of weeds in the soil, but yet mistakenly insist that a man's ruling over woman should continue. Instead, Christians should work for the equality seen at Creation, which represents God's intention and highest ideal.

Another result of the Fall meant that the man would have pain and difficulty in his work to feed his family (Gen. 3:17-19). Even though both parents would suffer pain, they would be given grace to have children and to feed them. Adam would have to sweat and toil. Does this mean that all men should be farmers or manual laborers? No, both men and women work in the fields and do physical labor. This passage is not talking about roles, nor does it address single women who don't bear children or men whose wives support them. If this were a passage on roles, it could be interpreted to mean that only males will die. Poetry is not precise; it is meant to be artistic. Although addressed to the man, death is predicted for all human beings. Both came from the ground; both will return to it (3:19).

The desire for power over others is the very essence of moral evil. Jesus said, "But you are not to be like that. Instead the greatest among you should be like the youngest, and the one who rules like the one who serves" (Luke 22:26). Both males and females are called to be servants, not to exercise lordship over each other. The rule of man over woman is a result of the Fall. Both men and women have the stamp of God's image on them, because they were created by God. And He wants to recreate believers into Christ's image as they walk with Him. "Just as we have borne the likeness of the earthly man, so shall we bear the likeness of the heavenly man" (1 Cor. 15:49).[16] According to the Bible, authority or leadership should not be granted according to gender but according to gifts and Christ-likeness (Rom. 12:3-8).[17] Christians are to live in mutual submission to other members of the body of Christ[18] (Eph. 5:21), not in rulership over them.

After the entrance of sin, equality was replaced with subordination. The male's ruling replaced mutual responsibility. Unity was severed as blame was shifted from one to the other. And intimacy gave way to shame and power struggle. God shed animals' blood to make garments of skin to clothe Adam and Eve. In grace and mercy, God covered their shame. But He put them out of the Garden so they would not eat from the Tree of Life and live forever. Both the man and the woman disobeyed and were thus equally guilty.

GOD'S IDEAL SEEN IN CREATION	GOD'S IDEAL MARRED BY SIN
Equality	Equality ignored
Mutuality	Subordination imposed: he ruled her
Unity	Unity severed: guilt brought accusations
Intimacy	Intimacy thwarted: sin exposed their shame

New Testament authors have much to say about erasing the effects of the Fall. "For since death came through a human being, the resurrection of the dead comes also through a human being. For as in Adam all die, so in Christ all will be made alive" (1 Cor. 15:21-22). This will be the focus of Chapters 6 to 12.

CONCEPTS AND SCRIPTURES CONSIDERED IN CHAPTER 3

GOD'S IDEAL AND HOW SIN MARRED IT

Note the truth about Eve: she was not alone when the serpent tempted her. Adam and Eve were together; both made the same choice to disobey God; and both men and women share the consequences of their original sin.

Creation, a defining moment of the Bible, demonstrates God ideal for men and women. Four characteristics of God's divine design are:

- Equality. Adam and Eve were created equally in God's image and equal to each other in being and function.
- Mutuality. They were commanded to rule over the earth together in a shared way.
- Unity. They were to be as one flesh.
- Intimacy. They concealed nothing from each other.

God was pleased with His design and promised to bless relationships that fulfilled His ideal.

But sin marred God's ideals.

- Instead of celebrating their similarities, equality was ignored.
- Instead of ruling together, subordination was imposed.
- Unity was severed as guilt brought accusations.
- Intimacy was thwarted as sin exposed their shame.

In spite of God's grace to cover their shame, the consequences of sin brought much suffering. But one day He would send a Savior to restore His ideal again.

Genesis 1:26-31
Genesis 2:18-25
Genesis 3 (Luke 22:25-26)
1 Corinthians 15:21-22

CHAPTER 4

MALENESS AND FEMALENESS IN THE OLD TESTAMENT

MOST PEOPLE THINK OF GOD AS "HE." Prayers and devotional writings use male pronouns to emphasize the fatherhood of God. Bible translations refer to "Him" and "His" in passages about Yahweh. So isn't God obviously a male? And didn't God come to earth in the male form of Jesus? Surely that proves something, doesn't it? Such questions often lead to emotional discussion and confusion, but the answers can be found. Though English grammar may be limited to using the pronoun "He," this does not limit the theological understanding of God.

Nature of God Relative to Gender

Writers of the Hebrew Bible, which Christians call the Old Testament, wrote in a male-centered culture. Men dominated society in general and religion in particular. The Hebrews' understanding of Yahweh, however, was not that He is male. Deuteronomy 6:4 describes God as one, complete, whole. He is another order, in contrast to the pagan gods and idols of other peoples. He is spirit, neither male nor female, but having both feminine and masculine characteristics. Although humans may talk about God's eyes or everlasting arms, it is clear that these are only picture language to help limited human understanding. Yahweh, the God of Israel, is far above our human conceptions, and says, "For I am God, and not man—the Holy One among you" (Hos. 11:9).

The Bible even uses female imagery for God in many places. In Hosea 11, Yahweh is the mother figure who taught Israel to walk, who healed him, and bent down to feed the hungry child.[2] Providing food and water to their families was the woman's work, yet Yahweh supplied the manna and water for the Israelites wandering in the desert (Exod. 16-17; Num. 11, 20; Neh. 9:15).

Psalm 22:9 pictures God as a midwife—"Thou art he who drew me from the womb, who laid me at my mother's breast" (*New English Bible*, NEB).[3] Isaiah records Yahweh saying, "Like a woman in childbirth, I cry out, I gasp and pant" (Isa. 42:14). And again, "As a mother comforts her child, so will I comfort you" (Isa. 66:13).[4]

New Testament writers record Jesus' picturing God as a woman. God is likened to a woman searching for a lost coin (Luke 15:8) and a woman mixing bread (Luke 13:20-21). Jesus compares himself to a hen gathering her chicks (Matt. 23:37).[5] Even in the word picture given to Nicodemus, "You must be born again," (John 3:8), Jesus describes God in a feminine role. "'How can anyone be born when they are old?' Nicodemus asked, 'Surely they cannot enter a second time into their mother's womb to be born!'"(John 3:4). It is a divine womb that produces New Birth.

Even modern people, such as John Stewart, have experienced God as both masculine and feminine. Stewart was an American of mixed European and African descent who lived in Virginia in the early 1800s. He accepted Christ and began to worship with Methodist believers. He joined in the singing, prayer, and Bible study of the class meetings and became a strong Christian. Stewart enjoyed walking into the fields or woods to meditate, pray, and read his Bible.

One Sunday evening, as he sat by a small stream, he heard a male voice speaking to him—seemingly from the sky. Astonished at the sound, Stewart believed God was talking directly to him, saying, "Thou shalt go to the Northwest and declare my counsel plainly." As he waited and looked around, sort of a halo of light appeared and seemed to fill the Western sky. Then, to his surprise, he heard the words spoken to him again, "Thou shalt go to the Northwest and declare my counsel plainly." The second time the words were spoken by a female voice.

Stewart was convinced that God had called him. Though at first he felt both unprepared and unworthy, he did go to the Northwest in 1816. (At the time, this meant the unsettled part of what became Ohio.) In the face of great opposition, he established a group of believers among the fierce Wyandot tribe of Native Americans.[6] Though his account of the halo and "what seemed to be the masculine and feminine voices of God" made some Christians uncomfortable, his church-planting example "helped inspire the establishment of the Methodist Missionary Society."[7]

Patriarchy[8] or Equality?

So one may ask, "Does the fact that the Bible was written in a male-dominated society mean that patriarchy and hierarchy were pleasing to God? Or did God merely choose a people who happened to be that way—not approving their behavior, but working within the limitations of the culture to bring them to a better understanding of His will?"

The Bible answers those questions. All peoples, the whole human family, have been marked by sin. God chose Abraham and his children, intending to cleanse them from their faults.[9] Scholars don't read God's intent back into Israel's sins of adultery, violence, polygamy, idolatry, nor abusive patriarchy. Almost all Old Testament people farmed the land or raised herds of animals. Yet the Bible is not seen as teaching that all Christians should be farmers. Israel also had a king for many years, but followers of God today live under many kinds of government.

The patriarchy of the Old Testament is not normative. It is not an absolute structure for followers of God. Thus, there were many exceptions to male-dominated practices. God's egalitarian[10] intent at creation stood in tension with the death and distortion of relationships at the Fall. He called Abraham to begin to resolve this tension. God took the nation of Israel where it was, chose it, and gradually led the people to get rid of their sins. The redemption *already* promised in Genesis did *not yet* appear until the death of Jesus and the birth of the Church.

CREATION	FALL	REDEMPTION
Genesis 1-2	Genesis 3	Genesis 12 until Christ's coming
Egalitarianism—God's intent	Hierarchy—sin's result	Tension—God's plan unfolding

Many Old Testament laws cannot be taken as God's highest ideal. One must look at the context and see that some laws, like the Ten Commandments, were absolute, timeless, and eternal. Other laws were regulations for where the people were at the time. For instance, in ancient times when a child was "stubborn and rebellious," the parent could pierce him or her through with a spear or kill them by stoning (Deut. 21:21). The law given in Exodus 21:23-24, "eye for eye, tooth for tooth," was actually more merciful than the prevailing conditions. Israelites could only take what had been taken from them.

Jesus reinterpreted that law, however, and showed that Exodus was not God's highest ideal for His people: "You have heard that it was said, 'Eye for eye, and tooth for tooth.' But I tell you, do not resist an evil person. If anyone slaps you on the right cheek, turn to them the other cheek also" (Matt. 5:38-39). A closer way to God's will is to mix mercy with justice. Christ's teaching supersedes the Old Testament. Abusive hierarchy becomes obsolete where people live by the Golden Rule that Jesus taught: "So in everything, do to others what you would have them do to you, for this sums up the Law and the Prophets" (Matt. 7:12).

Roles of Women and Men in the Old Testament

God used both women and men as leaders of the people even in the strictest of patriarchal societies.[11] God showed that He valued women as leaders. During one period of Israel's history, judges were the highest rulers. God himself called them to their office and empowered them to deliver His people (Judg. 2:16-18). Deborah, a very successful judge, served as God's spokesperson to her people. Whereas Samson's rule was confined to one tribe, her authority "transcended tribal divisions" (Judg. 5).[12]

Deborah spoke as a prophet and led troops with the military commander. Judges 5 records the song of victory she composed and sang.[13] Canaan had oppressed Israel for twenty years, but the land had peace for forty years under Deborah's rule (Judg. 5:31). The next judge, Gideon, also triumphed in battle against great odds with God's help (Judg. 6-8).

Both men and women played important parts in the freeing of Israel from slavery in Egypt. The midwives, Shiphrah and Puah, feared God and disobeyed Pharoah. They allowed the Hebrew male babies to live, and God rewarded them with families of their own (Exod. 1:15-22). Miriam, Moses' sister; and Jochebed, his mother; helped save his life by hiding him in a basket among the reeds (Exod. 2:1-10). The daughter of Pharoah defied the unjust decree to murder all Hebrew male babies. She rescued the infant Moses, raising him as her own child. God later used Miriam as a prophet (Exod. 15:20).[14] Many centuries later the prophet Micah recognized her significant role. Together with her brothers, Moses and Aaron, she was called by God to lead Israel out of bondage (Micah 6:4).

Both women and men spoke as prophets. Huldah, who lived at the same time as Jeremiah and Zephaniah, strongly influenced the great religious reform in the days of King Josiah. Israel had gone into idolatry. Both the king and the high priest recognized Huldah as the most authoritative prophet of God at the time and came to her for counsel.[15] They wanted to know the future of the nation. She denounced the religious corruption and predicted judgment. This caused King Josiah to burn the pagan objects of worship and begin reform. God used her to reveal His will and she greatly affected the history of the nation as the men submitted to her counsel (2 Kings 22:1-23:25; 2 Chron. 34:22).

Thirteen women are identified in the Bible as prophets, along with dozens of male prophets.[16] In fact the highest Old Testament religious office was not the priest, but the prophet. The priests represented the people to God, but "the prophet went forth from the presence of God to the people."[17] God spoke to people through them. They were correctors of priests, judging them when they went wrong (Jer. 7; Amos 5:21-27; Isa. 1:10-17). They appointed kings and denounced their sins. Samuel corrected Saul. Nathan confronted David. Only a prophet could declare, "Thus saith the Lord." Although the Hebrew religion had no female priests, it did have women who prophesied with the same kind of authority as male prophets.

Both males and females participated in the religious service of the community. Duties included preparing the tabernacle (Exod. 35:20-29), composing laments in honor of the dead (2 Chron. 35:25), and singing in the temple choir (Neh. 7:67). Pagan religions of the time had women priests, temple prostitutes, and female idols and deities. But God was moving Israel back to His creation intent, while working within the cultural pattern of the time. God established strict laws of uncleanness for that time in history. Having female priests would not have been compatible with these laws. Thus, having no female priests was a temporary situation as part of the Old Covenant. But in time, Christ's once-for-all sacrifice replaced the animal sacrifice in Yahweh worship (Heb. 9-10). Jesus' declaration of all foods "clean" (Mark 7:19), replaced the Levitical food laws. In the same way, the New Testament priesthood of all believers replaced the all-male priesthood (1 Pet. 2:4-10).

Those people who favor hierarchy today say that God sometimes used a woman because no man was available. No, if female leadership were wrong, God would never use it. God is now working through the Church and He wants to use women as well as men to lead.

The naming, care, and instruction of children were joint responsibilities of fathers and mothers. Children were commanded to honor both father and mother alike (Exod. 20:12)—the only commandment with a promise. God asked both parents to teach His laws to their children (Deut. 6:6-9, 20-25). The Proverbs instructed children to listen equally to their father's and mother's teaching (Prov. 1:8, 6:20, 30:17).

In some of the Hebrew marriages, wives acted on their own initiative and God commended them for doing so. Hannah decided to dedicate her only son Samuel to the Lord (1 Sam. 1:9-11, 21-24). The ideal wife of Proverbs 31 received the praise of her husband and children for running a business, overseeing a farm and vineyard, buying and selling real estate, teaching, doing social work, and keeping a vast household operating smoothly. She supported her family in ways beyond the domestic sphere while serving in a variety of busy roles.

Abigail saved her community by secretly taking food to David and his army after her husband, Nabal, had refused to give them any (1 Sam. 25:2-38). She apologized for her unkind husband, but advised David not to kill him. David praised God for sending Abigail to keep him from shedding innocent blood. Her drunken husband died ten days later. If hierarchy were meant to be absolute, God should have allowed Nabal to live and killed this woman who defied her husband's wishes, but He didn't.

Tragedy took place when Sarah blindly obeyed her husband Abraham instead of doing what was right (Gen. 12:11-20) and when Abraham obeyed Sarah instead of doing what was right (Gen.

16:2-6). God spoke personally to Sarah, Hagar, and Abraham in this story. In Genesis 21:12, God told Abraham to obey Sarah. If a husband's authority over his wife were an absolute, God would not have done that.

Consider the wise woman of Tekoa, who took the initiative and saved her city. When she asked Joab, the leader of the troops, to spare the city, he told her he was really chasing only one man who had opposed the king. The wise woman offered a compromise, "I'll give you the man's head if you will leave the city alone." When Joab agreed, she persuaded the rest of the people in the city to turn over the man (2 Sam. 20:15-22).

A similar story recalls how Rahab, the prostitute and resistance leader who feared God, saved herself and her family from death. She took a risk and helped Joshua's spies escape from Jericho (Josh. 2; 6:23). She later had a family and came to hold a place among the ancestors of Christ (Matt. 1:5). Though she stepped out of a traditional female role, she was commended for her actions (Heb. 11:31).

The sexual relationship portrayed in the Song of Solomon models mutual respect and delight between the lovers: "My lover is mine and I am his" (Song of S. 2:16). There is evidence of the beginning of the recovery of the one-husband-one-wife egalitarian marriage, even in a society that allowed men to have several wives.[18] The man and woman show mutual admiration and reciprocal actions, not domination, manipulation, or any difference in rank or status.

God considered women competent to handle family inheritance. Numbers 36:1-13 and Joshua 17:1-5 relate how God commanded that the inheritance of Zelophehad be given to his five daughters, since he had no sons. Job's daughters inherited a share of their father's wealth equal to their brothers' (Job 42:13-15). God chooses whom He will.

Miriam was a single woman leader. Tamar, Rahab, Ruth, and

Bathsheba all were included in the list of the ancestors of Jesus (Matt. 1:3-6). The courageous Jael, who crushed the head of Sisera, is called "blessed of women" (Judg. 5:24). God used Deborah, a wife and mother, as a spiritual and just leader. He spoke to a king through Huldah, the prophet. The wife of Proverbs 31 held multiple careers. Gretchen Hull concludes,

> Like Abigail, these women were not locked into some sort of artificial role playing nor were they limited by the men in their lives. They lived in a patriarchal society, but they operated in nonpatriarchal ways, and the Bible text commends them for their actions.[19]

Conclusion

The Scriptures show that God's nature transcends (is above) maleness and femaleness. The feminine and masculine images of God demonstrate that His character embraces aspects of both. References to God with male pronouns should not limit the reader's theological understanding that God is spirit. When the New Testament describes God's coming to earth, it is Christ's humanness, not His maleness, that is the focus.

Because of His nature, God chose to work with the Hebrew people and to lead them back toward His pattern of egalitarianism as revealed in Eden. God's actions reveal timeless truths. He at times overruled patriarchy by choosing and anointing women in the roles of civil judge, prophet, community and religious leader, and wise partner in family settings. It is clear that God often contradicted hierarchical structures to show His ideals—monogamous marriage, equal authority for male and female prophets, leadership roles for both women and men. God blessed women who acted in faith and obedience to Him, taking risks guided by the Spirit.

In the Old Testament, God accommodated[20] the old patterns. His purpose was to lead people into a new pattern with the coming of Christ and the establishment of the Church. Priestly succession and hierarchy marked the Old Covenant. Ministry according to giftedness and egalitarian relationships in home, church, and society mark the New Covenant. Examination of Christ's treatment of women in the culture of His day further reveals God's values. Peter, empowered by the Holy Spirit on the Day of Pentecost, proclaimed God's desire to anoint all believers as prophets. And Peter, inspired by the Holy Spirit in his first letter, proclaimed God's desire that all believers be His priests.

CONCEPTS AND SCRIPTURES CONSIDERED IN CHAPTER 4

THE OLD TESTAMENT AND GENDER

Though Hebrew society revolved around men, God emphasized to His people that He is not a man (nor a woman).

- God's nature is above sex and includes characteristics identified with both genders.
- The life and teachings of Jesus reinforce this truth.

The patriarchy of the Old Testament is not normative but one of the results of the Fall.

- God chose Israel, not approving of that culture, but working with those people to gradually get rid of their sins.
- Jesus is the highest example of God's goal to restore Creation ideals.

The Old Testament records that God used both men and women as leaders in religion, society, and the home.

- By the time of the New Testament, when people led according to their giftedness, even the hereditary ban on the priesthood was lifted.
- Every role of ministry is open to every race, class, and gender today.

Deuteronomy 6:4; Hosea 11:9; Isaiah 42:14; 66:13
Luke 13:20-21; 15:8; Matthew 23:37; John 3:8
Judges 4-5
Exodus 1:15-22; 2:1-10; 15:10, 20; Micah 6:4

2 Kings 22:1-23:25; 2 Chronicles 34:22
Isaiah 8:3
Luke 1:36-38, 41-45, 46-55
Acts 21:9
Exodus 35:20-29; 2 Chronicles 35:25; Nehemiah 7:67
1 Peter 2:4-10
Exodus 20:12; Deuteronomy 6:6-9, 20-25;
Proverbs 1:8; 6:20; 30:17
Proverbs 31:10-31
1 Samuel 25:2-38
Genesis 21:12
2 Samuel 20:15-22

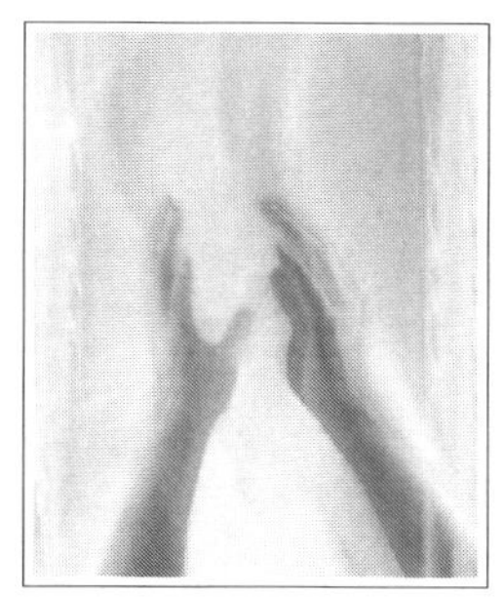

Unit Three

NEW TESTAMENT FOUNDATION

CHAPTER 5

GRECO-ROMAN, JEWISH, AND CHRISTIAN CONTEXTS

THE BIBLE SAYS THAT BOTH ADAM AND EVE sinned and both were punished for their disobedience by being put out of the Garden. The Old Testament does not mention Adam and Eve after Genesis 4:25 and 5:1-5. Neither these passages nor any others in Scripture suggest that women are weak, easily deceived, or responsible for sin in the world—especially sexual sin. Yet such interpretations have risen from particular cultural settings.

While it is the study of the Bible itself that brings release from the bondage of traditions or false teachings, knowing the cultural contexts in which Bible writers lived helps the student understand what they wrote. And knowing the cultural contexts of later interpreters of Scripture reveals the true origin of traditions that devalue women. Though anti-women sources are not biblical, they arose from within the Judeo-Christian context. Thus, they have influenced many Jews and Christians to view women in a negative way.

For example, in the Old Testament many laws concerning women addressed their virginity and marriage. In the ancient Near-Eastern context, where women had few rights, these laws in Scripture served to protect women. Yet, later writers used these very laws, as *they* interpreted them, to lay blame more heavily on the woman than the man for sexual abuses. The original reason for the certificate of divorce discussed by Moses (Deut. 24:1,2) was to protect the welfare of the unattached woman, permitting her officially to marry again. But by the time period between the Old and New Testaments, however, interpreters of this passage considered divorce to be a male prerogative to be exercised at will. A husband could divorce his wife for talking too loudly, for burning his food, or just because he had found another woman more attractive.

In order to see the impact of Christ's words for women, one must see the religious setting into which He came. This chapter focuses its study on the writings outside the Old and New Testaments and how they have negatively influenced Jews and Christians.

It must be noted also, however, that cultural views recorded in literature, though prevalent in the thinking of a certain time period, are not always strictly enforced. For example, even though the Old Testament specifies putting to death anyone who cursed his father or mother (Lev. 20:9), evidence does not support that this regulation was regularly practiced.

The same is true for cultural views about gender. Gender stereotypes are widespread in the writings of the Greeks, Romans, and Jews. Yet in ancient Mediterranean society, among both Jews and non-Jews, women often played quite powerful social and political leadership roles. Such roles were rooted in these women's authority at the household level. Much business and commerce centered around households of the wealthy. These households could be sizable domestic communities including immediate family, extended family members, servants/slaves, and employees.[1] In the ancient world, both men and women could be householders and patrons. Women's experience as managers of these households, their "social authority, economic power, and political influence"[2] established their leadership in other domains in Greco-Roman society and even synagogue leadership in Jewish society.[3] In spite of the fact that there were women such as these who exercised leadership authority, the writings of this period demonstrate how commonly held and deeply rooted in culture were the negative attitudes toward women.

Greco-Roman Context

The Greco-Romans left many written records of their views on women.[4] These perspectives—identified as those of first-century pagans[5]—influenced ancient Jews and Christians so strongly that their effect is still felt today. Rome conquered the world's empires with armies, but Greece conquered the world's thinking with philosophies and cultural theories. Though the Greeks came first, they exerted a much stronger influence than the Romans and have continued to do so well past the Roman era.

What was the Greek attitude toward women? Greek women had very little status unless they were born wealthy. From early times, Greeks taught that women were in all ways inferior to men. Parents often abandoned female babies outdoors to die or to be collected by strangers and brought up as slaves or prostitutes. Women could not participate in the official religion, but found many opportunities in the mystery religions and cults.

Socrates, a Greek philosopher (470-399 BC), said, "All the pursuits of men are the pursuits of women also, but in all of them a woman is inferior to a man."[6] Plato (428-378 BC) recorded Socrates' teachings and passed them on to his pupil, Aristotle (384-322 BC). Perhaps the most influential thinker of ancient times, Aristotle believed "the male is by nature superior, and the female inferior, and the one rules, and the other is ruled."[7]

Roman society held similar views of and standards for women. They remained completely under the control of the male head of the extended family or, in certain conditions, under their husbands' control. Public assistance often excluded women. In most cases women were expected to remain indoors and not be involved in public affairs. The average woman who lived in the first century was the teenaged wife of a 35-to-50-year-old husband. She would be attached to his family and bear a child every two years until about age 49.[8]

Judaism and Its Literature[9]

As Yahwism, the original religion of Israel, developed into Judaism, women's status declined. Judaism was more institutionalized[10] and more secularized[11] than the Old Testament religion of the Jews (Yahwism). God's ideals for woman (from Gen. 1) were replaced with an inferior view of her status.

What caused this change? In the latter part of the Old Testament, the Jews were suffering God's punishment for their idolatry. The Northern Kingdom of Israel fell to the Assyrians (722 BC), never to exist as a people again. The Southern Kingdom of Judah fell to the Babylonians (597-587 BC). Following 70 years of exile, only a remnant (a small portion) of its people returned to their homeland. During this period[12] Alexander the Great conquered much of the world and spread Greek culture, called Hellenism. In order to resist the pull of paganism during the period of Hellenization,[13] conservative Jews became more and more strict in their interpretations of the Torah.[14] They added many more regulations to God's laws, becoming more rigid, exclusive, and male-biased.

At the same time, other Jews were impressed with the Greco-Roman intellectuals. To prove they were enlightened and not culturally backwards, these Jews adopted many of the philosophers' worldviews. Jewish intellectuals, like Philo, replaced God's ideal (women created in the image of God) with the pagans' view (that women are less than human).

A variety of Jewish writings from the period reflect this low view of women: the Old Testament Apocrypha,[15] the Pseudepigrapha,[16] the works of Philo and Josephus, and the Talmud.[17] Though Christians do not consider these to be accurate sources of theology, these writings do reflect the history of Jewish thought.

Rabbinic Literature. The ancient rabbis from the fifth century before Christ began a new method of oral instruction and memory work. The process of interpreting the written Law[18] may have been started by Ezra and his companions and is called *midrash*. This method followed the order of the Scriptures themselves. In the two centuries just before Christ's birth, Jewish rabbis began to arrange their interpretations of the laws by topics, not in scriptural order. The "traditions" began to grow as teachers addressed issues, often without referring to the biblical text. They asserted that the text supported their teaching, but interpretations often appear to be very subjective.[19] The schools of various rabbis collected these oral materials and put them in writing from about 100 BC to AD 200. This collection became known as the Mishnah.

During the next 300 years rabbinic scholars continued to add explanations and interpretations of the Mishnah to deal with problems Judaism encountered in its changing cultural situation. Their work is called the Gemara. The Mishnah and Gemara were then combined to form the Talmud,[20] the second greatest literary work in Hebrew and Aramaic, around the year AD 550.

One chapter in the Old Testament (Lev. 15) is devoted to uncleanness caused by bodily discharges. Half of the chapter contains rules about a man's uncleanness (vv. 2-18), and half of the chapter contains rules about a woman's uncleanness (vv. 19-33). Here's an example of how the Talmud treats women. When the Talmud discusses this kind of uncleanness, one has difficulty finding a single reference to male discharges. But it devotes an entire tractate of ten chapters (over 500 pages) to the topic of women's uncleanness.[21] Such disproportionate emphasis reveals the authors' perspective that women are more unclean than men, and that women's uncleanness is much more of a concern than men's.

An example from the oral law prohibited speaking to a woman in public: "'Speak not much with a woman.' Since a man's own wife is meant here, how much more does not this apply to the wife of another? The wise men say: 'Who speaks much with a woman draws down misfortune on himself, neglects the words of the law, and finally earns hell.' (Mishnah Aboth 1, 5)."[22] A three-fold daily prayer recommended for Jewish males shows the position of women in the society: "Praised be God that he has not created me a gentile; praised be God that he has not created me a woman; praised be God that he has not created me an ignorant man. (Tosephta Berakhoth 7, 8)."[23]

To summarize, many in Rabbinic Judaism[24] held the view that women should stay in their homes, wear veils, and refrain from eating with or talking to men. Some texts reveal a perspective that women are inferior and evil. Others taught that men should avoid contact with women and should not talk even to their wives or daughters in public. Rabbis restricted women even further in religious affairs, not permitting them to recite prayer at meals or study the Torah. Women were not obligated to attend festivals, nor did they count in the number of persons required to have a synagogue. They were generally not given an education. Thus, this period of Judaism severely limited women's roles in both society and religion.

Old Testament Apocrypha and Pseudepigrapha. One example of apocryphal writing comes from Ben Sira, in the book Ecclesiasticus (or Sirach), dated about 180 BC. His writings contain the first reference to Eve after Genesis: "From a woman sin had its beginning, and because of her we all must die" (25:24).[25] Scholars think his writings began the ideology that shaped the emerging Pharisees. He reflects the Jewish attitudes of the time in saying, "It is a disgrace to be the father of an undisciplined son and the birth of a daughter is a loss" (22:3),[26] and "Any iniquity is small compared to a woman's iniquity; may a sinner's lot befall her!" (25:19a).[27]

Pseudepigraphic writings also demonstrate a similar bias against women based upon a distorted view of history. In *The Life of Adam and Eve,* Eve is heard mourning over the sin she caused. Near the beginning of the story she says to Adam,

> "My lord, would you kill me? O that I would die! Then perhaps the Lord God will bring you again into Paradise, for it is because of me that the Lord God is angry with you" (*The Life of Adam and Eve, Vita* 3.1).[28]

And at the end of Adam's life she is still saying,

> "I have sinned, O God; I have sinned, ... and all sin in creation has come about through me" (*The Life of Adam and Eve, Apocalypse,* 32.1,2).[29]

In the *Testaments of the Twelve Patriarchs,* Reuben, in the Testament of Reuben, calls his sons together and tells them to instruct their wives not to wear jewelry or cosmetics, because he believes those are the devices that women use to seduce men. "For women are evil, my children ... . Indeed, the angel of the Lord told me and instructed me, that women are more easily overcome by the spirit of promiscuity than are men" (5:1,5).[30]

Philo. Philo, a Jew who lived in Alexandria, Egypt (one of the intellectual capitals of the ancient world) at the time of Christ, wrote six times as much material as is found in the New Testament. His writings attempted to build a bridge between Old Testament Jewish teachings and those of the philosophers Plato and Aristotle. In *Questions and Answers on Genesis,* Philo asks, "Why does the serpent speak to the woman and not to the man?" His answer: Because "woman is more accustomed to be deceived than man. ... But the judgment of woman is more feminine, and because of softness she easily gives way and is taken in by plausible falsehoods which resemble the truth."[31]

In *Special Laws,* Philo insists on male superiority:

> In the first place the victim of the whole-burnt-offering is a male because the male is more complete, more dominant than the female, ... for the female is incomplete and in subjection and belongs to the category of the passive rather than the active.[32]

Josephus. Josephus, a Jewish historian who died about AD 100, lived in Palestine until the destruction of the Temple. He first served as a Jewish general, then switched sides and worked for the Romans. He wrote more than 20 volumes of Jewish history. He read Greek interpretations into the Old Testament. In *Against Apion* 2.25, Josephus wrote:

> For, saith the Scripture, "A woman is inferior to her husband in all things." Let her, therefore, be obedient to him; not so that he should abuse her, but that she may acknowledge her duty to her husband; for God hath given the authority to the husband.[33]

New Testament Apocrypha. In the early Christian period following the New Testament, an apocryphal gospel about Mary called the Protevangelium of James (AD 150) reveals Judaistic tendencies. It is possibly the earliest reference to Eve's being alone in the Garden. Though absent in the original Genesis 1-2 account, from AD second century on, it is assumed Eve was alone. In the story at 13.1, Joseph has just come in to his betrothed, Mary. He has discovered for the first time that she is pregnant. He becomes very angry and says,

> "Who has deceived me? Who has done this evil in my house and defiled her [the virgin]? Has the story of Adam been repeated for me? For as Adam was absent in the hour of his prayer and the serpent came and found Eve alone and deceived her and defiled her, so also it has happened to me."[34]

This is another text that clearly gives the false impression that Eve bears all the responsibility for the Fall.

What do all of these texts say to us today? Rabbinic Jews wrote negatively about women; their writings were accepted, spread widely, and endured long. Succeeding generations of Jewish teachers built their traditions on the negative foundation that had been laid. Their views reflect the prevailing attitude of their times.

Yet history bears the record of one exceptional female Talmudic scholar. Beruriah lived in Tiberias in the second century AD, was daughter of the martyr Rabbi Hananiah ben Teradion, and the wife of Rabbi Meir the Tanna. The Talmud mentions Beruriah's superior intellect, virtue, and wit, based on her skills in biblical interpretation. Rabbi Judah endorsed a decision of hers that went counter to the view of "the wise" (Tosef., Kelim, B. M. i. 6). Several stories tell how she corrected misinterpretations resulting from portions of Scripture pulled out of context. "Look to the end of the verse," taught Beruriah. This principle of interpretation, which became an exegetical rule among later sages, is attributed to her.[35]

Recent scholarship and archaelogical discoveries point to the fact that in spite of the prevalence of this negative view there were women leaders. Bernadette Brooten documents that there were a number of women leaders in ancient synagogues.[36]

Still, to summarize, in the literature of Judaism of the late first century on, women were viewed as inferior socially, religiously, culturally, sexually, and in every other way. Their role was to be in the home, not in public life in any way. In the view of these writers, women were considered responsible for all sexual sin, all deviation, and most of the problems in the world.

Early Church Fathers

The pagan influence that affected Judaism is also seen in the writings of some of the early Church Fathers. Tertullian, an early Christian writer (AD 160-230), became a famous, influential preacher. He wrote, addressing women,

> And do you not know that you are (each) an Eve? The sentence of God on this sex of yours lives in this age; the guilt must of necessity live too. *You* are the devil's gateway; *you* are the unsealer of that [forbidden] tree; *you* are the first deserter of the divine law; *you* are she who persuaded him whom the devil was not valiant enough to attack. *You* destroyed so easily God's image, man. On account of *your* desert—that is, death—even the Son of God had to die.[37]

The Church Father Augustine (AD 354-430) said, "Marriage is a covenant with death." He contradicted Scripture in saying,

> the woman, together with her own husband, is the image of God, ... but when she is referred to separately ... then she is not the image of God, but, as regards the man alone, he is the image of God as fully and completely as when the woman too is joined with him in one (Augustine, *De Trinitate, 7.7, 10*).[38]

The theologian Thomas Aquinas (AD 1224-1274) tried to harmonize Aristotle's teaching with the Christian faith. Thus the Greek attitude toward women became imbedded in Christian theology. He wrote,

> As regards the particular nature, woman is defective and misbegotten, for the active force in the male seed tends to the production of a perfect likeness in the masculine sex, while the production of woman comes from a defect in the active force or from some material indisposition, or even from some external change, such as that of a south wind, which is moist.[39]

Not all of the Church Fathers were so negative about women. Bonaventura, a leading scholar of the thirteenth century, for example, has a much higher view. He argued, "The soul of woman—no matter what restrictions or inhibitions philosophers might offer—is the perfect equal of the soul of man. And hence, woman is man's equal in nature, grace, and glory."[40]

Generally speaking, however, the perspective of paganism continued to negatively influence the view of women in the Church through the Middle Ages. Even the Reformation era betrays this bias. Not until the era of evangelicalism,[41] and its revival movements, when the role of the Holy Spirit in equipping for ministry was again recognized, was women's status raised. Still, the negative perspective, so deeply rooted in culture through time, continues to the present day.

Renaissance and Reformation Interpreters

Without exception Renaissance and Reformation interpreters

portray woman as the one who tempts in Genesis. Notes in the Geneva Bible (AD 1560) comment, "The woman seduced by the serpent, enticeth her husband to sin." Adam ate of the fruit, "not so much to please his wife as moved by her persuasion." And further: "The woman was first deceived and so became the instrument of Satan to deceive the man ... woman was guilty of the transgression."[42]

Martin Luther wrote in *Table Talk*:

> Men have broad shoulders and narrow hips, and accordingly they possess intelligence. Women have narrow shoulders and broad hips. Women ought to stay at home; the way they were created indicates this, for they have broad hips and a wide fundament to sit upon [keep house and bear and raise children].[43]

The Rheims-Douay Bible used marginal notes to quote Chrysostom, who used Genesis to justify the position that women should not teach: "The woman taught [the man] once … and ruined all."[44] It also quotes Ambrose, who viewed Eve as sinning and Adam as innocent: "Well does the Scripture omit specifying where Adam was deceived; for he fell, not by his own fault, but by the vice of his wife."[45]

Even twentieth-century interpreters like C. I. Scofield believed that women were unfit for leadership or teaching. Scofield comments on Genesis 3: "The entrance of sin, which is disorder, makes necessary a headship, and it is vested in man." He states, regarding women in general: "A woman, *in the bad ethical sense,* is always a symbol of that which, *religiously,* is out of its place. The 'woman' in Matt. 13:33 is dealing with *doctrine,* a sphere forbidden to her … . In Thyatira a woman is suffered to teach (Rev. 2:20)."[46] Scholars have recognized that Scofield's notes have had "a profound effect on conservative evangelical opinions on biblical teachings about women."[47]

Evangelical Revival Movements

Janette Hassey conducted a well-documented study of the advocacy of women in ministry by evangelicals around the turn of the last century, from 1880-1930.[48] She explains that two strong convictions of evangelicals of that time resulted in equal opportunities for service in ministry for men and women. Those early evangelicals believed that the Holy Spirit equipped women and men equally for ministry. They also believed that Jesus Christ was coming back soon and every voice was needed to spread the news. Hassey dispels two myths about biblical equality. The movement is *not* a misguided effort to follow secular feminism. Denominations with a high view of Scripture have *not* always prohibited women's call to serve in ministry leadership. Women were pioneer pastors and missionaries in many denominations that have nearly none today.

Just look at the evidence from that period Hassey has uncovered. During Moody Bible Institute's (MBI) founding years there were scores of women preachers, pastors, and evangelists trained at MBI and publicized in *Moody Monthly* magazines. A. J. Gordon, the founder of what are now Gordon College and Gordon-Conwell Theological Seminary, wrote in defense of women's right to preach. The Keswick movement in Great Britain was then greatly impacted by a woman, Hannah Whithall Smith. A. B. Simpson provided equality for women at his Nyack school and in the Christian and Missionary Alliance.

Eyewitnesses, interviewed at Maranatha Village in the 1970s, claimed that the Assemblies of God had more ordained women than men in attendance at its first General Council. Another large Pentecostal denomination, the International Church of the Foursquare Gospel, was founded by a woman—Aimee Semple McPherson. Early on, the Evangelical Free Church of America, the Independent Fundamental Churches of America, and the Baptist General Conference all endorsed women's ministry. The Wesleyan-holiness movement had scores of women ministers.

Unfortunately, many of these same denominations take a very different stance on women today.[49] Some evangelicals argue that traditional Christian roles exclude women from leadership in ministry over men. Excluding women may be the *current* practice in many evangelical churches today, rooted in the negative views of Christians and Jews influenced by ancient paganism. But it is *not* the original evangelical perspective. Evangelicalism emerged as a movement of equality.

Conclusion

What these writings tell us very clearly and uncomfortably (since we recognize some of these attitudes today) is that women were viewed as inferior among many people in the first century. God's creation ideals continued to be distorted. The Fall into sin continued to be a prevailing part of the culture of Jews and non-Jews who later influenced Christian views on women that have continued through many centuries. Some of these attitudes are still prevalent in twenty-first-century Judeo-Christian culture. It is most important to note, however, that they do not derive from Scripture, but from sources outside of the Bible.

The next chapter focuses on Jesus and women. In light of these Greco-Roman and Jewish socio-cultural contexts, Jesus' treatment of women was revolutionary. Jesus and His first-century followers radically challenged the gender systems of Greco-Romanism and Judaism. The Early Church was a community of equality in which women led at all levels.

Eventually, however, the same ideologies about gender that had affected Judaism came to influence the Church as well. As the Church became Romanized and institutionalized, and emerged from the domestic to the public sphere women were relegated to lesser roles.

CONCEPTS CONSIDERED IN CHAPTER 5

CULTURAL CONTEXTS SURROUNDING THE NEW TESTAMENT

- The literature of the Greeks and Romans reveals a very negative attitude about women. A culture that holds an opinion that women are inferior may use it to justify devaluing and mistreating them.
- As Judaism developed, its regulations became more and more male-biased. Its theological basis became more like the philosophies of the Greeks and Romans and less like the ideals of the God of the Bible.
- Christian writers after the New Testament have also been strongly influenced by this negative view. So strong is its influence that in many settings it is considered the traditional Christian perspective.
- Yet all of these negative interpretations of women's status and role are from outside the Bible.
- Jesus said of such interpreters:

  "You have let go of the commands of God and are holding on to human traditions. ... "You have a fine way of setting aside the commands of God in order to observe your own traditions. ... Thus you nullify the word of God by your tradition that you have handed down. And you do many things like that" (Mark 7:6b-9, 13).

CHAPTER 6

JESUS' TREATMENT OF WOMEN AND MEN

IN SUCH A SOCIAL AND RELIGIOUS context as has just been described, Jesus' treatment of women was revolutionary! Nowhere in the gospels do we see Jesus treating women as inferior beings. Instead, Jesus treated women as equal to men even when it meant breaking social customs to do so.

Jewish girls could not go to school to learn to read and write. Nor could they study the Torah like their brothers. Some rabbis said it was evil to teach girls.[1] Yet Jesus taught both men and women using methods similar to the rabbis. Both male and female disciples followed Him as He taught (Luke 8:1-3). Only males over the age of 12 could go into the court of Israel in the temple. Women were restricted to the women's court—which is one of the places Jesus chose to do His teaching.

Wherever the values of heaven were put into practice, Christ's kingdom began to be established on earth. For Christ's followers the effects of the Fall were canceled by the surpassing effects of the Cross; and woman's status was restored to God's ideal—as originally created fully in the image of God, she is finally redeemed fully by the work of Christ. Jesus' example had a positive impact on the status of women.

His Ministry Practice

Note the egalitarian nature of Jesus' ministry. While His contemporaries regarded women as sex objects, He treated them as persons (Luke 7:36–50; John 8:2–11). Christ directed His ministry to male and female alike, whether it was in preaching, miraculous provision, healing, deliverance ministry, or raising the dead (Matt. 8:14–15; 9:18–26; 15:21–28).

Men and women were treated the same in Christ's healing ministry. He healed the unclean woman who sought Him in the crowd (Mark 5:25-34) and blind Bartimaeus by the roadside (Mark 10:46-52). He healed on the Sabbath both the man with the shriveled hand and the woman crippled for 18 years (Mark 3:1-5; Luke 13:10-17). Luke gives the account of Jesus' raising to life both a widow's son (7:11-17) and the daughter of Jairus (Luke 8:40-56).

Though Palestinian social customs strongly disapproved of men conversing with women, Jesus interacted with them personally—even when they were strangers or despised people (Matt. 9: 18–26; Luke 10:38–42; John 4:7, 27). Against socio-cultural restrictions, Jesus touched a female corpse in order to raise her from the dead (Mark 5:41) and He rejected the blood taboo[2] in order to heal the woman with the issue of blood (Luke 8:43-48).

Jesus showed women great courtesy, compassion, and honor. He treated His mother with great tenderness (John 19:26–27). He received the tears and anointing of a sinful woman and said to her, "Your faith has saved you; go in peace" (Luke 7:37–50). Neither did He condemn the woman taken in adultery (John 8:2–11). He appealed to the best in both the accusing males and the woman.

Some of the greatest revelations of Christianity Jesus made to or about women. To the Samaritan woman at the well, He gave the first announcement of His Messiahship, "I, the one speaking to you—I am he" [the Messiah] (John 4:7-42). She became the first evangelist. Seeing the widow who gave only two small coins, Jesus said, "This poor widow has put more into the treasury than all the others. They all gave out of their wealth; but she … put in everything—all she had to live on" (Mark 12:43–44). To Martha, Jesus first entrusted the message of comfort, "I am the resurrection and the life. Anyone who believes in me will live, even though they die;

and whoever lives and believes in me will never die" (John 11:25-26). The angel at Jesus' tomb even reminded the women of the teaching Jesus had given them about His death and resurrection (Luke 24:6-9). That was "inner circle" teaching, not part of the sermons Jesus gave to the crowds. The risen Christ appeared first to women. And for the great news of His resurrection after it had taken place, He sent women to go and tell the eleven male disciples (Matt. 28:10; John 20:17-18).

Jesus taught women. He commended Mary for sitting at His feet (Luke 10:38–42), teaching that following Him must be one's first priority and "learning about Him is the most important occupation in life."[3] Jesus had female disciples who traveled with and supported Him and the Twelve (Mark 15:40–41; Luke 8:1-3). He also commissioned them to testify in His behalf (Matt. 28:10). Although rabbinic traditions forbade both the teaching of the Hebrew scriptures to women and the acceptance of the testimony of women, Jesus did both.

His Teaching Manner

Note the egalitarian style of Jesus' teaching. It applies equally to women and to men. He balanced the parables with male and female activities so that both genders would receive the message. For example, He compared the kingdom of God to a mustard seed which a man planted and then to the yeast that a woman mixed in her dough (Luke 13:19–21). When teaching about lost sinners, Jesus used first a male shepherd who loses a sheep and then a woman who loses a coin as examples (Luke 15:3–10). He matched the parable of the persistent widow with the parable of the Pharisee and the tax collector to teach about justice (Luke 18:1–14). And He used both the story of the ten virgins and the story of the three servants to teach about the kingdom of heaven (Matt. 25:1–30).

Jesus used the examples of both women and men to teach

spiritual truths. In Mark 10:17-22, from the rich young ruler, Jesus taught about giving to the poor. In Mark 14:3-9, it was the lavish gift of a woman's perfume that He used to teach about giving.

Jesus frequently coupled illustrations in pairs enabling easy identification for persons of each sex: "the tax collectors and the prostitutes" (Matt 21:31–32); Jonah as a sign and the Queen of the South as a sign (Luke 11:29–32); and two men in the field and two women grinding (Matt. 24:40–41). Jesus used feminine imagery in describing himself and His Father (Luke 13:20–21, 34; 15:8–10).[4]

Jesus addressed mixed groups using "complementary discourse": a term used to refer to the repeating of statements twice (changing the gender each time) in order to make application to each sex.[5] Although such was completely out of step with the grammatical norms of His culture, Jesus frequently spoke using the following pairs: "men and women," "husbands and wives," "fathers and mothers," "fathers-in-law and mothers-in-law," "sons and daughters," and "sons-in-law and daughters-in-law." In Luke 12:53 Jesus refers to "father against son ... and mother against daughter." To the crowds He said, "If anyone comes to me and does not hate father and mother, wife and children, brothers and sisters—yes, even life itself—such a person cannot be my disciple" (Luke 14:26).[6]

His Doctrinal Content

Note the egalitarian quality of Jesus' doctrine. No instructions in Jesus' theology applied only to women or only to men. He explained that there are no sexual distinctions in eternity. He did not confine women's role to the domestic sphere, but He himself frequently served in those ways (Luke 10:38–42, cooking, serving, feeding).

In all the gospel records, there is no teaching or preaching of subordination for women. When a woman praised His mother for giving Him birth and nursing Him (womanly duties), Jesus corrected her values: "Blessed rather are those who hear the word of God and obey it" (Luke 11:27-28). He also corrected Peter (Matt. 16:21-23) and James and John (Luke 9:51-55). Neither did Jesus tolerate double standards when it came to divorce (Matt. 19:3-10) or adultery (John 8:1-11—both offenders were to be stoned according to Lev. 20:10). The good news of the gospel is that there is freedom and equality for *all* people in Christ's kingdom!

Jesus came to cancel the consequences of sin, to reverse the effects of the Fall, and put right-side-up a world whose values were up-side-down.

His Specific Attitude Toward Women

David Scholer, in analyzing the impact of Jesus' example on the status of woman, enumerates five things that Jesus did for women. The discussion that follows comes from his work.[7]

Jesus challenged the sexual put-down of women. (1) The Divorce Debate. Jesus was asked for what reason a man may divorce his wife (Matt. 19:3-9). He answered that Moses allowed divorce only because of the hardness of hearts. God had said that a man and a woman would leave their parents and cleave to each other, they would become one flesh, and what God has put together should not be broken apart. By quoting Genesis 2:24, Jesus was saying that marriage was a mutual partnership. The text says nothing about superiority—its whole point is that the woman is identical in essence to the man. The impact of Jesus' statements in the context of this debate was to neutralize the male prerogative of divorce. It is to say, "I will have nothing to do with this abuse by men."[8] Instead, Jesus stressed that there should be equality in the marital state.

(2) The Look of Adultery. Jesus said that if a man looked on a woman and lusted after her in his heart he had already committed adultery (Matt. 5:28). There is no other text in antiquity that places that level of responsibility on a man. The impact of this statement must have been awesome—Jesus rejected the idea that women are

responsible for all sexual sin! Instead, He says that if a *man* looks with sin in his heart, *he* has committed adultery.

Jesus reached out to women who were despised and rejected. (1) The Woman with the Issue of Blood. Leviticus 15 contains the Jewish laws about uncleanness. About half the chapter (vs. 1–18) has to do with male emissions and about half the chapter (vs. 19–32) has to do with a woman's menstrual cycle. But in the days of Jesus, only the part that dealt with women was discussed—and the rabbis wrote a long book about it. During her period a woman was considered unclean. This woman had been shunned by her society for twelve years. But in the press of the crowd she reached out to touch Jesus, and Jesus blessed her. He accepted her. Her told her that her faith had made her whole (Luke 8:43-48).[9]

(2) The Woman Who Anointed Jesus. At another time, Jesus was in the home of Simon, a Pharisee who had Him over for dinner. A woman came in who was known as a sinner, probably a prostitute, and during the entire dinner that woman kissed, and anointed Jesus' feet. Simon thought, "Now I know He can't be the Messiah. No prophet would let a woman like this touch Him." Yet here again Jesus said, "Your faith has saved you" (Luke 7:36-50).

(3) The Samaritan Woman. This woman was both socially and ethnically despised. She was living in sexual sin and she was a "half-breed Jew"—not to mention the fact that she was female. Yet Jesus took the time to demonstrate that He valued her as a person enough to share with her the Water of Life (John 4:7-42).

(4) The Woman Taken in Adultery.[10] Jesus offered this guilty woman love and forgiveness (John 8:2-11). What did Jesus write in the sand? Scholer suggests that maybe it was the regulation from Deuteronomy, that is, that both offenders—male and female—are to be stoned.

Jesus said, "Truly I tell you, the tax collectors and the prostitutes are entering the kingdom of God ahead of you" (Matt. 21:31). Jesus reached out to people who were marginalized—rejected and neglected by society. One of the largest groups of such people in His day was women.

Jesus included women in His larger group of disciples. Though there were no women among the Twelve, there were women among Jesus' followers.[11] The average believer today may think that "disciple" means one of the twelve apostles, but that is not true. Jesus had a larger band of followers. We read of the 70 He sent out, the 500 who witnessed the ascension, and the 120 who remained in the Upper Room for the promise. In describing that group of followers in Acts 1:14, Luke names some of the men present and then notes that women were among the 120 too. He says, "They all joined together constantly in prayer, along with the women and Mary the mother of Jesus, and with his brothers." Jesus had a larger group of disciples and among those were women.[12]

(1) Mary and Martha. In first-century Judaism it was not appropriate for a Jewish male teacher to teach women, but Jesus did. Not only did He teach Mary, but He commended her for her learning. He defended her and said that by sitting at His feet and learning the lessons of faith, she was doing what was most important (Luke 10:38-42).

(2) The Samaritan Woman. Jesus taught the Samaritan woman some of the highest theological concepts He ever explained, such as "God is spirit, and his worshipers must worship in the Spirit and in truth" (John 4:24). The Samaritan woman is the only person we have record of to whom Jesus made a clear statement that He was the Messiah. That is remarkable!

(3) Others Mentioned by Name. Other followers of Jesus mentioned in Luke 8:1–3 are Mary Magdalene, Joanna, Susanna, and many others. These women followed Jesus in Galilee (during

His first year of ministry), continued all the way to the Cross, were the first ones at the tomb, and are the ones who appear in Acts 1:14–15 among the 120 who gathered in the upper room and were filled with the Spirit. They were not just "Jerusalem tag-alongs"—they had been with Jesus all along. They were part of Jesus' group of disciples during His ministry and they continued faithful even after His ascension.

Jesus valued the discipleship of women over their biological function. Twice when Jesus' mother was mentioned or blessed for being His mother, Jesus said, "Whoever does God's will is my brother and sister and mother" (Mark 3:35); and "Blessed rather [than being my biological mother] are those who hear the word of God and obey it" (Luke 11:28).

As lofty and honorable as the roles of wife and mother are, Jesus was asserting that one value stands still higher. He was not denying or diminishing maternity, He was saying that discipleship is of even greater value. This is the Gospel version of Paul's statement that in Christ there is no male or female (Gal. 3:28). In Christ, in the area of discipleship and of relating to God, there is a higher value than one's gender identification and the roles determined thereby. A higher value is obeying God. The highest role is serving God—discipleship surpasses even motherhood.

Jesus included women among those who proclaim the gospel. The first proclaimers of the death and resurrection of Christ—which is Paul's definition of the gospel—were women. It is remarkable that in a culture where women's testimony was not even accepted in court, the first to proclaim Christ's resurrection were women.[13] And this was not just by chance. Jesus, himself, commissioned them as His authentic witnesses. This intentional assignment helps one to appreciate the context and power of what Jesus did for women.

Jesus did not appoint any female elders—but He never

appointed male elders either. What He did do was call and commission disciples. And within that band of faithful disciples were both men and women.

Jesus' model is relevant; it is important. It was the foundation that led the Early Church to understand that the Holy Spirit had come to both men and women in fulfillment of the prophecy of Joel. And it led to the statement of Paul that in Christ there is no male or female. Jesus treated men and women equally in discipleship and that is the first basis of ministry.

Conclusion

Jesus' disciples were so impressed by Jesus' example that they were faithful to record it as it was even though it was at variance with their own personal social customs. Women must have been important sources for the Gospel accounts (Luke 1:1-4). Much of the description of the birth of Christ could have come only from Mary, His mother (Luke 1-3). When all the disciples but John had fled the scene of the Cross, the women stayed (Matt. 27:55-56; Mark 15:40-47; Luke 23:26-56; John 19:25-27). Afterwards they shared their stories. Details about the Resurrection must have come from the women who witnessed them.

Men and women gathered in an upper room and waited for the promised Holy Spirit. "All of them were filled with the Holy Spirit and began to speak in other tongues as the Spirit enabled them" (Acts 2:4).

Jesus' example also had great influence on subsequent church history. The Church in its early, original state, followed Jesus' example, celebrating it as the incarnation of the good news.

CONCEPTS AND SCRIPTURES CONSIDERED IN CHAPTER 6

JESUS, WOMEN, AND MEN

In light of the contexts of first-century Greco-Roman and Jewish cultures, Jesus' equal treatment of women and men was revolutionary.

- His ministry reached out to men and women equally.
- His teaching was directed to women and men equally.
- His doctrine applies to men and women identically.

What did Jesus do for women?

- Jesus challenged the sexual put-down of women.
- He reached out to women who were despised and rejected.
- He included women in His larger group of disciples.
- He valued the discipleship of women over their biological function.
- And He included women among those who proclaim the gospel.

Jesus' example is normative. The disciples taught, practiced, and recorded His teachings; and the Early Church followed His model.

Luke 7:36-50; 8:1-3
John 8:2-11
Mark 5:22-43
Matthew 15:21-28
Luke 10:38-42; 13:10-17
John 4:4-26
Mark 3:31-35; Luke 11:27-28
Mark 12:43-44
Luke 13:19-21, 15:3-10, 18:1-14
Matthew 25:1-30
Matthew 5:28, 19:3-9
John 19:26-27
Mark 15:40-47
John 20:17-18; Luke 24:1-11
Acts 1:14-15

CHAPTER 7

WOMEN IN THE NEW TESTAMENT CHURCH: THEOLOGICAL TEXTS

THE BEST PLACE TO GO TO FIND God's answers to today's questions is the Bible. It is the one sure record and promise of God's involvement with humanity from eternity past to eternity future. Though its story spans the ages, its message is for today. The Old Testament is the backdrop for the drama of salvation history. The first century sets the stage. And Jesus steps on the scene as the main character. Christ entered human history to satisfy God's righteous requirements by sacrificing His life for the world's sins. His death canceled the penalty of the Fall into sin for believers and restored the possibility of a right relationship with the Almighty Creator God. And Jesus' life provides the perfect example for our lives.

What about women in the Church? What were their roles *then,* in the first churches? And what should be their roles *now,* in this day and age? The New Testament spotlights Jesus as the model. He treated women with respect and dignity, included them in spiritual matters, and involved them in religious work. New Testament theology—giving God's words about women and their roles—teaches that the Holy Spirit equips all people (male and female) for God's work. The New Testament history depicts the first-century church at worship. It describes women as full participants in the services, equal recipients of spiritual gifts, and leaders at all levels—

even identifying female church workers by the same titles as male ministers. And the New Testament states its correctives concerning certain women in certain church situations.

As mentioned in Chapter 2, there are different categories of Bible texts. Every verse is inspired, but not all passages apply equally to every situation. S. Scott Bartchy organized every New Testament text about women into one of three categories. In this book, his three categories are identified as *theological statements* that teach "the way things ought to be;" *historical statements* that describe "the way things were;" and contextual *corrective statements* that deal with "local problems that needed correction."[1]

This chapter and the following three chapters will not only discuss those New Testament verses by category, but will train a person to recognize the marks that characterize each category. This way, no matter what questions a reader brings to the Bible, he or she will be able to interpret and apply the verses as they were originally intended.

Jesus' treatment of women in light of the contexts of Judaism and paganism has been discussed in previous chapters. The next consideration is the influence of Jesus' model in shaping the theology of the Early Church relative to women. What did the church consider to be normative roles for women? That is, what standards did it prescribe? The first church was so impressed by Jesus' example that they followed it in their practice of Christianity—even though it differed greatly from their Jewish and pagan cultures.

Acts 2:17-18

"In the last days," God says,
"I will pour out my Spirit on all people.
Your sons and daughters will prophesy,
your young men will see visions,
your old men will dream dreams.
Even on my servants, both men and women,

I will pour out my Spirit in those days,
and they will prophesy."

The Day of Pentecost was the birthday of the Church. It changed everything! It was such a significant event in the entire salvation-history drama that nothing would ever be the same again. Jesus had promised His disciples the Holy Spirit would come. He had told them to wait for the promise, and that the Spirit would empower them to be His witnesses (John 14:16-18, 26; 15:26; 16:7-14; and Acts 1:4-8).

When the Day of Pentecost arrived, people witnessed the same kind of supernatural signs and wonders that were always linked with the Day of the Lord[2] (Acts 2:2-3, 19-20). Peter recognized the event as a turning point on the timeline of eternity. With the insight and anointing of a prophet himself, Peter identified the outpouring of the Spirit as the end-time fulfillment of Joel 2:28-32. Egalitarianism was proclaimed; the fulfillment begun. Peter's sermon (Acts 2:17-18) provides the key text of the theology of the Holy Spirit in the "last days." As such, it lays the foundation for women's role in Christian ministry.[3] The promise of Jesus, the supernatural signs, and the apostle Peter's specific interpretation of the

CREATION	FALL	REDEMPTION	PENTECOST
Genesis 1-2	Genesis 3	Genesis 12 until Christ's coming	Acts 2 until Christ's return
Egalitarianism—God's intent	Hierarchy—Sin's result	Tension—God's plan unfolding	Promise—Fulfillment in process

event as normative (a timeless truth) confirms that this passage should be recognized as a theological text.

Throughout the book of Acts women's participation in the church (in fulfillment of this text) is evident. Women, including Mary the mother of Jesus, were among the 120 who spoke in tongues on the Day of Pentecost (Acts 1:14). The pronoun "these" refers to both men and women, not just men. Note: "Aren't all these [men and women] who are speaking Galileans?" (Acts 2:7); and "These people [women and men] are not drunk as you suppose" (Acts 2:15).

Both women and men were constantly added to the new community (Acts 5:14; 8:12; 17:4, 34). Both male and female individually bore guilt for lying to the Holy Spirit (Acts 5:7-10). And Saul later dragged both men and women off to prison (Acts 8:3; 9:2). Luke also wrote about Lydia, "a worshiper of God" whom Paul baptized (Acts 16:13-15), and Philip's four daughters who prophesied (Acts 21:9).

What is the theological significance of Acts 2:17-18? Peter, quoting Joel on the Day of Pentecost, declared to those in Jerusalem that they were seeing the fulfillment of prophecy. The new era of the Spirit had come. In these "last days," all people—regardless of age, social status, or gender—qualify to preach Christ, because from that day on it has been the Holy Spirit that equips people for ministry.

1 Corinthians 7:4-5, 7

> The wife does not have authority over her own body but yields it to her husband. In the same way, the husband does not have authority over his own body but yields it to his wife. Do not deprive each other except perhaps by mutual consent and for a time, so that you may devote yourselves to prayer. Then come together again so that Satan will not tempt you because of your lack of self-control. ... I wish that all of you were as I am. But each of you has your own gift from God; one has this gift, another has that.

The idea of a wife's ruling over her husband's body is unheard of in Jewish literature. Yet here, in 1 Corinthians 7, Paul explains that Christian marriage is a relationship of mutuality and reciprocal[4] authority.

Also, in Christ there is equal respect for both the married and single states. Personal wholeness and fulfillment come from a relationship with Christ, not from a marriage partner. Therefore, a single believer is no less a whole person than a married believer. Though Paul recognizes that both a spouse and singleness are gifts from the Lord, in verse 7 (in sharp contrast to Jewish custom) he affirms singleness as the state he personally prefers.

Note how extremely egalitarian is the New Testament teaching on marriage. Ten times in this chapter, as Paul addresses marital issues, he applies the same standards to each spouse. Thus he describes the rights and responsibilities for both the husband and the wife as identical (compare verses 2, 3, 4, 10–11, 12–13, 14, 15, 16, 28, 32–34).

Just as some of Jesus' teachings replaced old laws and traditional Jewish ideals with Christ's higher ones, so also Paul does the same thing. His open declaring of a standard above the ordinary, marks this as a new norm for Christ-followers, a timeless truth meant to apply from his day on. This chapter of 1 Corinthians has a ring of authority. Paul is not suggesting or recommending in this chapter; he is teaching. Furthermore, in verse 7, Paul contrasts his subjective opinion (that singleness is the best way to serve the Lord) with the objective doctrine of equality in marriage. These are evidences of the theological nature of this text.

1 Corinthians 11:11-12

> Nevertheless, in the Lord woman is not independent of man, nor is man independent of woman. For as woman came from man, so also man is born of woman. But everything comes from God.

What theology does this passage present? It teaches the interdependence of male and female. It also serves to lessen any apparent importance of creation order—for even though the first woman came from a man, every man since Adam has come from a woman (his mother). The whole passage seems to be focused on origins, and concludes that the true source is God. This passage then is normative, underscoring the same ideals seen in Genesis—both male and female come from God and share His image. The *interdependence* of this New Testament passage mirrors the *unity*, *equality*, and *mutuality* of the Old Testament creation account.

Understanding the significance of 1 Corinthians 11:11-12, clarifies the often misunderstood context in which it is found, 1 Corinthians 11:3-12. First Corinthians 11 and Ephesians 5 are the primary passages in Scripture dealing with what has been called in popular theology "male headship." Much of the basis of the teaching for male authority stems from a common, but inaccurate, interpretation of 1 Corinthians 11:3, 7-9:

> But I want you to realize that the head of every man is Christ, and the head of the woman is man, and the head of Christ is God.
>
> A man ought not to cover his head, since he is the image and glory of God; but the woman is the glory of man. For man did not come from woman, but woman from man; neither was man created for woman, but woman for man.

The Greek word for head is *kephale*. Its literal meaning is identical to its English translation—the top part of the body in most higher animals. A problem arises, however, when the term is used figuratively.[5] Though there are more than twenty figurative meanings for the term in both languages, there is not a one-to-one correspondence between the figurative meanings of "head" in English and those of *kephale* in Greek.

A very common figurative English meaning of head is "a foremost person; leader, ruler, or chief."[6] The New Testament Greek lexicon suggests that *kephale* has the same metaphorical meaning: "In the case of living beings, [*kephale* is used] to denote superior rank." This lexicon cites father, husband, Christ, and God as examples associated with this meaning for *kephale*.[7] The even more comprehensive lexicon of classical Greek, however, offers no such meaning.[8] It presents forty-eight meanings for *kephale*, but not one of them is "a foremost person, leader, ruler, chief, or one of superior rank."

The meaning of *kephale* has been a battleground between Greek experts.[9] One by one, scholars are cataloging every occurrence of this word in ancient Greek literature. Not only does the debate affect the issue of male-female relationships, it touches on Christology.[10] A subordinationist[11] view of Christ's position in the Godhead is equivalent to the Arian heresy.[12] The issue has not yet been settled conclusively because new texts continue to be discovered and discussed. But based on the mounting evidence many (including the authors of this book) are persuaded that *kephale* does *not* denote superior rank.[13] Interpreters have incorrectly read into the ancient Greek texts a modern English meaning that was foreign to the original concept of *kephale*.

The correct meaning of *kephale* here in 1 Corinthians 11 is more likely "source or origin," one of the common metaphorical meanings of the Greek term.[14] Modern English shares this meaning also. For example: "The *head* waters of the Mississippi River are Lake Itasca." Paul uses *kephale* as "source" here in his discussion of creation. How well that meaning of *kephale* fits its literary context! (Recall from the comments above on 1 Corinthians 11:11-12 that the whole passage [1 Corinthians 11:3-12] seems to be focused on origins and concludes that the true source is God.) Here is an amplified, interpretive paraphrase of verse 3.

> The head of man is Christ, that is, Adam was created by Christ—Christ is man's source or origin. The head of woman is man, that is, Eve was taken from Adam's side—Adam was Eve's source or origin. And the head of Christ is God, that is, Christ's being issues forth from God's.

Philip Payne writes that Paul is referring to Christ's coming to do His saving work and to give us direct access to God: "The eternal second person of the Trinity came forth from the Godhead in the Incarnation (John 1:14; 8:42). Thus it is proper to speak of his source as God."[15] This interpretation fits the context perfectly, for verses 11–12 are Paul's balancing of the scales on the issue raised in previous verses. He is saying, in essence:

> Even though there is a sequence of origins (God ... Christ ... man ... woman) in the Lord, neither man nor woman are independent of each other. For just as the first woman came from the man [her head, source or origin, was Adam], all men since Adam have come from women [their head, source or origin, was their mothers]. But all of this is inconsequential! What really matters is that all things come from God [He is the head, source or origin, of us all].

Thus, 1 Corinthians 11:3 has nothing to do with male authority or rulership over females. Such an understanding of "headship" forces an unlikely metaphorical meaning of the English word "head" on the Greek word *kephale* and ignores the significance of the literary context.

The original text of the entire passage (1 Cor. 11:2-16) in the Greek is unclear at several points. Scholars have struggled to understand whether it is teaching about hairstyles or head coverings. They have wondered why there are references to "angels" and to "nature." Most of all, what do such things have to do with "authority"? (The lengthy commentaries on this passage and many journal articles written about it demonstrate the challenges to interpreters this passage has caused.[16])

Trying to find a cultural application, many people assume verse 10 concerns a veil to cover a woman's head, thinking that a literal headcovering is the sign of a woman's submission. At least one translation has even inserted the word "veil" (for example, the RSV), though it is not in the original text. Assuming this meaning, other translations try to make things clearer, by adding the words "a sign of" or "symbol of" to verse 10 (for example, the NIV, ASV and NRSV). ("The woman ought to have *a sign of* authority on her head" (1 Cor. 11:10, NIV [emphasis added].)

Based upon that translation, still others try to find a theological principle in this passage. In their thinking "the covering" is a metaphor for a husband's spiritual authority and covering over his wife. This passage is taught as part of the biblical basis for male headship—a husband's authority over his wife. Some have gone so far as to say that an unmarried woman must also find a male for her covering.

The addition of the words "a sign of" turns the meaning of the original Greek text upside-down. The original text (as the TNIV translates it) says, "The woman ought to have authority over her own head." In this verse the apostle Paul is rejecting the chain-of-command teaching of patriarchal households. Against anyone else's authority over her, Paul says "a woman ought to have authority over her *own* head" [emphasis added].[17]

This passage presents many difficulties to understanding. But it does not refer to a husband's authority over his wife or any man's authority over a single woman. (It does not provide biblical support for the teaching that a man is like an umbrella, offering spiritual covering to the woman.) It is a big leap to spiritualize[18] the passage in this way.

1 Corinthians 11:3-12 states that the head (source or origin) of both sexes is Christ. And it affirms that a woman has authority over her own head. Even though more work remains to be done on the meaning of *kephale,*

> in reality, the case for equal partnership of men and women in the Church's ministry does not rest on the kephale debate. The biblical case rests, rather, on the total biblical teaching on women and ministry, on the specific and full context and intent of each New Testament kephale passage, and on the first century AD cultural setting of these kephale texts and the hermeneutical issues involved in their appropriation today.[19]

The New Testament lists three categories of spiritual gifts in three passages of Scripture. Though each category is distinct in its purposes, all gifts share the following elements in common: (a) Each gift represents a unique way God's grace *enables* individuals to effectively do His work in the world and in the church. (b) God's gifts are no reason for boasting; they are not given as a badge of honor to those who deserve them, but are *unmerited* gifts of grace. (c) Spiritual gifts are not for the benefit of the recipient, but are given for the common good, that is, to serve the needs of *others*, for the building up of the body of Christ, and for ministry in the marketplace. (d) Thus, all gifts are to be operated with *love*.[20] (e) And, from the Day of Pentecost on, God has poured out His Spirit on sons and daughters alike, equipping *both genders* in every category of gifts.

1 Corinthians 12-14

> Now about the gifts of the Spirit, brothers and sisters, I do not want you to be uninformed. …
>
> There are different kinds of gifts, but the same Spirit distributes them. …
>
> Now to each one the manifestation of the Spirit is given for the common good. To one there is given through the Spirit a message of wisdom, to another a message of knowledge by means of the same Spirit, to another faith by the same Spirit, to another gifts of healing by that one Spirit, to another miraculous powers, to another prophecy, to another distinguishing between spirits, to another speaking in different kinds of tongues, and to still another the interpretation of tongues. All these are the work of one and the same Spirit, and he distributes them to each one, just as he determines (1 Cor. 12:1, 4, 7-11).

First Corinthians 12-14 discusses the nine *supernatural* gifts of the Spirit: a message of wisdom, a message of knowledge, faith, gifts of healing, miraculous powers, prophecy, distinguishing between spirits, speaking in different kinds of tongues, and the interpretation of tongues. The Holy Spirit makes the choice of which gifts He gives to which individuals (1 Cor. 12:11). And those spiritually-gifted persons comprise God's gifts to the church. "God has placed the parts [in this context, (spiritually-gifted) people] in the body, every one of them, just as he wanted them to be" (1 Cor. 12:18). There is no evidence in Scripture that gender has any bearing on the choices He makes.

The members of the body of Christ and their spiritual gifts are diverse, yet together they form a unified whole. God's plan is that "there should be no division in the body" (1 Cor. 12:25). Every part (person, including their gifts) is needed; every part is to be valued; every part is to be honored and cared for—and every believer is a part of the Body (1 Cor. 12:27). Scripture warns against devaluing God's gifts (1 Thess. 5:20; 1 Cor. 14:39). Disregarding the "people-gifts" (that is, the persons God has supernaturally equipped for service) would grieve the Holy Spirit.

The supernatural gifts are so beneficial to the Church that Scripture encourages all of Christ's followers to seek them, especially certain gifts. Paul writes, "Eagerly desire the greater gifts;" that is, "those [gifts] that build up the church;" "eagerly desire spiritual gifts, especially the gift of prophecy" (1 Cor. 12:31; 14:1, 12 [compare 6-11]). "Therefore, my brothers and sisters, be eager to prophesy" (1 Cor. 14:39). If the apostle Paul is suggesting any ranking of supernatural gifts, the "greater" kind of gift seems to be prophecy. Does the Holy Spirit gift women with prophecy?

Yes, prophecy is a spiritual gift with which the Holy Spirit gifted women in the New Testament (1 Cor. 11:5). First Corinthians 11:5 gives evidence that prophesying women were active in the worship service. Female prophets were among those the Holy Spirit gifted to the New Testament Church (Acts 21:9). Scripture explains that though not every person is a prophet (1 Cor. 12:29), *any* person (male or female) can be gifted by the Holy Spirit to prophesy (1 Cor. 14:31). Furthermore, prophets are the ones authorized to judge the authenticity of utterance gifts (1 Cor. 14:29). Thus those who prophesy have authority in the supernatural gifts.

And because prophecy, as an intelligible utterance gift, has real potential to build up the Body, it is a supernatural gift that is highly esteemed. Since the Holy Spirit gifted women in the New Testament with prophecy—perhaps the highest of supernatural gifts— it follows that all the rest of the supernatural gifts are available to women too.

Romans 12:3-8

> For by the grace given me I say to every one of you: Do not think of yourself more highly than you ought, but rather think of yourself with sober judgment, in accordance with the faith God has distributed to each of you. For just as each of us has one body with many members, and these members do not all have the same function, so in Christ we, though many, form one body, and each member belongs to all the others. We have different gifts, according to the grace given to each of us. If your gift is prophesying, then prophesy in accordance with your faith; if it is serving, then serve; if it is teaching, then teach; if it is to encourage, then give encouragement; if it is giving, then give generously; if it is to lead, do it diligently; if it is to show mercy, do it cheerfully.

Romans 12:3-8 discusses the six *motivational* gifts. Like spiritual temperaments, the motivational gifts are the reason a certain Christian has zeal for one ministry rather than another. These gifts are the inner inclinations that influence why individuals think and act the way they do. They are the very core of what motivates a person.

These motivations are spiritual gifts, graciously given by God to each member of the Body in order to serve Him with great joy. For example, the motivational gift of prophesying involves a drive to perceive the will of God and speak it out to others. Serving involves the joy of helping meet the needs of others. Teaching involves a love for research and communicating truth in an effort to see lives changed. Encouraging involves enjoying being a positive influence to help people live victoriously. Giving involves finding joy in investing resources to benefit others and advance the gospel. Leading involves thriving on organizing, facilitating, and directing. Showing mercy involves compassion that desires to heal hurting hearts.

As with all spiritual gifts, it is God who distributes them as He pleases. The Church is most strengthened when each of its members makes use of these gifts fully: prophesying with faith, giving with generosity, leading diligently, showing mercy cheerfully, etc. To paraphrase the apostle Paul, "Whatever your motivation, exercise it for all you're worth!" (Rom. 12:6-8). All Christ's followers, male and female, have been graciously gifted with unique motivations.[21] It would grieve the Holy Spirit to reject the passionate involvement in the Lord's work of a person He had spiritually motivated.

Ephesians 4:4-16

> But to each one of us grace has been give as Christ apportioned it.
> This is why it says:
> "When he ascended on high,
> he led captives in his train
> and gave gifts to his people."
>
> ...It was he who gave the apostles, the prophets, the evangelists, the pastors and teachers, to equip God's people for works of service, so that the body of Christ may be built up until we all reach unity in the faith and in the knowledge of the Son of God and become mature, attaining to the whole measure of the fullness of Christ. ... From him the whole body, joined and held together by every supporting ligament, grows and builds itself up in love, as each part does its work (Ephesians 4:7, 11-13, 16).

Ephesians 4:4-16 discusses the *equipping* gifts. Scripture specifies in this gift passage, just like the others (describing supernatural and motivational gifts), that it is the grace that Christ gives to a believer (Eph. 4:7) that qualifies him or her to be Christ's gift to the Church. In this list the five[22] gifts (sometimes called "offices") are identified as apostles, prophets, evangelists, pastors, and teachers.

The way God gives grace to meet the Church's needs with these gifts is through the people God sends as their leaders. These leaders' work is to equip the members of the Body for ministry, so that the Church might grow in unity, orthodoxy,[23] and maturity—growing into complete Christ-likeness. Apostles establish works for God. Prophets speak as mouthpieces for God. (A person who prophesies with regularity and is judged to be accurate and anointed may come to be recognized as a prophet.) Evangelists proclaim the "good news," helping people come to Jesus in salvation. Pastors care for the flock of God. Teachers train the flock of God.

In the New Testament, the highest spiritual leadership gift is an apostle. If a woman could serve as an apostle, it would follow that she could serve in any other office. Were there any women apostles in the New Testament? Yes, Junia in Romans 16:7. (See Chapter 8 under "Romans 16:1-7, 12-13, 15.")

What is the New Testament theology of spiritual gifts and women? As Robert Clinton, noted author on leadership, explains, God gifts both men and women with natural abilities; God helps both men and women to acquire leadership skills; and God gifts both men and women with spiritual gifts. Clinton concludes concerning gender and leadership, "Definitions of leader, leadership, and power bases for influencing including giftedness are not gender biased. And I have strongly emphasized that both males and females can lead and exercise leadership with gifted power."[24] The New Testament also teaches that those gifted by God are responsible to employ their gifts for one another as good stewards of God's great grace (1 Pet. 4:10).

Destined to become one of the greatest female evangelists ever, Maria Underwood [Woodworth-Etter] felt God's call at age thirteen (1858). She said,

> I heard the voice of Jesus calling me to go out in the highways and hedges and gather in the lost sheep. ... I had never heard of women working in public except as missionaries, so I could see no opening—

> except as I thought, if I ever married, my choice would be an earnest Christian and then we would enter upon the mission field.[25]

Her marriage to an ex-soldier/farmer did not result in ministry, so she struggled with her call. They lost five of their six children to illnesses before Maria's rededication to the Lord in 1879. She was "baptized with the Holy Ghost, and fire."[26] Still she hesitated and tried to study further, even as she prayed for her husband's permission to go out in ministry. In her struggle, she thought, "If I were a man it would be a pleasure for me, but for me, a woman, to preach, if I could, would subject me to ridicule and contempt ... and bring reproach upon our glorious cause."[27] After seeing a vision of Jesus, finding examples in the Bible of how God used women to lead, and studying Acts 2, Maria was convinced that "women are required to work for the advancement of Christ's cause."[28]

She began holding revival meetings in Ohio and planting churches (about age thirty-six). During the first year and a half, she

> held four revivals, organized two churches—one of them with about seventy members—and a Sabbath-school of about one hundred scholars ... had preached in twenty-two meeting houses and four school-houses, for eight different denominations, and had delivered two hundred sermons.[29]

In 1885 Maria Woodworth began conducting healing services as well, eventually traveling widely with an 8,000-seat tent, attracting publicity and winning converts around the country. She preached powerfully to a crowd of 25,000 in Indiana and then to thousands in California in 1889. From the time of her five-month crusade in Dallas in 1912 (at age sixty-eight), she remained a highly respected evangelist in the Pentecostal movement the rest of her life.

Her books went out as missionaries; as many as 25,000 copies sold between 1912 and 1921. Abridged versions were translated into French, Italian, Danish, Swedish, Egyptian, Hindustani, and other dialects of India and South Africa. In the preface to the fifth edition of *Signs and Wonders* in French, a national minister said, "The Pentecostal revival in France can be attributed in certain measure to the ministry of Woodworth's books."[30]

The complete title of her autobiography is *Signs and Wonders God Wrought in the Ministry for Forty Years*. In it Woodworth-Etter explains the reason for her bold obedience to God. Here's a paraphrase of her reasoning: When a woman is called by God, how can she be obedient without answering the call? How can you doubt the call when God himself confirms it with miraculous power?[31] The logic she used to conclude that women may minister and lead in the Church is the same logic the first-century "apostles and elders" used to conclude that Gentiles may become Christ's followers—the evidence of the Holy Spirit's work of grace and power (Acts 15:6, 7-9, 12). How did the Jerusalem Council perceive that God makes no distinctions between people? They witnessed God's grace in salvation and God's power in signs and wonders. They saw God's intent confirmed in Scripture (Acts 15:15-18). So they concluded, "We should not make it difficult for the Gentiles who are turning to God" (Acts 15:19).

Woodworth-Etter experienced God's grace and was convinced from examples in Scripture that God used women to lead. She resolved that she must obey. And God himself confirmed His calling with forty years of signs and wonders. As the first church concluded, may today's church also say, "We should not make it difficult for the women who are obeying God."

Galatians 3:26-29

So in Christ Jesus you are all children of God through faith, for all of you who were baptized into Christ have clothed yourselves with Christ. There is neither Jew nor Greek, neither slave nor free, neither male nor female, for you are all one in Christ Jesus. If you belong to Christ, then you are Abraham's seed, and heirs according to the promise.

This passage (and especially verse 28) has been called the Magna Carta[32] of Christian Equality. Amidst the Judaizers'[33] propaganda, Paul says all people who believe on Christ—Jews and Greeks, slaves and free persons, males and females—are all children of God. The curious use of "sons" instead of "children" (at verse 26) in some translations is not sexist, gender-exclusive language. Paul calls believers "all sons of God through faith in Christ Jesus" (NIV) to emphasize maturity. "Sons" are those who have left spiritual infancy and are mature, full-fledged saints—heirs, with direct access to God. Gentile believers are no longer "shirt-tail relatives of God" who are judged to be inferior. Believing slaves are no longer servants who do not qualify for the rights and privileges of the free born. Female believers are no longer excluded from inheritance rights. Instead, through faith in Christ Jesus, all believers are "sons" of God.

Through baptism, believers are clothed in Christ. Baptism is a rite in which women can participate as freely as men. It replaces circumcision as the sign of Christ's New Covenant. Our former identities and the hierarchical biases based upon them matter no more. Believers are covered with a new identity—that of "Christian."

Those who belong to Christ are Abraham's offspring. Gentile converts are not direct, physical descendants of Abraham. Under Judaism, they would only be "second-class" Jews at best. Even if they were to do all they possibly could do to convert to Judaism—including males' submission to circumcision—they would still be only proselytes. But if they belong to Christ, though they are not descendants in the flesh, they are his *true* seed—the spiritual descendants of Abraham—"heirs according to the promise" (3:29).

In Christ there is neither Jew nor Greek, neither slave nor free person, neither male nor female. We are all one in Christ. What does this mean? It does not mean that we lose our gendered identity and become unisex any more than Christian Jews stop speaking Hebrew. The importance of those differences, however, *as a basis of discrimination* is wiped out. Hierarchical distinctions are abolished, done away with, in Christ Jesus. It is obvious, by the fact that this text transforms traditional Jewish thinking, that this passage is normative—a timeless truth. The apostle Paul wrote it with the specific purpose of putting right any teaching that has strayed from truth.

Ephesians 5:21

Submit to one another out of reverence for Christ.

The verse following this normative text, is a text often quoted all by itself: "Wives, submit yourselves to your own husbands as you do to the Lord" (Eph. 5:22).[34] When a text is quoted by itself, one may actually be misrepresenting its true meaning in its original context.

Context is absolutely critical to this verse, since Ephesians 5:22 is not a complete sentence in the original. It has no verb. Literally, the verse reads, "wives to your own husbands in the Lord." What is missing must be supplied from the preceding verse, that is, the first half of the sentence. This means that verse 22 must always be interpreted in light of verse 21. And what is verse 21? "Submit to one another out of reverence for Christ." The pattern for the Christian home is *mutual* submission.

Note the surrounding context in which we find this pattern for Christian family life. Paul presents mutual submission (5:21-6:9) as one of the four evidences of living in the Spirit (5:18-6:20), along with spiritual worship (5:19), perpetual thanksgiving (5:20), and spiritual warfare (6:10–20). The section on living in the Spirit (5:18-6:20) finds itself within a larger literary context as one of the four characteristics of the believer's walk (5:15-6:20), including walking in wisdom (5:15), redeeming the time (5:16), and understanding the will of the Lord (5:17). Paul's placement of this passage in this setting shows that mutual submission is an essential characteristic of walking in the Spirit and even of living in Christ!

5:15-6:20 THE BELIEVER'S WALK

(1) WALKING IN WISDOM 5:15

(2) REDEEMING THE TIME 5:16

(3) UNDERSTANDING THE WILL OF THE LORD 5:17

(4) LIVING IN THE SPIRIT 5:18-6:20

- (a) Spiritual Worship 5:19
- (b) Perpetual Thanksgiving 5:20
- (c) Mutual Submission 5:21-6:9
- (d) Spiritual Warfare 6:10-20

This portion of Scripture (Eph. 5:21–6:9) is actually a *Haustafel* (a domestic code). In the first century many Gentiles had these domestic codes, or tables of rules concerning the household, posted on the walls of their homes. Paul took this code and Christianized it. The great changes he made can be seen when this passage is compared with other household codes from the first century.

In Paul's domestic code, "Submit to one another out of reverence for Christ" (Eph. 5:21) is the topic sentence, setting the tone, for the whole discussion that follows. Individuals in three pairs of relationships, are to relate to each other out of reverence to Christ. Mutual submission is expected of husbands and wives. The role of the wife is to show honor and respect to her husband; the role of the husband is to love *(agapein)* her. In the other two pairs of relationships (slaves and masters, children and parents), Paul changes the verb from "submit" to "obey," but he still expects the same kind gracious behavior out of reverence to Christ to be part of those relationships (in both directions). Slaves are to work diligently; masters are to treat slaves with the same respect they expect to receive. Fathers are to nurture their children; and children are to obey their parents. Where these guidelines are followed, abuse is nonexistent. Life under the Golden Rule is fair, just, and peaceful for all.

Even though it was not customary in first-century society,[35] this scripture tells husbands to *love* their wives. This is a striking command in its historical setting. And the model for a husband's love is Christ's *agape* (love). *Agape* is self-giving love. Paul teaches husbands to love their wives "just as Christ loved the church and gave himself up for her" (v. 25). *Agape* is giving up one's own desires for the best good of another. What a fine definition of submission! Respect and honor from the wife and true *agape* love from the husband are descriptions of the mutual submission expected of all Christians in relationships (compare verses 21 and 33).

In this passage, also, the term *kephale* is found (v. 23). The husband's role as *head* of his wife is likened to Christ's relationship with the Church. Here also, the word *kephale* is used figuratively. The metaphorical meaning "source" for *kephale* fits this context, although not in terms of source or origin in creation, but in terms of source or origin of grace, favor, or enablement.

Agape is love for the sake of the object (not for the sake of the subject). It is what one person does for another person, not what they get out of the other. It is knowing what someone needs and willingly giving it. The goal of Christ's love for the Church is "to make her holy, … and to present her to himself as a radiant church, without stain or wrinkle or any other blemish, but holy and blameless" (Eph. 5:26–27). This is the analogy for the husband's being "the head of the wife as Christ is the head of the church, his body, of which he is the Savior" (5:23). "In this same way, husbands ought to love their wives as their own bodies. … After all, people never hated their own bodies, but they feed and care for them, just as Christ does the church" (5:28–29).

As the head of the Church, our Savior, Jesus Christ, gave up His life to bring us into divine perfection (v. 25). So also the role of the husband, as head, is to express mutual submission. He surrenders his desires (v. 27), in order to bring his wife to her highest fulfillment. When the husband is the source of his wife's enablement, when he is the one who encourages her personal growth, then he is being the head of his wife as Christ is the head of the Church. This is the biblical view of headship.

A wife married to such a husband, finds it much easier to fulfill her part of the command to mutual submission. Out of reverence to Christ, she reverences her husband in all things. She doesn't need to be subjected by her husband, but willingly submits herself and her desires to him in the same way she does to the Lord. When both spouses practice mutual submission there is harmony in the home.

Ephesians 5:21 gives a strong theological corrective to the abuses of patriarchy, harsh parenting, and tyrannical slave masters. Although the world has endured these kinds of practices for thousands of years, mutual submission has been the goal of Christ for all His followers' relationships since the Church began. Out of their reverence to Christ, His followers are to submit themselves as is appropriate of their own free will. This verse is a theological text of timeless truth. Its normative nature is seen in the way the apostle Paul transformed a tradition. His first readers would have recognized the literary form, the *Haustafel*, and Paul's radical change of it. In this way Paul confronted the chaos of his culture to set forth God's creation ideals.

1 Peter 2:5, 9 (and Revelation 1:5b-6[36])

> You also, like living stones, are being built into a spiritual house to be a holy priesthood, offering spiritual sacrifices acceptable to God through Jesus Christ.
>
> But you are a chosen people, a royal priesthood, a holy nation, God's special possession, that you may declare the praises of him who called you out of darkness into his wonderful light.

In the Old Testament, women were excluded from the priesthood in the religion of Israel. In the New Testament, however, women are a part of the priesthood of all believers. No longer is a human go-between necessary for God's people to communicate with Him. Since Christ came, He is the only mediator needed (1 Tim. 2:5). All believers have direct access to God. All believers are thus priests in their own right. The Church is a new nation of priests, mediating the light of Jesus Christ to this dark world.

In this text the apostle Peter teaches the New Testament theology regarding priests. This, too, is a normative text, which takes precedence over the Old Testament restrictions. No longer is priesthood an exclusive role, limited to a few males (from a certain family in a certain tribe) qualified by heredity. In Christ's new nation every man or woman, boy or girl, can be a priest unto God.

Conclusion

As the New Testament teaches theology, the end times are emphasized. In these last days God's blessings and ministries are equally available for women and for men.

These normative texts declare that in Christ's new creation sexual hierarchical distinctions are abolished. Marriages are to be egalitarian; submission is to be mutual. Ministry and church leadership are open to all whom the Holy Spirit so gifts. And headship, as modeled by Christ, is the encouragement of personal and spiritual fulfillment.

CONCEPTS AND SCRIPTURES CONSIDERED IN CHAPTER 7

NORMATIVE TEXTS IN THE NEW TESTAMENT

The teachings of the Early Church regarding women are grounded in the example of Jesus. The theological texts address "the way things ought to be."

- **Acts 2:17-18** teach that the Holy Spirit equips all kind of people for ministry, regardless of gender, age, class, etc.
- **1 Corinthians 7** teaches that Christian marriage is a relationship of mutuality and reciprocal authority.
- **1 Corinthians 11:11-12** teach the interdependence of male and female.
- **1 Corinthians 12-14 (Ephesians 4:4-16; and Romans 12:3-8)** expand on Acts 2, demonstrating the diversity of spiritual gifts available to any person to whom the Holy Spirit chooses to give them.
- **Galatians 3:26-29** emphasize that hierarchical distinctions based on gender, race, or class are abolished in Christ.
- **Ephesians 5:21** gives the pattern for Christian relationships—mutual submission.
- **1 Peter 2:5, 9 (Revelation 1:5b-6)** explain that the Church is a new nation of priests. All God's people now serve in what was once an exclusive role.

CHAPTER 8

WOMEN IN THE NEW TESTAMENT CHURCH: HISTORICAL TEXTS

THE OLD TESTAMENT reveals foundational truths regarding God's women as it shows God's original design in creation. Though sin distorted that ideal, Jesus came to reverse the effects of the Fall.

Among the New Testament passages that express theology on the women's issue, a key text is Acts 2:17-18, which asserts that the Holy Spirit equips all kinds of people equally (including male and female) for God's work. In full agreement are 1 Corinthians 12-14, Romans 12:3-8, and Ephesians 4:4-16, which do not specify any restrictions of spiritual gifts on the basis of gender. Paul, in Galatians 3:26-29, echoes equality when he explains that in Christ "there is neither male nor female." Paul goes on to the theology of mutuality in marriage in 1 Corinthians 7. Verse 4 explains that the husband has authority over his wife's body and that the wife has authority over her husband's body. In Verse 5 the Apostle commands couples' intimacy in marriage. Ephesians 5:21 commands mutual submission; and 1 Corinthians 11:11-12 negates the independence of either gender, mandating their interdependence and unity.

The creation account describes God's ideal for male-female relationships with four characteristics: equality, mutuality, unity, and intimacy. The Fall into sin distorted them: equality was ignored, subordination was imposed, unity was severed, and intimacy was thwarted. But Christ reversed the effects of the Fall by paying sin's penalty with His death. The New Testament makes this clear in its theological texts on male-female relationships. Note how all four ideals were restored: equality (Acts 2:17-18; Gal. 3:26-29), mutuality (1 Cor. 7:4), unity (1 Cor. 11:11-12), and intimacy (1 Cor. 7:5).

God's Ideal Seen in Creation	God's Ideal Marred by Sin	New Testament Theology Restores God's Ideal
Equality	Equality ignored	Equality restored in Christ and by the Holy Spirit Galatians 3:26-29; Acts 2:17-18
Mutuality	Subordination imposed	Mutuality Reestablished 1 Corinthians 7:4; Ephesians 5:21
Unity	Unity severed	Unity Reinforced 1 Corinthians 11:11-12
Intimacy	Intimacy thwarted	Intimacy Encouraged 1 Corinthians 7:5

The focus of this chapter is the historical record of the way things were in the first-century church. The texts of this chapter simply describe the kinds of things women did in the earliest church.

The following four texts, from each of the four Gospels, record how women were commissioned and testified of the Resurrection.

Matthew 28:9-10

Suddenly Jesus met them [Mary Magdalene and the other Mary]. "Greetings," he said. They came to him, clasped his feet and worshiped him. Then Jesus said to them, "Do not be afraid. Go and tell my brothers to go to Galilee; there they will see me."

Mark 16:7, 9-11

[And the young man, wearing a white robe, said to Mary Magdalene, and Mary the mother of James, and Salome] "But go, tell his disciples and Peter, 'He is going ahead of you into Galilee. There you will see him, just as he told you.'"

When Jesus rose early on the first day of the week, he appeared first to Mary Magdalene, out of whom he had driven seven demons. She went and told those who had been with him and who were mourning and weeping. When they heard that Jesus was alive and that she had seen him, they did not believe it.

Luke 24:10-11

It was Mary Magdalene, Joanna, Mary the mother of James, and the others with them who told this to the apostles. But they did not believe the women, because their words seemed to them like nonsense.

John 20:14-18

At this, she turned around and saw Jesus standing there, but she did not realize that it was Jesus.

He said to her, "Why are you crying? Who is it you are looking for?"

Thinking he was the gardener, she said, "Sir, if you have carried him away, tell me where you have put him, and I will get him."

Jesus said to her, "Mary."

She turned toward him and cried out in Aramaic, "Rabboni!" (which means Teacher).

Jesus said, "Do not hold on to me, for I have not yet ascended to the Father. Go instead to my brothers and tell them, 'I am ascending to my Father and your Father, to my God and your God.'"

Mary Magdalene went to the disciples with the news: "I have seen the Lord!" And she told them that he had said these things to her.

Acts tells of the female disciple, Dorcas, and of Philip's four unmarried daughters who prophesied.

Acts 9:36 and 21:8-9

In Joppa there was a disciple named Tabitha (in Greek her name is Dorcas); she was always doing good and helping the poor.

Leaving the next day, we reached Caesarea and stayed at the house of Philip the evangelist, one of the Seven. He had four unmarried daughters who prophesied.

First Corinthians discusses the behavior expected of women who participate in public prayer and prophetic ministry in the congregation.[1]

1 Corinthians 11:4-5

> Every man who prays or prophesies with his head covered dishonors his head. But every woman who prays or prophesies with her head uncovered dishonors her head—it is the same as having her head shaved.

The next two passages list some of Paul's co-workers in the gospel. Paul's high regard for his female co-laborers in the ministry is in sharp contrast to the traditional Jewish limitations placed on women's social and religious involvements. Paul mentions a host of female Christian workers and offers them highest praise.

Philippians 4:2-3

> I plead with Euodia and I plead with Syntyche to be of the same mind in the Lord. Yes, and I ask you, my true companion, help these women since they have contended at my side in the cause of the gospel, along with Clement and the rest of my co-workers, whose names are in the book of life.

The verb for "contended at my side," "shared my struggle," "struggled together," or "co-labored," *synatheleo,* is a common descriptor of those involved in ministry. Euodia and Syntyche worked hard for Christ and Paul recognized them for such.

The term "fellow-worker" or "co-worker," *synergos,* is the word Paul usually used for his male colleagues in full-time ministry, for example, Timothy, Barnabas, Apollos, Luke, Demas, Epaphroditus, Clement, and himself. By including Euodia and Syntyche among his "co-workers," Paul identifies them as ministers. Some people believe that Euodia and Syntyche, along with Lydia, were probably wealthy women who hosted and led congregations in their homes (house churches).[2]

Romans 16 names a multitude of ministering persons. Ten of them were women.

Romans 16:1-7, 12-13, 15

> I commend to you our sister Phoebe, a deacon of the church in Cenchrea. I ask you to receive her in the Lord in a way worthy of God's people and to give her any help she may need from you, for she has been the benefactor of many people, including me.
>
> Greet Priscilla and Aquila, my co-workers in Christ Jesus. They risked their lives for me. Not only I but all the churches of the Gentiles are grateful to them.
>
> Greet also the church that meets at their house. …
>
> Greet Mary, who worked very hard for you.
>
> Greet Andronicus and Junia, my fellow Jews who have been in prison with me. They are outstanding among the apostles, and they were in Christ before I was.
>
> Greet Tryphena and Tryphosa, those women who work hard in the Lord. Greet my dear friend Persis, another woman who has worked very hard in the Lord.
>
> Greet Rufus, chosen in the Lord, and his mother, who has been a mother to me, too.
>
> Greet Philologus, Julia, Nereus and his sister, and Olympas and all the believers with them.

Phoebe. Phoebe was the letter carrier of the epistle to the Romans. As such she was given great responsibility—as Paul's forerunner to Rome. Paul requested a hearty reception for her—"give her any help she may need from you" and "receive her in the Lord in a way worthy of God's people." He gave her a high endorsement—"I commend (stand beside, express solidarity with, recommend, give approval, show, demonstrate, prove her value, display as an ideal) to you our sister Phoebe." All these facts show her high position of ministry in the church.

Unfortunately, biases of modern English translators have sometimes obscured this fact, calling her a "servant," "helper," or "dear

Christian lady." Yet Phoebe was *diakonos* of the church at Cenchrea. This is a term often used by Paul for a minister or leader of a congregation. Paul used it in referring to Jesus Christ, Apollos, Tychicus, Epaphras, Timothy, and to his own ministry (Rom. 15:8; 1 Cor. 3:5; Eph. 6:21; Col. 1:7; 1 Tim. 4:6; 1 Cor. 4:1). When the term appears in the plural and in conjunction with bishops (overseers) or elders, it is translated "deacon." When it appears in isolation from bishop/overseer or elder or when it is in the singular, it is translated "minister." Yet, because of a prejudice of many modern translators against female ministry, her leadership status is often hidden.

To render *diakonos* as "deaconess," as do the *Phillips* paraphrase, *Jerusalem Bible* (JB), and the *Revised Standard Version* (RSV), is not quite accurate either.[3] The term in this text (Rom. 16:1) is not the feminine, *diakonissa*, but a masculine noun. Though it is irregular for a woman to be described by a masculine noun, it is not a grammatical error. When, in Greek, a female is associated with a masculine noun the term is an official or ecclesiastical title. Paul called Phoebe *diakonos* of the church at Cenchrea because he was precisely identifying her as its "minister" (or, though less likely, "deacon").

In the past several decades, much scholarly effort has been focused on women deacons and deaconesses in the Early Church. It has been learned that the order of deaconess *(diakonissa)* was not even present at Phoebe's time, but was the creation of the later Roman (Catholic) church to restrict the role of ministering women to serve women only. If Phoebe were a deacon (as opposed to a minister), however, her role was the same as any deacon of the first century. It is inaccurate and belittling, therefore, to call her a deaconess.[4]

The translation "helper" (NASB, RSV) for *prostatis*, is poor and biased also. The verb from which it comes, *prostasso*, means "to rule, order, command, be put in charge over," and was used for significant church leaders. Similarly, the noun (appearing in both masculine and feminine forms in ancient Greek, both pagan and

Christian literature, as an official title for particular religious leaders) is a strong word which means "leader, governor, ruler, patron,[5] commander, guardian, defender, succourer." Montgomery's translation here is "overseer."

What a model to female ministers, this woman Phoebe![6]

Priscilla. Priscilla and Aquila are listed next. They are also (as were Euodia and Syntyche) described as Paul's "co-workers in Christ Jesus." Four out of the six times this couple is mentioned in the New Testament, the wife's name precedes her husband's (Acts 18:1–3, 18, 24; Rom. 16:3–4; 1 Cor. 16:19; 2 Tim. 4:19). This is highly irregular in an ancient text, where the husband's name is "supposed" to come first. Why is this not the case with Priscilla and Aquila?

Acts 18:1-3 is the first time Luke mentions this couple. True to cultural convention, when Luke introduces them by name, it is husband first, then his wife. But as the story unfolds, Paul gets so close to these his co-workers that when he leaves Corinth to embark on the next leg of his missionary journey the couple accompanies him (v. 18). Already, Luke (recording Paul's story) switches the order of names and lists Priscilla first. (The couple was with Paul when he had his hair cut in Cenchrea because of a vow he had taken. That means Priscilla got acquainted, there, with another female minister whom Paul admired—Phoebe who ministered in Cenchrea.) When Paul moved on from Ephesus, he left Priscilla and Aquila (wife's name first again) to minister in his absence (v. 19). When the couple met up with Apollos it is Priscilla and Aquila (wife's name first, vv. 24-26) who "explained to him the way of God more adequately." Luke, a polished Greek author, careful and accurate, would not break literary traditions without purpose. He was so impressed with Priscilla, that he listed her name first intentionally.

Paul mentions or addresses the couple three times in his writings. These are the references in *chronological order*: 1 Cor. 16:19; Rom. 16:3–4; 2 Tim. 4:19. Only in 1 Corinthians (his first reference to them) does Paul list Aquila's name first (1 Cor. 16:19). The more Paul gets to know this couple, the more he loves them both, and the more he respects Priscilla (Rom. 16:3–4). In his last farewell of his final epistle, Paul breaks with cultural convention again, to honor Priscilla by greeting her first.

What was it about Priscilla that so impressed both of these Bible authors? It was most likely her ministry and leadership. Of the two, Priscilla and Aquila, she played the more prominent spiritual role. Note well that there is no disgrace in that fact. Both Aquila and Priscilla were fine Christians. The couple, and Aquila in particular, is not put down for letting his wife exercise her leadership. Both women and men in the New Testament fully used all of their gifts in God's service, even if a wife's gifts might have surpassed her husband's in a given area. Such a scenario seems not to have disturbed Paul in the least. Instead of Priscilla's actions prompting a rebuke from Paul, her spiritual leadership received his warm affection and hearty affirmation.

Priscilla must have been a very capable person. Ancient Church Father, Origen, was so impressed by her that in his commentary on 1 Corinthians (paragraph 74), he said that Priscilla's example legitimated women's teaching ministry.[7]

German scholar, Adolf Harnack, suggested Priscilla might be the unknown author of the anonymous epistle to the Hebrews.[8] And there is good evidence to support it. Prisca/Priscilla is a name associated with Greek women of wealth. As such she was most likely very well-educated. The epistle to the Hebrews is written in the sophisticated, polished Greek of an upper-class educated person. Priscilla had converted to Judaism, and later with her husband, converted to Christianity. Hebrews reflects an intimate understanding of Judaism, the Temple, and the Jewish sacrificial system. Since this couple had lived with and labored together (both professionally, as tent-makers, and in the ministry) with the apostle Paul, Priscilla would have known Paul very well. The style and content of Hebrews is very similar and yet distinguishable from Paul's.

Even the fact that the epistle is anonymous is an argument in her favor. What motivation would lead a New Testament author to leave a letter unsigned? Had someone like Paul, Luke, Barnabas, or Clement written Hebrews, including his signature on the epistle would have increased the likelihood of its reception by the Church at large. Perhaps *not* leaving a clue as to its authorship, however, was the only way for a woman's work to be accepted (especially amid the Judaistic tendencies prevalent among the recipients of the letter to the Hebrews). But by leaving it anonymous, the epistle would have the opportunity to become circulated and accepted on the merit of its contents, in spite of the mystery of its authorship.

Thus, Priscilla has all the earmarks of the author of Hebrews—and perhaps to a degree superior to the other contenders.

Junia. Junia's name appears in verse 7. This person is considered foremost among the apostles. Her name has been commonly masculinized (that is, to *Junias*) in English translation. Many Christian scholars have been unwilling to admit that there could have ever been an apostle—the highest office in the Early Church—who was female.

Judging from grammatical case, *Iounian,* as the direct object of a verb could be either masculine or feminine. But in all ancient records and name lists there is "no evidence that Junias was used as a male name at this time."[9] Edwin Judge of Macquarie University in Sydney, Australia, perhaps the greatest scholar of papyri[10] today, states that in all extant records there has *never* been a male Junia.[11]

There was no doubt in the mind of the ancients that Junia was a female apostle. Church Father John Chrysostom (who died in AD 407)—though he was an opponent of women's ministry—was very impressed with Junia's commendation as a *woman apostle.*[12] It was not until Aegidius of Rome (1245-1346) masculinized her name in his commentary that it became the common reading.[13] And ever since then, Christians who deny ministry leadership to women have considered this apostle to be a man.

The *King James Version* maintains Junia's femininity, as does the *English Standard Version* (2001), the *New King James Version*, the *New Living Translation* (NLT), the NRSV, the *Revised English Bible*, and the TNIV. Most other modern translations,[14] in spite of the evidence, have kept her identity male. Such is the power of tradition and the presuppositions of translators.

Other women named. The sixteenth chapter of Romans names at least seven women who ministered with Paul as well as at least three others to be greeted. In addition to Phoebe, Priscilla, and Junia, verse 6 mentions Mary and verse 12, Tryphena, Tryphosa, and Persis. Julia, the sister of Nereus, and the mother of Rufus (and perhaps the mother of Paul) are also greeted. Paul describes the ministries of these women with verbs and nouns used exclusively of persons in official church leadership; and he offers these women highest praise.

Most scholars would agree that there was a fluidity of roles in the Early Church, meaning that titles were not yet fixed and functions were overlapping. The institutionalized hierarchy which did not allow women, however, was a later development of the Catholic church.

In the Pastoral Epistles there was recognition of both male and female leadership in the service of the church. Where leadership qualifications are listed, there are statements which apply equally to men and women, some which relate specifically to male candidates, and some which relate specifically to women. First Timothy 3:11 seems to address female deacons, and Titus 2:3 female elders.[15]

1 Timothy 3:11

In the same way, women who are deacons are to be worthy of respect, not malicious talkers but temperate and trustworthy in everything.

Most of the third chapter of 1 Timothy is devoted to a discussion of church offices. The first part of the chapter (verses 1–7) contains qualifications for the office of overseer (or bishop). The second part of the chapter (8–13) contains qualifications for deacons.

By *adding* a masculine qualifier (to verse 8) which is not present in the Greek,[16] (thus rendering the verse, "Deacons, likewise, are to be *men* worthy of respect") many English translations and paraphrases leave the impression that deacons must be male.[17] The KJV, TNIV, RSV, and TEV are accurate in *not* making these verses refer strictly to males.

Verse 11, in the original text, is unclear about which women the apostle is addressing. Most versions assume they are wives, but the NASB is literal in its translation: "Women must likewise be dignified, not malicious gossips, but temperate, faithful in all things" (1 Tim. 3:11). Who are these women?

Three options present themselves.[18] The Greek word refers either to (1) all Christian women in general, (2) deacons' wives, or (3) female deacons. Judging from context, option one seems most unlikely, since this verse falls in the center of a paragraph concerning deacons. Option number two has been the traditional interpretation based upon the false assumption that women were not allowed to serve in New Testament offices of ministry. That tradition remained largely unchallenged up to the rise of the early Fundamentalist/ Evangelical movement,[19] the birth of Pentecostalism,[20] and contemporary discoveries concerning the Early Church.[21]

Now that scholars have so much evidence for female deacons in the Early Church, consensus is shifting in favor of option number three. This can be seen in Bible footnotes (compare NASB, NIV, NEB) and serious commentaries. It seems very clear, therefore, that the words of 1 Timothy 3:11 are qualifications for female deacons.

Titus 2:3

Likewise, teach the older women [or better, women elders] to be

> reverent in the way they live, not to be slanderers, or addicted to much wine, but to teach [literally, "be teachers of"] what is good.

The New Testament displays a flexibility in roles and titles. The Holy Spirit equipped both men and women for leadership. Later, when the church became more institutionalized, criteria valued by the culture (such as class, status, political connections, or gender) became prerequisites for official church leaders. In the earliest period women are described in the same roles and identified with the same titles as men in leadership, including elders. This is often obscured by translators who look at texts from a perspective of later history.

One single word may be translated either as "female elder" or as "older women." (The same is true of the Greek word for "elder" and "older man.") Therefore, many times in the Pastoral Epistles, translators have to make a judgment as to how to render these terms. This is the issue in Titus 2:3 and perhaps 1 Timothy 5:2.

It is clear that an ecclesiastical position of elder emerged in the Early Church. There are ancient records of women serving in that office.[22] Titus 2:3 identifies certain women as "good teachers" or "teachers of what is good" with the masculine noun *kalodidaskalous*. Thus these women also seem to serve in an official role and bear an ecclesiastical title. The comments in Titus 2:3 (and perhaps 1 Timothy 5:2) may be comments applicable to female elders.

Conclusion

What do the historical texts of the New Testament teach about God's women then? The history of the first-century church confirms its theology. In other words, Christ's early followers "practiced what they preached." The first-century Christian community was very conscious of women.[23] As the New Testament describes church life, women are pictured as full participants in the church's services, equal recipients of all charismatic gifts, functioning in all the ministries and sharing the same titles from the level of saint, to and including the level of apostle.

In summary, then, the Church has, does, and will continue to encourage the full use of women's gifts in all levels of ministry, to the degree that it is convinced of their supernatural call and anointing for ministry.

CONCEPTS AND SCRIPTURES CONSIDERED IN CHAPTER 8

DESCRIPTIVE TEXTS IN THE NEW TESTAMENT

The New Testament serves as the historical record of the kinds of roles women played in the Early Church—"the way things were."

- **Matthew 28:9-10; Mark 16:7, 9-11; Luke 24:10-11; John 20 14-18** record that Jesus commissioned women to give the Resurrection message.
- **Acts 9:36; 21:8-9** tell about a female disciple, known for her good works, and four single women, known for their prophecies.
- **1 Corinthians 11:4-5** discuss the way women take part in public prayer and prophesying.
- **Philippians 4:2-3** describe two of Paul's co-workers in ministry, Euodia and Syntyche, possibly leaders of house churches.
- **Romans 16:1-7, 12-13, 15** list ten more esteemed women (as well as men), who served in a variety of roles: deacon/minister, teacher, church leader, apostle, and diligent workers with Paul in the cause of Christ. Especially exemplary are Phoebe, Priscilla, and Junia.
- **1 Timothy 3:11** gives qualifications for female deacons.
- **Titus 2:3 (1 Timothy 5:2)** describe female elders and teachers in the church.

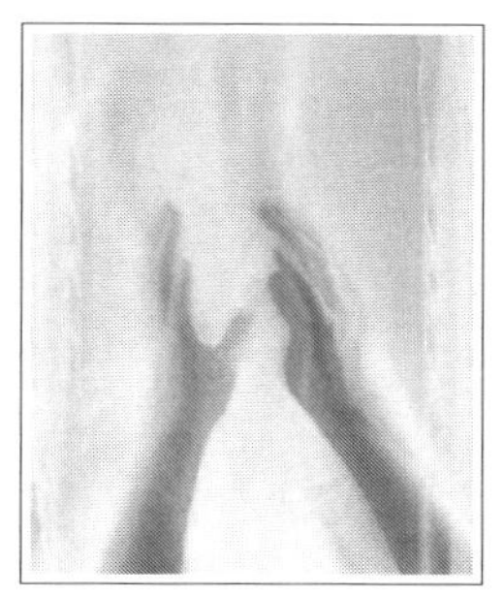

UNIT FOUR

SPECIFIC ISSUES IN LOCAL CHURCHES

CHAPTER 9

THE SITUATION IN CORINTH

WHAT ARE PROPER ROLES for God's women in the church, society, and the home? May they be leaders? These kinds of questions, often clustered under the term "the women's issue," are best answered from the Bible.

The Old Testament sets the foundation for God's high view of women. God created women in His own image, just as He created men. Throughout history, people who follow God have held women in higher regard than many of the surrounding pagan peoples. The New Testament displays Jesus as a model for us all. His life echoed God's high view of women, and His death reversed the effects of the Fall into sin.

The New Testament states clear theology on the women's issue. As for ministry, Acts 2:17-18 explains that the Holy Spirit equips all kinds of people (male or female) equally. Nowhere in the spiritual gifts passages (1 Cor. 12-14; Rom. 12:3-8; and Eph. 4:4-16) is there any indication that God's gifts are restricted by gender. The New Testament includes women in the priesthood of all believers (1 Pet. 2:5, 9, 10). As for marriage, 1 Corinthians 7 tells husbands and wives to share authority. First Corinthians 11:11-12 teaches men and women to see themselves as partners. Ephesians 5:21 urges both husbands and wives to submit to one another. And as for life in the Church, Galatians 3:26-29 explains that in Christ "there is neither male nor female." Though fallen cultures may follow a scripturally unsupported hierarchy, such distinctions do not hold in the new community Christ is creating among His followers.

Historical records describe the kinds of things God's women did in the New Testament church. Women witnessed the Resurrection first, before the men. Jesus commissioned the women to proclaim that news to His male followers. Women served in ministry without regard to their marital status. The New Testament identifies single, married, and widowed women in ministry. Women served the church as prophets. Women were permitted to pray publicly in church services. Women were ministers, leaders in the church. Females are described as serving in the same roles and identified by the same titles as male ministers. The apostle Paul highly praised numerous female leaders for their service unto the Lord. And historical records indicate that women's leadership continued in the Early Church after the New Testament era.[1]

Of all the passages in the New Testament that have any relation to the women's issue, only two remain to be considered here: 1 Corinthians 14:34-35 and 1 Timothy 2:11-12. In light of Jesus' high regard for women, and the New Testament's positive theology and glowing history of women's leadership in ministry, these two passages stand out from the others. Numerous texts examined in Chapter 8 evidence the apostle Paul's high praise of many women in ministry, by name. Yet in these final two texts, that same apostle Paul appears to be limiting women's leadership in the church.

How can a reader understand the seeming contradiction between these last two texts and all the others? What did these two texts mean to the original audience? How do they apply to women in churches today? How should they speak to believers of all times? Do these texts contain timeless truth or were they instruction for a particular time and place?

One principle of interpretation is *internal consistency*. That means, a document or an author agrees with themselves. Neither does the Bible contradict itself, nor would the apostle Paul contradict himself. Scripture has unity and integrity. When, in the Bible, students locate what appears to be a contradiction, they must look further. Studying the words, the grammar, the literary context, and historical setting is very beneficial. These help the student to keep both the big picture and all the details in view at the same time.

In-depth study of these two passages uncovers isolated issues that troubled these two specific local congregations. Though some details may remain unclear, the student can offer understandable solutions to what seem to be contradictions. Knowing the kind of problems Paul was dealing with in Corinth and Ephesus clarifies what these passages meant to the original audiences. Only when one sees what they meant then and there, can the texts be accurately applied here and now.

These final two passages are cases of biblical instruction directed to a particular time and place. What proves that the message of these two texts is limited to specific local problems? If these texts were to be taken out of their historical setting and applied to all women everywhere, they would be in conflict with timeless truths: the example of Jesus Christ, the theology of the Early Church, and the New Testament record of history. These passages, therefore, are *not* once-and-for-all prohibitions against women in ministry everywhere for all time, but corrections of specific local problems.

Just what kind of problems was the apostle Paul correcting? The texts themselves have left enough evidence to answer that question. The careful student of Scripture must take note of all the clues on the journey to discover the answer. The study of these passages comprises a short course in *hermeneutics,* that is, the art and science of interpretation.

1 Corinthians 14:34-35

> Women should remain silent in the churches. They are not allowed to speak, but must be in submission, as the law says. If they want to inquire about something, they should ask their own husbands

at home; for it is disgraceful for a woman to speak in the church.

Insights from the Book Itself

A careful student of Scripture reads verses not only by themselves, but also within the setting that surrounds them. This setting is called the *literary context.* When a small stone is dropped into a pool, it makes circles inside of circles. These are called *concentric circles.* Context—both literary and historical—consists of concentric circles. Verses near the one being studied are more closely related than verses far away. And, because each Bible author writes with an intentional purpose, the context of the whole book influences how one understands individual verses. In fact, the Bible as a whole is the largest of the concentric circles of literary context. The principles of internal consistency, unity, and integrity affirm that Scripture itself provides the primary context for interpretation.

What evidence from literary context sheds light on the meaning of this verse? That is, what specific problem in Corinth was Paul addressing? All of the following clues are present in the Bible.

Scriptural Precedent. New Testament theology and history have commended the speaking ministry of women in the church. Could Paul be prohibiting in this passage what he commended in others?

Internal Consistency of the Letter. Within the very book, the first epistle (letter) to the Corinthians, just three chapters earlier (11:5), the apostle Paul permitted women to pray and prophesy publicly in the church. First Corinthians 11:5 is in the context (verses 2-16) of a discussion on hairstyles or head coverings considered culturally proper for men and women who minister in public church services. (Note the reference to churches: v. 16.) The kinds of ancient hairstyles and head coverings Paul referred to are not precisely clear to us today. But such is no problem, because those restrictions were for a specific time and place. The timeless truth of this text, however, is that both then and now, Scripture permits women to pray and prophesy publicly in church services. If Paul allowed women to pray and prophesy in the church in 1 Corinthians 11:5, what kind of speaking was he prohibiting in 1 Corinthians 14:34-35?

Repetition in the Chapter. In the very chapter, 1 Corinthians 14, three times Paul asked certain kinds of people to be silent. Each category was commanded to be silent, *not* always, but under specific circumstances. Compare Paul's three instructions for silence within the context of this chapter:

(v. 28)	*Tongues speakers*	must be silent if	*there is no interpreter present;*
(v. 30)	*prophets*	must be silent if	*another prophet has a revelation;* and
(v. 34)	*women*	must be silent if	. . .

Under what circumstances were women to be silent?

Insights from the Time and Place

Information surrounding the occasion of the writing of a book sets the biblical text in its *historical context.* Historical context means the setting in time and place. Bible tools, such as a study Bible, Bible handbook, dictionary, encyclopedia, atlas, introduction, or commentary can shed light on the events of history in the place a text was written to or from.

Historical information based on original ancient documents and records, called *primary sources,* is most reliable. And primary sources composed near the time and place of the biblical passage are more relevant than those from far away. Clues from history can send a reader back to the biblical text with new eyes to see what might have been missed without them. What historical clues shed light on the meaning of this verse?

Geography. Ancient Corinth was located on the narrowest part of the southern Greek peninsula, called Achaia, which separated

Asia (to the east) from Europe (to the west). By dragging small ships and the contents of large ships over land near Corinth, many days of dangerous travel could be avoided. Therefore, from the seventh century BC on, Corinth controlled the Italian and Adriatic trade routes. While their ships were being hauled west over land from the Aegean Sea (through the seaport of Cenchrea) to the Adriatic Sea (through the seaport of Lechaeum) or in the opposite direction, the sailors, merchants, and travelers had several days to spend in the city.

Corinth's east-coast seaport, Cenchrea, was home to Phoebe. She was Paul's chosen representative to hand-carry his epistle to the Romans, an illustrious leader, the deacon or minister of that congregation.[2] The people receiving Paul's first epistle to the Corinthians were probably close friends of Phoebe's. They knew of Paul's admiration for her ministerial leadership in the Cenchrean congregation. What kind of silence could he have been asking of women in the Corinthian church?

Urban Setting. Corinth was a bustling commercial city. There was much wealth and many ways to spend it. Alcohol and sexual immorality were among Corinth's vices. Because of its international contacts, this cosmopolitan city was host to many pagan religions and mystery cults.

Religious Setting. Corinth was also home to a Jewish synagogue. Stating "as the law says," as the basis for silencing women in the church, sounds more like something Judaizers[3] would say than like Paul. First Corinthians 1:12 lists the factions in the church. Those who identified their leader as Cephas, the apostle Peter's Hebrew name, might have been Judaizers.

What is the apostle Paul referring to when he silences women in Corinth? First, look at four weaker interpretations, in order from less likely to more likely. And finally, examine a strong interpretation, the mostly likely of interpretations.

Four Weaker Interpretations (Possible, but Less Likely)

Interpretation Number 1. This interpretation holds that women may serve the Church, but only in special circumstances, that is, in certain *parts* of the service or in certain *kinds* of church services. But women may not speak with authority in public worship gatherings.

Those who hold this interpretation suggest, for example, that women may be involved in music ministry, congregational singing, or personal testimonies. And, they may speak in private home meetings or teach children. But they should not teach male adults or lead public worship services. In other words, women may be participants in the service but must not have an authoritative, speaking role in ministry.

Problems with this theory are so many that it is the least likely of interpretations. First, there is no support for more than one kind of service (that is, public versus private) in the earliest church. *All* the services were held in homes. (It was not until the third century, when the Roman Empire became Christianized, that church buildings were permitted.)

Second, the hosts of the house churches were most often their leaders. And there were numerous female hosts of house churches: Mary, the mother of John Mark, presided over a Hellenistic house church in Jerusalem (Acts 12:12-17); Apphia presided, with two other leaders, over a house church in Colossae (Philem. 2); Nympha in Laodicea (Col. 4:15); Lydia in Thyatira (Acts 16:14-15); Phoebe at Cenchrea (Rom. 16:1); and Priscilla with her husband Aquila in Ephesus (Acts 18:19, 26; 1 Cor. 16:19) and Rome (Rom. 16:3-5).[4] These female leaders played an active, authoritative role and were praised by Paul for it.

Third, neither this text nor any other in the New Testament indicates any ministry role restrictions by gender. In fact, on the contrary, Paul permits women to pray and prophesy, and such roles were obviously very high-ranking ministry functions. Prophecy is esteemed as a spiritual gift to be desired,[5] and the New Testament addresses the topic of women prophesying in the church as if it were common and accepted in the first-century church (1 Cor. 11:5).

And fourth, those who prophesy in the church are qualified to judge the utterance gifts (validity and accuracy).[6] This authoritative ministry role (prophesying) was permitted to women in the New Testament. Thus this passage cannot be interpreted as Paul's limiting women's speaking in the church to private, non-authoritative participation.

Interpretation Number 2. These verses are referring to newly-converted women, teaching them what behavior did not belong in the church.

Though the state religions of the upper class Greeks and Romans restricted the participation of women, the pagan religions of the common people, called mystery cults, permitted it. State worship was formal and conducted mostly by professional male priests. Female priests (such as the Pythia at the oracle of Delphi) played a more trance-like, inspired role. The unintelligible prophecies of these women had to be interpreted and delivered by men. The worship of the mystery cults was enthusiastic and all those present—including women—took part. Hysterical shouting and wailing of women was a valued part of the meetings. Ancient texts record even the sounds and syllables they uttered.

Some scholars suggest that the apostle Paul may have been silencing the disruptive shouting of pagan women who had recently become Christians.[7] It is thought that these women were excited about participating in Christian worship but did not yet know how to behave properly in the church. So they acted the way women were supposed to act in pagan religions and cults.

Some lexical[8] support exists for this interpretation. The precise verb used for "to speak" in this text is not the most typical verb *(lego*[9]*)* but a slightly less common verb *(laleo)*. One use of the verb *laleo* meant non-regular speaking, such as hysterical cries and shouts which could not be understood. It is a verb the pagans used to refer to the loud "speaking" of women in mystery cults.

First Corinthians 11 shows that women were allowed to pray and prophesy in the Christian worship service. Appropriate participation was always welcomed. It must have been some kind of behavior that was causing chaos that Paul opposed. Perhaps the problem Paul was dealing with in Corinth is that newly converted women were expressing their spiritual zeal in inappropriate, pagan ways. Interpretation number 2 suggests that Paul was silencing this kind of shouting and wailing by women, which was disrupting the services.

There is a weakness of this interpretation, however. It is too narrow—referring only to formerly pagan women. Jewish or proselyte women might have made up the larger part of the congregation. It is not likely that they would have been involved in such kinds of shouting.

Interpretation Number 3. These are not the words of the apostle Paul, but words of his opponents that he quoted in order to refute them.[10]

The literary context of 1 Corinthians shows that Paul was writing the Epistle in response to oral reports of problems in the church brought by Chloe's people (1 Cor. 1:11), as well as in response to a letter delivered by Stephanas, Fortunatus and Achaicus (1 Cor. 16:17) detailing some of the congregational difficulties in Corinth. A number of times in the letter, Paul begins sections of his teachings with the words "now concerning" or "as you wrote" (5:1; 7:1, 25; 8:1, 4; 12:1; 16:1). Then, before offering his advice, response, or rebuke, he sometimes quotes their correspondence or oral reports. The verses surrounding 1 Corinthians 14:34-35 fit this possible scenario very well.

Text criticism further supports this interpretation. It is important to remember that, just as there were no chapter or verse markings in the ancient manuscripts, neither were there punctuation marks, capitalizations, paragraph indentations, or quotation marks. All of these were added later at the discretion of the editors.

The text of 1 Corinthians 14:33b–39 could be translated as follows:

> [Paul's quotation of his opponents:]
>
> As [you claim is true] in all the congregations of the people of God:
>
> "The women should remain silent in the churches. They are not allowed to speak, but must be in submission, as the law says. If they want to inquire about something, they should ask their own husbands at home; for it is disgraceful for a woman to speak in church."
>
> [Paul's refutation of their position:]
>
> [What?] Did the word of God originate with you? Or are you the only ones it has reached?
>
> If any think they are prophets, or otherwise gifted by the Spirit, let them acknowledge that what I am writing to you is the Lord's command. [And just three chapters earlier in my passage on worship behavior for women, I permitted their ministry in prayer and prophecy in the worship service].
>
> Those who ignore this [that is, my authority on this matter], will themselves be ignored.
>
> Therefore, my brothers and sisters, be eager to prophesy, and do not forbid speaking in tongues [even by the women]. But everything should be done in a fitting and orderly way (TNIV, except for bracketed remarks).

Such an interpretation turns the traditional understanding of this text on its head and makes Paul consistent with his other statements about women in ministry as well as his encouragement of the exercise of charismatic gifts. It has several points in its favor.

First, this interpretation deals well with the issue of "the law/Law" and with the so-called "un-Pauline" characteristics of this passage. Nowhere does the Old Testament make any statement that women "are not permitted to speak, but should be subordinate" or that "it is shameful for a woman to speak in public assemblies." Yet such teaching was very common in traditional materials of the time—such as has been seen in the writings of Josephus, Philo, and rabbinic literature. The "Cephas party" (one of the factions in the Corinthian congregation, 1 Cor. 1:12, see vv. 10-31) may have been Judaizers. As such, they would have held to the "traditions of the elders/fathers" (that is, the oral law), and thus required silence of women. In such a case, Paul (just as Jesus had in the Gospel arguments with the Pharisees) strongly opposed their raising of oral traditions to level of "law." Instead, he maintained that it was *he* who wrote the Lord's command. There is a real challenge to authority here—Paul was denying the validity of the *logion* (saying) they had claimed to be "law."

Second, perhaps the reason why Paul dealt twice (first in 1 Corinthians 11 and now in 1 Corinthians 14), with the issue of women speaking in church is that he was responding to two separate reports. For example, maybe Stephanas, Fortunatus, and Achaicus arrived subsequent to the delegation of Chloe's people. Though Paul had already responded to questions on worship behavior (that is, concerning woman's head covering in chapter 11), he had to return to the issue when the second aspect—women's silence—was raised (here in chapter 14).

There is, however, one weakness with this interpretation. The grammar of this passage is not quite consistent with the other known quotations in 1 Corinthians. Without the actual oral sources or written documents that Paul was responding to, one cannot be sure that all the quotations in 1 Corinthians have been identified. But in the case of the quotations that are more certain, Paul introduced them with a formula such as, "now concerning" or identified the source of his information about the problem he addressed. In the case of 1 Corinthians 14:33b-40, these telltale features of quotations are absent.

Interpretation Number 4. First Corinthians 14:34-35 records not the words of the apostle Paul, but of another party, such as the Judaizers. These words are not original to Paul's letter, but were added by someone else later, such as a scribe. An addition into an ancient manuscript is called a *textual interpolation.*

Scholar Robin Scroggs writes[11] that this statement (1 Corinthians 14:34–35) does not sound like Paul. Most notably the phrase "as the law/Law says" seems un-Pauline since the statement "women are to be in submission" does not appear anywhere in the five books of Moses which, to Paul, is "the Law." Also, Paul (the "Apostle of Grace") is not prone to base his arguments on "the Law."

Literary context and text criticism[12] lend support for considering these verses to be a scribal insertion. First, these two verses stand as a complete grammatical unit. That means they could have circulated independently as a *logion* (saying), perhaps attributed to Paul, to be inserted later by a scribe. Second, the text reads fine without verses 34–35 (*more* smoothly, in fact, without them, since they repeat several words). Third, ancient manuscripts contain these verses in a variety of different locations. Some manuscripts include the passage after verse 33, some after verse 40, still others include it twice—in both places, and sometimes the verses appear in a marginal note. Eventually, the textual tradition was settled. All late manuscripts include the verses in their present location. Such a textual history prompts the question of whether or not Paul's *original* letter contained these verses.

And fourth, there is good reason, from a period of history later than Paul's, for a scribe to want to *add* this text. The scribe may have wanted to support the practices of his present day and his church's current understanding of Paul. Perhaps that is how this passage entered 1 Corinthians.

The weakness of this interpretation, however, is that it does away with the verses rather than seeking to deal with them in the context.

The Strongest (Most Likely) Interpretation

A fifth interpretation is that the apostle Paul was not prohibiting women's vocal participation in worship or ministry that contributed to the church service. Instead, he was silencing continual talking that interrupted the church service.

Insights from Lexicology.[13] This interpretation is supported by lexical insights. Another frequent use of the verb *laleo* had the negative connotation of "noisy jabber" or "chatter," that is disruptive talking.

Insights from Grammar. The tense of the verb *laleo*[14] is not the most common tense (the aorist), but the less common Greek tense (the present) which emphasizes linear (on-going) action. Thus it is better translated "to keep talking." Paul is saying in verse 34, "[Women] are not allowed to *keep on talking,*" and in verse 35, "It is disgraceful for a woman to *continually chatter* in church." The kind of verbal action indicates that it is not women's vocal participation but the perpetual disruptive rumble of noise that is disallowed.

One theory (a sub-option of Interpretation Number 5) is that the disruptive chatter of the women was discussion with their husbands from a great distance away. It has been often taught that the New Testament church met in ancient synagogues and in spaces arranged like them, which had separate seating sections for men and for women. It has been thought that wives seated in the balcony were shouting down to their husbands on the main floor, or that wives on one side of a divider were calling out over the divider to their husbands on the other side. This would certainly be disruptive to a worship service! If spouses couldn't sit together, any discussion between them would disturb the rest of the congregation.

Recent archeological evidence, however, has proven that the ancient synagogue (in the Roman era, that is, New Testament times) did not have divided seating sections. Bernadette Brooten's study of the sites and inscriptions of the nineteen extant ancient synagogues[15] has greatly diminished the strength of this argument. On the other hand, there are places around the world today where congregations are segregated by gender. Thus, while it is easy to imagine that this could have been the situation in Corinth, it is not probable.

Insights from Literary Context. As mentioned above, three times in 1 Corinthians 14 Paul instructed categories of people to be silent in certain situations. In each case, the whole classification of people was not silenced universally, but only in specific situations.

(v. 28)	*Tongues speakers*	must be silent if	*there is no interpreter present;*
(v. 30)	*prophets*	must be silent if	*another prophet has a revelation;* and
(v. 34)	*women*	must be silent if	*they are continually talking in church.*

The literary context (v. 35) offers two clear clues (found in the verbs emphasized below) as to the precise nature of the disruptive chatter these women were probably making. "If they want to *inquire* about something, they should *ask* their own husbands at home" [emphasis added].

Insights from Cultural Context. The secular cultural context of ancient Corinth provides clues as to why women might have more questions than men. Common women were greatly disadvantaged in the first century, both socially and educationally, and they were forbidden participation in most religions. In the Christian congregation, where women were given equality as full-fledged equal participants, they would likely have had many more religious questions and far fewer social graces than men. The surprising thing, however (considering the day and age in which Paul wrote), is that the Apostle wanted these women to learn! He encouraged wives to ask their husbands and expected Christian husbands to teach their wives about spiritual things—practices that were discouraged in Judaism.

Insights from Religious Context. The first-century Judeo-Christian religious context is most informative in its insights in support of this interpretation. Early Christian preaching was much different than preaching as it is presented in many places today. Jesus' preaching style (based on the rabbinic technique) was less of a monologue[16] and more of a group interactive discussion. Most of Jesus' teaching was in response to questions, and many were the questions that Jesus asked[17]—the more questions, the more teaching; the better the questions, the deeper the answers. But, if a certain segment of the congregation were to monopolize the discussion with questions that had no significance to others, the rest would not be edified.[18]

A biblical principle that the apostle Paul repeatedly emphasized in 1 Corinthians is that a believer must limit the exercise of their own freedom for the sake of others. See 1 Corinthians 6:1-20 (esp. 7b,12); 7:3-38 (esp. 10-12); 8:1-13 (esp. 9,12,13); 9:1-27 (esp. 12,15,19); 10:20-33 (esp. 23-24); and 11:33-34. Also in the spiritual gifts passages (chapters 12-14), Paul urges the body of Christ to care for all its parts, to operate the gifts in love, and to do all things to edify others.

In the case of tongues speakers, Paul says, "I would like every one of you to speak in tongues" (14:5). But "if there is no interpreter," the tongues "speaker should keep quiet" (14:28). In the case of prophets, Paul says, "You can all prophesy in turn so that everyone may be instructed and encouraged" (14:31). But if another prophet starts speaking, the first should stop (14:30). And in the case of women, Paul says that they may minister in prayer and prophecy in the church (11:5). But if they want to learn—and I sure want them to (see also 1 Tim. 2:11)—they should ask their own husbands at home; for it is disgraceful for women to be continually talking in church (see 14:35).

From 1981 to 1995 my family and I (Deborah) ministered among a group of people who had no previous connection with any church—or with American culture. They had recently arrived in our city from countries half a world away. How strange and different our ways seemed to them compared to the cultures of their homelands! In their background religious events were *social* gatherings, which involved bringing an offering or sacrifice to the place of worship and then chatting with friends.

We experienced such challenges communicating with each other. When they first arrived they knew no English; and we knew none of their languages. Yet the Lord was at work. Soon we had become dear friends to each other. We wanted so much to be able to understand each and learn each others' stories. The children and young people picked up English much faster than the adults and much faster than we learned their languages.

Among the adults the women seemed more interested in the Christian Faith than their husbands. They came faithfully, Sunday after Sunday, in spite of the struggles to understand. Sometimes in our services, especially in the early days, it was a challenge to just to keep the women from continually chatting with one another at a conversational volume.

Later, as they came to understand more, they had many questions. That thrilled us! But it also posed some problems. I remember at times a woman would interrupt the service calling out a question to her son while he was giving the sermon or interpreting it. She would carry on a conversation with him in her native tongue. The whole service would stop and the congregation wait while the dialogue went back and forth between the two of them. I remember thinking, "This is like the problem Paul was addressing in Corinth."

It was most effective when we could handle their questions in a Sunday school class of their own. There the discussions were lively; the mutual love and respect grew to be precious; and the learning was fruitful. In such a way the women would get their questions answered, and the congregation could be edified—"everything ... in a fitting and orderly way."

Conclusion

What did 1 Corinthians 14:34-35 mean to its original audience? It seems most likely that Paul was silencing the perpetual questions of new female converts in Corinth.

And how does it apply today? What is its message to readers of all times? This passage does not prohibit female leadership, but as does the rest of the chapter, it encourages that "everything [in Christian worship services] should be done in a fitting and orderly way" (14:40).

CONCEPTS AND SCRIPTURE CONSIDERED IN CHAPTER 9

WHY DID PAUL SILENCE THE WOMEN IN CORINTH?

Scripture agrees with itself; and the apostle Paul would not contradict himself. In light of God's ideals, Jesus' example, New Testament theology, Early Church history—and especially the praise of Paul for female leaders—1 Corinthians 14:34-35 could not be prohibiting women's speaking that contributed to the worship service. What, then, was the specific problem in Corinth that he was correcting?

These are the possibilities and their evaluations from least to most likely.

- Women may serve in the church, but only in certain parts or certain kinds of services.

  There is no biblical support for limiting women's participation in this way.

- Newly-converted women were interrupting the services with enthusiastic outbursts, appropriate in paganism, but inappropriate in Christianity.

Though this could be true of first-century pagan women, it has little application to women with a Jewish background.

- Paul was quoting words of his opponents in order to refute them.

  This passage does not have the clear evidence of other more certain quotations in 1 Corinthians.

- These are not the words of Paul, but of a later scribe.

  This interpretation removes the verses rather than interpreting them in their context.

- **Paul was not prohibiting women's speaking ministry, but the perpetual interruption of the service by their continual questions.**

  Paul did want the women to learn but not at the expense of the congregation.

And what is the application of this text to readers today?

- **Believers must limit the exercise of their own freedom for the good of others. The building up of the Body of Christ is to be a main concern of the members of His Body. That is why in the worship service all things must be done in a fitting and orderly way.**

CHAPTER 10
THE SITUATION IN EPHESUS

THE REMAINING TEXT FROM the New Testament related to women in the church is 1 Timothy 2:11-12. These verses, like 1 Corinthians 14:34-35, deal with an isolated issue specific to a local congregation. In this case, the church was in Ephesus. The pastor of the church in Ephesus at that time was Timothy. The one writing the corrective was the apostle Paul. And the nature of the problem Paul was correcting is the focus of this discussion.

I Timothy 2:11-12

> A woman should learn in quietness and full submission. I do not permit a woman to teach or to have authority over a man; she must be quiet.

Do all Christians agree with the interpretation that this text deals with a specific problem in the church of Ephesus? No, there are many Christians who hold a different opinion. Chapter 1: "The Bible and Women" illustrates two opposing views on women. Chapter 2: "Bible Answers to Today's Questions" explains how good people can come to different conclusions about Scripture. How then can the student of the Bible be sure which interpretation is correct? What did this text mean to its first readers and how does it apply today?

Reason for this Approach to the Text

What proves that the apostle Paul is correcting a specific problem in Ephesus and not prohibiting all women's leadership everywhere for all time? It is clear that this passage is a regulation limited to people where they were[1] for the following reasons. First, God's ideal in creation is equality. Second, though sin threatened to distort God's ideal, Jesus Christ restored it through His sinless life, sacrificial death, and resurrection. Jesus' life and teachings demonstrate that He valued and empowered women. Third, New Testament theology speaks to women. The Early Church held to norms consistent with Jesus' example. Passages teaching timeless truths[2] welcome the participation of women and endorse the full use of their gifts in ministry and leadership. Fourth, New Testament history[3] confirms that the Early Church practiced what it preached. The Book of Acts and the epistles record evidence of many women leaders in the Church. And the apostle Paul himself offers highest praise for his female co-workers in the ministry of the Church. Robert Clinton observes that prophecy is allowed for women in 1 Corinthians 14, pastoring in Romans 16 and Philippians 4, and also apostolic work and evangelism. He concluded, "If this [1 Tim.] passage were prohibiting leadership by women, it would have to deal with all the leadership gifts" not just the teaching gift.[4]

Thus, if Paul were prohibiting women's teaching and authority in this 1 Timothy text, he would be contradicting not only himself, but also New Testament theology, church history, and God's ideal, as expressed in many passages elsewhere. Since it is clear that Paul is correcting a specific local problem in Ephesus, the student of Scripture must dig deeper to determine the nature of the isolated issue addressed.

How is it possible to arrive at a different conclusion, that is, that these verses prohibit women's leadership? Note this powerful demonstration of the importance of the right starting point.

Everyone brings to Scripture a personal background that influences interpretation. This is called a presupposition. Careful students of Scripture must be objective. They should honestly recognize that one's history affects one's interpretation. At the same time, every student must be willing to evaluate and even change, if necessary, any opinion that is challenged by the evidence.

People who have made up their minds that women cannot lead or have influence over men see these verses as supporting their view. Such people select the two passages addressing isolated issues (1 Cor. 14:34-35 and 1 Tim. 2:11-12) as their foundation. They read the rest of the Bible's verses about women as exceptions in light of the only two texts that deal with local problems. In so doing, however, they disregard the mass of evidence of a far more normative nature: God's ideal, the nature of God relative to gender, Jesus' life and teachings, New Testament theology, and first-century church history. (This is one of the mistakes to avoid, discussed in Chapter 2.)[5] Relying uncritically on one's presuppositions often results in "proof-texting." That means, misusing the Bible by citing a small amount of evidence to try to confirm a position. Those who start with a view that women cannot lead, often base their whole argument on these two passages as proof-texts.

Here is the crux of the controversy regarding women in the church. To know with certainty the biblical position, a person must answer accurately these questions: What is normative; what is exceptional? What is God's ideal; which texts address local problems?

The right approach to Scripture is to start at the *beginning* and examine *all* the evidence. Let the Bible *itself* provide the verification as to which texts are timeless truths and which are not. Based on what the Bible presents as foundational, examine history for the records that have normative relevance. Interpret passages for people where they were in such a light. Let them speak to their original audience first. Only after gaining insight into what they meant to them then, can application be made to lives today.

Such errors of interpretation (that is, not challenging presuppositions and proof-texting) often go hand-in-hand with another error. Also mentioned in Chapter 2, is the mistake of taking verses out of context. It is often context that prompts the reader to dig deeper. What may appear to be a contradiction to a modern reader might be perfectly clear when set in its context (whether literary or historical). The original readers were fully aware of facts that a modern reader might have to research to find. The meaning of the passage can only be discovered after its setting is understood.

Several facts from the historical context of this text have a major bearing on what these verses meant to their original audience and thus how they apply to a contemporary audience today. There are three circles of context worth investigating for insights into this passage.

Insights from Context

Historical Context. The first significant context is the background of biblical history, specifically, the founding of the church in Ephesus. The Bible itself, in the Book of Acts, gives the reader the early history of the church in Ephesus.

Paul started the church in Ephesus near the end of his second missionary journey. He left Priscilla, along with her husband Aquila, in Ephesus to lead the new congregation in his absence. Paul intended to return to Ephesus if it were the Lord's will (Acts 18:19-21).

Priscilla[6] was one of Paul's favorite women in ministry. He knew her well, having lived in her and Aquila's home for a year and a half in Corinth (Acts 18:1-18, especially verses 3 and 11).[7] When Paul left Corinth, Priscilla and Aquila accompanied him to Ephesus (verse 18). She was one of Paul's most positive role models for women of all times.[8] Her husband, Aquila, was also a believer with a solid Jewish background. Yet both Paul and Luke seem to imply that Priscilla was a spiritual leader and the more prominent in public ministry of the two as a couple.[9] Scripture does not disparage the couple for these roles. Instead, Paul lauds them for their leadership, praises them both as models, and displays sincere affection for them as friends.

The church in Ephesus met in Priscilla and Aquila's home (Acts 18:19, 26; compare 1 Cor. 16:19-20). Later, after relocating back in their home city, Rome, another church met in their house there (Rom. 16:1). Scholars maintain that people who hosted New Testament house churches provided not only a place to meet, but also spiritual leadership for the congregations.[10]

While in Ephesus,[11] Priscilla and Aquila taught Apollos. God used her to adjust Apollos' theology. They "explained to him the way of God more adequately" (Acts 18:26). And who was Apollos? Luke records that he was a Jew, "a native of Alexandria," Egypt—one of the intellectual capitals of the Roman world:

> He was a learned man, with a thorough knowledge of the Scriptures. He had been instructed in the way of the Lord, and he spoke with great fervor and taught about Jesus accurately, though he knew only the baptism of John. He began to speak boldly in the synagogue (Acts 18:24-26).

That means Priscilla (a woman) taught a man (Apollos) under the commission of Paul (the apostle) in Ephesus (in the very church of the recipients of 1 Tim. 2:11-12). Priscilla's was a gracious manner. She did not address Apollos publicly in the synagogue, but invited him to her home (Acts 18:26). Perhaps during a service, among the Christian brothers and sisters that met there, she instructed him. Priscilla drew on her authority to spiritually influence another great leader of the church. This is the kind of ministry and leadership Priscilla exercised that the apostle Paul praised.

Because the original readers of 1 Timothy 2:11-12 knew Priscilla, they had insight into the limits of Paul's prohibition. Timothy and his Ephesian congregation were well aware of Paul's high regard for Priscilla's spiritual leadership. So were "all the churches of the Gentiles" (Rom. 16:3–4). And, by the time of Paul's second epistle to Timothy, Priscilla and Aquila had returned to Ephesus again (2 Tim. 4:19). Priscilla, in fact, might have been back in Ephesus and in Timothy's congregation at the time when this *first* letter was read to the church. Look at the text through the eyes of its first audience. They knew that the apostle Paul, who had left Priscilla to pastor this very congregation, was not prohibiting, once and for all, women as spiritual leaders. Historical context (especially, these details surrounding the founding of the church) disallows such an interpretation.

The Ephesian Christians also knew how much the apostle Paul despised the corrupting influence of false doctrine. What other historical insights on the situation Paul is dealing with in 1 Timothy 2:11-12 can be gained from context? Two more kinds of context are worth mentioning.

Literary Context. The second significant context is the literary context of the passage. Three concentric circles of literary context shed light on the kinds of problems Timothy was combating in Ephesus. Insights can be gained by reading verses 11-12 in light of: (1) the Pastoral Epistles[12] as a group (1 and 2 Timothy and Titus); (2) the epistle (1 Timothy) as a whole; and (3) their immediate context (verses 9–15, the paragraph in the Greek text).

(1) From reading Paul's Pastoral Epistles to Timothy and Titus as a group it seems that both Ephesus and Crete were experiencing similar problems with heresy (see Titus 1:10-11, 14-15; 2:11-15; 3:9-11). Even at the time of Paul's second epistle to Timothy, the problems continued (2 Tim. 2:14, 18, 23, 3:1-9, 13; 4:3-4). And those who had spread the heresies had done so among women. They had "[wormed] their way into homes and [gained] control over gullible women, who [were] loaded down with sins and [were] swayed by all kinds of evil desires" (2 Tim. 3:6). Heresy was not the domain of one gender: "Evil doers [the Greek text is gender-inclusive] and imposters will go from bad to worse, deceiving and being deceived" (2 Tim. 3:13). Male heretics were listed by name—Hymenaeus,

Alexander, and Philetus (1 Tim. 1:20; 2 Tim. 2:17, 4:14-15)—and it is likely that women also spread heresies.

(2) From reading 1 Timothy as a whole, it is clear that Ephesus was being plagued by false teaching (1 Tim. 1:3-11; 4:1-10; 6:3-5, 20-21). Again, those spreading the heresy had focused their efforts on women. As a corrective, for example, Paul (2:9–15) gives instruction on clothing, jewelry, teaching, and bearing children. A woman's jewelry, especially the wearing of gold and pearls in ancient times, indicated her freedom from a husband, that is, that she was sexually loose. Paul's extended teaching on widows (5:3-16) seems to be aimed at correcting a heresy that prohibited marriage and called for the women to meet together. In Paul's view, the lure of women to this heresy was so powerful that if widows did not remarry they would be taken captive by this trick of Satan. Paul was concerned that an unattached woman was helplessly vulnerable to these false teachers. Obviously, the widow injunction (that all widows *must* remarry) is not an "eternal word for the church" but was made at a particular point in time for a specific reason. The same is true of 1 Timothy 2:11-12. This text is not a timeless truth but a regulation for people where they were. But just where was the Ephesian church theologically? What error were false teachers spreading that needed to be corrected?

(3) Looking at the immediate context (the paragraph) surrounding 1 Timothy 2:11-12, a curious cluster of topics is found.[13]

What is the relationship between a woman's silence and learning, creation order and the fall into sin, and salvation in childbearing and characteristics of virtue? Though the topics of verses 9-15 appear disjointed to modern readers, to the original audience these ideas were interrelated. Concentric circles of context indicate that in the author's mind all of these seemingly unrelated topics made up one unified issue. Paul addressed them under the theme of "Women's Dress and Lifestyle" as a part of his corrective for errors

2:1-3:13 I. SETTING THE CHURCH IN ORDER: GENERAL PRINCIPLES FOR GROUNDING THE TROUBLED CHURCH IN EPHESUS

I.A. PRAYER FOR PEACE 2:1-8

I.B. WOMEN'S DRESS & LIFESTYLE 2:9-15

- (1) Preference for Their Spiritual Adornment 2:9-10
- (2) Command That They Be Taught 2:11
- (3) Command That They Be Silent 2:12
- (4) Creation Order Reiterated 2:13
- (5) Fall Into Sin Explained 2:14
- (6) Hope for Their Salvation Announced 2:15

I.C. OVERSEERS 3:1-7

I.D. DEACONS 3:8-13

of doctrine and practice in the Ephesian church ("Setting the Church in Order: General Principles for Grounding the Troubled Church In Ephesus"). But what specific doctrine and practice was the apostle Paul correcting? One other context helps to clarify the answer.

Cultural Context. The final significant context is the cultural background of first-century Ephesus. Compare the clues from the biblical text about Timothy's opponents with historical sources from the region[14] around Ephesus, near the time of the first century.[15]

This city, on the western coast of Asia Minor (modern Turkey), was the fourth largest city in the Roman Empire. In about 1000 BC, Ionian Greeks conquered the area. Ephesus became a world-class city and had a reputation for intellectual snobbery, oriental culture and tradition, and a predominance of goddess religion. By the mid-third century BC, Jews settled in the area around Ephesus, and by the first century AD, the Jewish population may have numbered 75,000.

Archeological evidence agrees, however, that the Jews in Asia Minor syncretized[16] the religion of Yahweh with paganism. They used magic and distorted the narratives from Genesis.

What kinds of heresies were known to be in first-century Asia? Ephesus was home to the Temple of Artemis (Diana in Greek), greatest of the seven wonders of the ancient world. She was a goddess of fertility, the Great Mother of Asia. The enormous statue of Caesar demonstrated the importance of the Emperor cult in first-century Ephesus. Besides these, there were the sexually unrestrained worship of the mystery cults and the very significant influence of the occult. The Acts account of this church's founding demonstrates how widespread was the interest in magic in Ephesus (Acts 19:18-19) and how central to the economy of the city was the Artemis cult (19:23-41). Some scholars see evidences of an early form of Gnosticism—a teaching that distorted Jewish ideas and opposed Christian ideas too.[17] Its dualistic[18] philosophy taught that material things are evil; only spirit could be good. Even though Gnosticism was not fully developed until the second century, primitive Gnosticism and its influences existed earlier. It is possible that the false teachers (1 Tim. 1:3–11; 4:1–10; 6:3–5, 20–21; 2 Tim. 2:14, 23; 3:1–9,13; 4:3–4; and Titus 1:14–15) and dualistic ideas (1 Tim. 4:3; 2 Tim. 2:18) can be attributed to gnosticizing elements infiltrating the church.

Understanding the cultural background of first-century Ephesus suggests the kind of specific problems Paul was writing to correct. The function of 1 Timothy 2:11-12 was not to theologically limit women's leadership in the church but to refute false doctrine and reaffirm orthodoxy. Though the precise nature of the heresies is not clear, it does seem clear that this passage was meant to silence them.

What did this text mean to its original readers and how does it apply today? First, look at four interpretations, from less likely to more likely. And finally, examine the application of this passage to readers today.

Four Possible Interpretations (from Less to More Likely)

Interpretation Number 1. This interpretation, based on the action of the present tense main verb in verse 12, *epitrepo,*[19] suggests that Paul's prohibition is limited to a temporary situation. Paul's words should be understood as: "[At the present time], I *am not permitting* a woman to teach or to have authority over a man" [emphasis added to identify the present tense main verb].

Grammar supports this translation. The nuances[20] of the two Greek tenses, present and aorist, differ not only in the time, but more importantly in the *kind of action* they represent. If this statement of Paul were in the aorist tense, it would have the force of a once-and-for-all prohibition, which would read: "I do not permit a woman to teach." The implication would be: "I never have and I never will." This is the way most English translations express the sentence, but such is inaccurate because the tense of the verb "permit" is *not* aorist in this verse. As it is, in the present tense, this sentence should be translated: "I am not permitting a woman to teach or have authority over a man." Which means, "[For the present time, under the circumstances in Ephesus], I am not permitting a woman to teach or have authority over a man."

Context lends support for this interpretation. The implication, based on the previous verse (1 Tim. 2:11 "a woman should learn," compare 3:6), is that when a woman has her theology straight and has something to offer—as Priscilla did—she too can share in a teaching ministry and have authority in the church. This interpretation is also in agreement with Paul's positive view of women in church leadership elsewhere.[21]

The weaknesses of Interpretation Number 1 are two. First, if Priscilla were back in the Ephesian congregation by the time this text was written, Paul would not have been prohibiting all women's teaching and authority in the church. She had returned to Ephesus by the time of 2 Timothy, and she might have been there by the time of 1 Timothy. Second, this interpretation provides no help in understanding the verses which follow this prohibition. Topics of creation, the Fall into sin, and childbearing seem totally unrelated to this interpretation.

Interpretation Number 2. This interpretation, based on the meaning of the rare verb in verse 12, *authenteo,*[22] suggests that Paul's prohibition is limited to a woman's abusive domination over a man, that is, "[Paul] does not permit a woman to teach or domineer over a man."

This interpretation has lexical and theological support. The Greek verb rendered, "to have authority over," appears only once in the entire New Testament.[23] Such an English definition is one that was chosen by translators based on this single literary context. There is no other New Testament support, therefore, for such a meaning. In the case of a word used only one time, going outside the biblical text is the only way to study its meaning.

Classicist[24] Catherine Kroeger has done over ten years of extensive research on this word[25] and has found that among its meanings is "one taking a very strong initiative."[26] Several ancient religions of Asia Minor featured such female dominance.[27] In Interpretation Number 2, "the condemnation is not directed against women participating in leadership but rather against a monopoly of religious power by women."[28] As Bartchy explains, "the verb *authentein* clearly bears the nuance of using such absolute power in a destructive manner, describing the activity of a person who acts for his or her own advantage apart from any consideration of the needs or interests of anyone else."[29]

The strength of this interpretation is in its theological agreement with God's creation ideal and the teachings of Jesus. It is understandable that women should not be domineering. Since creation, God intended equality, unity, and mutuality. Men and women are to rule together; neither is to rule over the other. Jesus taught that no follower of Christ is to dominate another. By His teaching and example He modeled that humble service is what Christian leadership is all about (Mark 10:42-45; Luke 22:25-27).

The weaknesses of this interpretation are three. First (as was the case with Interpretation Number 1), understanding Paul's prohibition as abusive domineering doesn't solve the mystery of connecting the verses that follow. Second, it offers no explanation of the relationship between a woman's teaching in the church and abusive domination over a man. And third, though the verb *authenteo* may have had such a meaning (abusive domination), it also had other meanings that may fit the context better.

Interpretation Number 3. This interpretation, based both on the meaning of the unusual verb *authenteo* (in verse 12) and on the significance of the verse's syntax,[30] suggests that Paul was prohibiting the teaching of a false version of the doctrine of creation. The syntactical construction could be rendered, "I do not allow [a] woman to teach or to present herself as author of man."[31]

Among ancient uses of the strange verb *authenteo*, Kroeger has found that it often, especially in religious texts, meant "to originate, to bring into being, to author," or "to present oneself as the author, originator, or source of something."[32] "*Authentein* is even used by the Early Church fathers for the creative activities of God."[33]

The unusual syntax of the Greek sentence (which contains two infinitive verbs,[34] and two negatives[35]) fits Interpretation Number 3: "I do not allow a woman to teach or present herself as author of man." Two other closely related translations also fit the syntax of the sentence and bear the same meaning (that Paul is prohibiting changing the creation story).[36] In Greek an infinitive can be used to indicate indirect discourse.[37] Therefore, the sentence could be rendered: "I do not allow a woman to teach *that she originated man*" [italics mark the indirect discourse]. A double negative (in this case *ouk* plus *oude*) can be used in Greek for the sake of emphasis. Therefore, the sentence could be rendered: "I *absolutely do not* permit a woman to teach" either "that she originated man" or "to represent herself as originator of man" [italics mark emphatic double negative].

This is an interesting interpretation, but what kind of Christian would ever teach such a doctrine—that woman originated man? A syncretistic or a heretical Christian. The native religions of Anatolia (the area surrounding Ephesus) taught that all life stemmed from the Great Mother. Goddesses Artemis/Diana, Cybele, and Isis were later identified with Eve. Syncretizing elements of paganism with orthodox teachings, heretical Christians might have taught this version of creation.

Some Gnostics (heretics) taught that Eve was created first and that Adam was taken from her side.[38] In their theology, she had not been deceived by the serpent, nor had she sinned in eating the fruit, but she was enlightened (saved) by *gnosis* (in this case, by the *knowledge* of good and evil).[39] Furthermore, some Gnostics did not want to have children. Childbearing was scorned and identified by their term "the works of femaleness."[40] Gnostics considered "the works of femaleness" powerful enough to condemn both a woman and her partner to spend their afterlife on earth instead of in the heavenly realms.

The great strength of Interpretation Number 3 lies in how well it fits the context of the verses following it.

> For Adam was formed first, then Eve. And Adam was not the one deceived; it was the woman who was deceived and became a sinner. But women will be saved through childbearing—if they continue in faith, love and holiness with propriety.

First Timothy 2:11-12 could be seen as a silencing of heresy, and verses 13-15 as a point-by-point refutation of error and reaffirmation of orthodox Christian doctrine and practice. Note the interpretive paraphrase below:

> I do not permit [a] woman to teach or represent herself as originator man; [if she does not know better than that—] she must be quiet!
>
> [Such may be the heretical (Gnostic?) version of the creation story being taught in Ephesus, but it is certainly not the orthodox one that I demand be taught by Christians.]
>
> [Now let's get this straight, once and for all—] For Adam was formed first, then Eve. And Adam was not the one deceived; it was the woman [far from being enlightened!] who was deceived and [this act of disobedience did not result in her rise to divine status—] she became a sinner.
>
> But women will be saved even though they bear children, ... if they continue in faith(fulness), love, and holiness with propriety.

The only weakness of Interpretation Number 3 is the speculation it involves. The meaning of *authenteo*, the rendering of the syntax, and the historical reconstruction are all possible but cannot be proven with absolute certainty at this time. Although it best solves the mysteries of the passage, is there an interpretation that is more simply understood?

Interpretation Number 4. This interpretation, based on the distinct change in grammatical number from plural (women) in verses 9-10 to singular (a woman) in verses 11-15a, and back again to plural (women) in verse 15b, suggests that Paul was silencing *one* female promoter of the false teachings troubling the Ephesian church in order to correct her teaching and restore her and the entire church.[41]

Several times in 1 Timothy Paul refers to the false teachers with gender-inclusive pronouns (1:3,6; 4:1; 6:21). David Hamilton points out that Paul identifies by name men that had been involved in deception (Hymenaeus [1 Tim. 1:20; 2 Tim. 2:17], Alexander [1 Tim. 1:20; 2 Tim. 4:14-15], and Philetus [2 Tim. 2:17]), and other men that had deserted him (Phygelus, Hermogenes, and Demas [2 Tim. 1:15; 2 Tim. 4:10]). But in the case of the woman who was teaching false doctrine (as well several other men in error in the

Pastoral Epistles), he did not mention her name. Hamilton suggests that perhaps such was because Paul had given up on the men he had named, whereas, he was hoping to restore those he had not named.

> Perhaps Paul did not name these individuals—the contentious person in Crete [cf. Titus 1:5, 11; 3:10], the man committing incest in Corinth [1 Cor. 5:1, 5], and the woman teaching heresy in Ephesus—because he hoped they would be restored. His pastoral heart longed for each of these people to be reconciled to the church. Maybe he avoided using their names to make it easier for them after they repented.[42]

Even before silencing her error Paul gave the solution to the problem— she must learn (1 Tim. 2:11). "This is not just a suggestion but an imperative. It is very important to realize that this is the *only* direct command Paul gave in this whole chapter."[43] "Paul did not simply say that [woman] *'may* learn' or *'should* learn' or that woman should be *'allowed* to learn.' Woman *must* learn. By implication, [this woman] must be instructed."[44] Because women (whether Jew or Gentile) were at an educational disadvantage, they were more susceptible to false teaching. Thus Paul extended to the female false teacher more grace than he did to Alexander, Hymenaeus, and Philetus. "These three men had sinned knowingly. So Paul 'handed [them] over to Satan.' But he handed the woman over to a teacher."[45]

And the way she should learn is "in quietness and full submission" (2:11)—that is, in "compliance with the law rather than resistance" and in "peace rather than argumentation."[46] Silence and submission, representing a teachable attitude, was a frequent formula for the ideal rabbinical student.[47]

But why the reference to Eve and to childbearing in the verses following? Paul sees this woman as *deceived*—that is why she needs to be taught the truth. Here is the connection with Eve—another deceived woman. Paul's point to Timothy is that Adam sinned knowingly, but Eve's error was that of deception.[48]

While Paul is on the subject of Eve's deception, it reminds him also of a woman's (as well as a man's) salvation. Hamilton suggests that being "saved through childbearing" (verse 15) refers back to Eve and the Genesis 3:15 promise of the bearing of the Christ-child. "The issue at stake here was salvation, not motherhood. Women aren't saved by getting pregnant and having babies. They're saved by the child who was born—Jesus!"[49]

Thus Interpretation Number 4 answers the question, "What specific problem was Paul dealing with in Ephesus?" One heretical woman. It fits the historical, literary, and cultural contexts. And it makes sense without requiring much speculation. Its meaning is a simple, straightforward reading of the text. Yet it highlights several new insights that clarify the issue. In light of what is known with certainty today, it seems the clearest interpretation of the text.

Conclusion

First Timothy 2:11-12 is not a universal timeless prohibition of women's leadership. Such an interpretation would contradict the biblical position on women, other statements made by the author of the passage, and Priscilla's history with the church of Ephesus. Her teaching and her leadership in the church were commissioned and commended by the apostle Paul himself.

Instead, 1 Timothy 2:11-12 (like 1 Cor. 14:34-35) deals with an isolated issue specific to a local congregation.

What was the issue, and how did the Apostle deal with it? In this passage, Paul was forbidding a false teacher with whom Timothy was struggling at that time, not all females forever. This text commands that a heretical woman must not teach false doctrine. Instead, she must be taught truth.

And what are the applications of this text to the readers of all time? First, Paul silenced a woman teacher in Ephesus *not* because she was *female*, but because she was *teaching false doctrine*. According to Paul, both men and women are to teach. Compare the following passages of Paul regarding Christian teachers: 2 Timothy 2:2 (where both men and women are included); 1 Timothy 3:2 referring to "overseers;" 2 Timothy 2:24 referring to "the Lord's servant;" and Titus 2:3 referring to women elders (or older women, the same Greek word). Thus, the problem addressed in 1 Timothy 2:11-12 was *not* a matter of *gender*, but of *deception*.[50]

Second, the *cure* for false doctrine is *orthodox teaching*.

> The antidote to deception is learning the truth. Therefore, Paul demanded that this woman be taught, opening a door of opportunity that society had shut. As we have already seen, this was a revolutionary stance for Paul, who completely broke with the double standard of the Greeks, Romans, and Jews. The Gospel not only permitted but also required equal education opportunity for women.[51]

CONCEPTS AND SCRIPTURE CONSIDERED IN CHAPTER 10

WHY DID PAUL PROHIBIT A WOMAN'S TEACHING IN EPHESUS?

The starting point of Scripture reveals God's creation ideals. They are later reaffirmed in the life and teaching of Christ. The theology of the New Testament echoes the teaching of Jesus, and its history proves the Early Church practiced what it preached. Paul had left a female role model in Ephesus to pastor that congregation. Thus, in 1 Timothy 1:11-12 Paul could not be silencing the spiritual teaching of all women and their leadership in the Church. What, then, was the specific problem in Ephesus that Paul was correcting?

These are the possibilities and their evaluation from least to most likely.

- Paul's prohibition is limited to a temporary situation—"at [his] present time he was not permitting a woman to teach or have authority over a man."

Yet if Priscilla were back in Ephesus by the time he wrote this passage, this is probably not what the apostle meant.

- Paul's prohibition referred to abusive domineering over a man.

  But then, what about a woman's teaching—where's the connection?

- Paul's prohibition referred to the teaching of a false version of creation.

  But can we be sure of the elements of this historical construction?

- **Paul was prohibiting one female false teacher in order to correct her and to restore her and the church.**

  The solution to her heresy is that she must learn.

And what is the application of this text to readers today?

- Though not a prohibition of women's participation in the church, this passage in its context is a condemnation of false teaching in general, whether by men or women. The apostle's cure is timeless in its application. Emphasize character over clothing. Assert biblical doctrine over popular theology. Replace loose morals with Christian virtues. And make sure that believers are grounded in the Faith[52] before permitting them to teach it.
- **Paul's approach to the problems in ancient Ephesus applies anywhere in the world today. Putting things right in the church requires determined discipleship.**

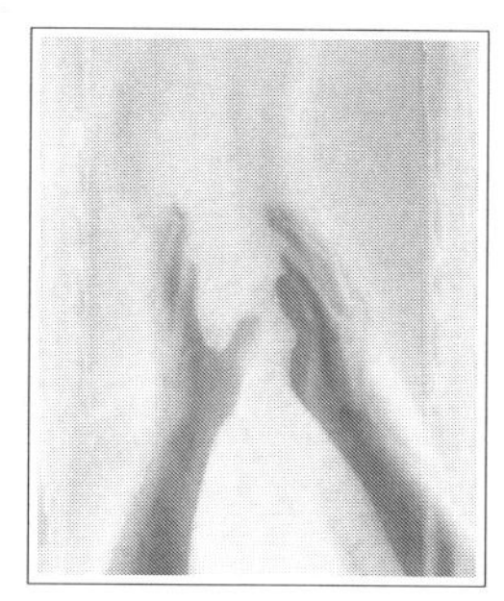

U N I T   F I V E

PRACTICAL APPLICATIONS FOR TODAY

CHAPTER 11

HUSBAND-WIFE RELATIONSHIPS

THIS BOOK'S EMPHASIS THUS FAR has been mostly the accurate interpretation of Bible passages in their original context. Being a student of Scripture, however, includes both correct interpretation of truth and correct application of those truths to one's life context. This chapter and those following it focus on how a Christian can live out what the Bible teaches. Practical questions will be considered. How do Old Testament and New Testament principles affect husband-wife relationships today? How do Jesus' first-century teachings on marriage apply to couples in the twenty-first century? How can biblical marriage principles be applied in the home of a Christian believer married to an unbeliever? How do spiritual gifts impact the ministry of women who are married?

Who's in charge?

In order to answer that question for today, one must begin by tracing it through the Bible and historical settings. God created Adam and Eve and gave them shared rulership in the Garden of Eden. God emphasized their oneness—equality in being and in function. A man was to leave his parents and be joined with his wife, to become "one flesh" (Gen. 2:24). The divine principle of a one-husband-one-wife home, established in the Garden of Eden, reinforced God's ideals of equality, unity, mutuality, and intimacy. The love poem of the Song of Solomon also shows mutual respect, reciprocal love, and initiative on the part of each lover.

With the coming of sin into the world, however, also came the exploitation of women by men.[1] A wife became a convenience, an object to be used by a husband to meet his needs. She was available to satisfy his physical desires. She was useful to produce many children to work in the fields. The Old Testament records how soon even the people of God strayed from God's one-man-one-woman principle. Esau took three wives (Gen. 26:34; 28:8-9). Jacob had twelve sons born of four mothers (Gen 29-30). And Solomon married a record 700 wives and kept 300 other women for his pleasure (1 Kings 11:3). When the husband treats his wife as property, he elevates himself as her owner. When he acts as her master, she becomes his slave.

By the time of the first century, Jewish marriage norms included the full power of fathers over their daughters. Up to the age of 12 and a half, a girl could not refuse any marriage decided by her father. Marriage contracts transferred a girl from her father's control to her husband's. The husband's duty was to support his wife and her duty was to serve him. Polygamy—having more than one wife—was still practiced. Current interpretations of the Torah limited a woman's religious rights and duties. Divorce could be a man's choice, but not a woman's. Men were not to speak to women in public, even their wife or mother. Jews considered a woman inferior to a man.[2]

Among first-century non-Jews, wives had a little more freedom. A wife was expected to be faithful to her husband, even though he shared drunkenness, immodesty, and sex with prostitutes. Prostitution had become highly organized. Unwanted female babies were collected and raised by houses of prostitutes. Religious cults, like the one that worshipped the creator goddess Isis, welcomed women's participation. But husbands severely punished their wives if they were caught attending strange religious services. A few women initiated divorces, but were criticized for using a "male" choice. Pagans held a double standard; women were less than men. Some men taught that women were not even human.[3]

How should students of Scripture today deal with a historical record of behavior that falls so far short of the ideal? Does history make it right? It that how they should live in a fallen world today? Absolutely not! The practice of having more than one wife violates the "one flesh" principle originated by God in Genesis and emphasized by Jesus (Mark 10:6-9). The husband as master or owner contradicts the equality God intended between husbands and wives and gives wives the status of servant or property. The inferior status and treatment of a woman by a man is at odds with the biblical view. Paul called her "the glory of man" (1 Cor. 11:7). Someone so precious should not be devalued.

In the first-century setting, Scripture sought to set things right again. Like the Old Testament, the New Testament emphasized equality and mutuality in marriage. When Paul taught about husbands and wives in 1 Corinthians 7:1-16, he gave specific instructions for their mutual relationship. Husbands are to give themselves freely to their wives and wives to their husbands. "The wife's body does not belong to her alone but also to her husband. In the same way, the husband's body does not belong to him alone but also to his wife" (1 Cor. 7:4, NIV). Paul's words clarify attitudes for Christian couples.

Though the Bible demonstrates that at times even God's people were not faithful to God's plan, that is no excuse to abandon it. God's Word consistently calls God's people back to His ideals. How then are these Old and New Testament principles to be applied today? The Church must call God's people back to God's ideals in this day. As part of the New Covenant people, Christian believers are called to resist the sins of patriarchy and to work to change them in the world.

Unfortunately, even among Christians, some teachers have tried to find a verse to show that the husband should manage the home and the wife should submit in all situations. Teaching the wifely submission of Ephesians 5:22 without the mutual submission of Ephesians 5:21 has often resulted in mental and physical abuse of one spouse by the other who wants to be "in charge."[4]

So who is in charge? Is the husband or wife to manage the household? Taking a verse out of context and making it an absolute rule is wrong. Consider the following two verses (emphasis added):

> Now the overseer ... must *manage* his own family well and see that his children obey him, and he must do so in a manner worthy of full respect (1 Tim. 3:2-4).

> I counsel younger widows to marry, to have children, to *manage* their homes and to give the enemy no opportunity for slander (1 Tim. 5:14).

"Who is in charge?" is the wrong question for a Christian to ask. The Scripture, in these passages, clearly says *both* the husband and the wife are to manage the house. If the husband is "giving himself up" for the wife (Eph. 5:25), and the wife is honoring and respecting her husband (Eph. 5:33), they will be working *together* to guide the household. Neither will be striving for control. The emphasis of Ephesians 5 is on the mutuality of the husband and wife, not on any hierarchy. The wife is not putting her husband in the place of God, but as *each* submits to the Lord, they will be able to submit to each other.

"But," some argue, "The Bible says women are supposed to submit to their husbands in everything, just as the Church does to Christ. Isn't that giving the husband absolute power over his wife?" The answer, as Paul goes on to explain, is "no." The Apostle is teaching the Ephesians one truth (the husband-wife relationship) by using another truth (the relationship of Christ and the Church) and the whole teaching concerns living in the Spirit.[5] The "household of faith" is, first of all, to be marked by the mutual submission of its members—not any one or any group being totally *controlled* by another.

In Christ, submission and love are tied together, and submission means voluntary deferring, not demanded subjection. Wives are to take the teaching about submission as seriously as the Church takes its submission to Christ, yielding her own rights and personal preferences to her husband (Eph. 5:24). A husband is also to take seriously Christ's relation to the Church by giving himself up as completely as He did—including yielding his own rights and personal preferences—because of love for his wife (Eph. 5:35).

Is Paul's comparing the husband's role to Christ's the same as equating the husband's status with Christ's? Does it mean a husband is spiritually superior or is the wife's savior? No, Christ's love is absolute and one-of-a-kind. He gave up His life to the death; He sanctifies and perfects His bride. He is the only one who has such abilities and authority—in His unique relationship to the Church. This is why *all* believers submit to *His* leadership. Husbands are to love their wives "as their own bodies" (5:28-29), but no husband can redeem his wife in the way Christ redeemed the Church. (The analogy should not be pressed beyond its points of contact.) A husband gives of himself in love; he cares for his wife as one who has become a part of his own flesh (5:31). But neither can he save his wife, nor be her absolute lord.

When Jesus (Matt. 19:4-6) and Paul (Eph. 5:31) taught on marriage, they both based their directives on the pre-Fall text. Thus, one can conclude that this passage—Genesis 2:24—contains God's defining ideal or standard for marriage. It speaks of unity, not hierarchy: "A man will leave his father and mother and be united to his wife, and they will become one flesh." Neither Jesus nor Paul quoted Genesis 3:16, the post-Fall passage that describes fallen behaviors. Neither Jesus nor Paul talked about male dominance and female subservience. That situation is the result of sin, not God's original perfect design.

Paul calls the relationship between Christ and the Church a "profound mystery," yet he uses it to help the Ephesians understand the profound relationship between spouses. The husband's level of caring and serving, giving and sacrifice, could never equal Christ's. But that's not the point—the point is mutuality, not hierarchy; the exercise of love, not of power.

David Scholer comments that the phrase "in everything" of verse 24 is restricted by the principle of "mutual submission out of reverence for Christ" in verse 21. "A wife's submission to her husband in the Church community is given a new and distinctive motivation: reverence for Christ (5:21)."[6] The identical spiritual motivation and command applies to husbands—"mutual submission out of reverence for Christ." For *love* to be a component of and application of mutual submission for Christians was revolutionary in the structure of Ephesian society. Such an attitude was unheard of in the pagan first-century culture. The principle of mutual submission in marriage, and the text it is based on stress love, not authority or chain-of-command hierarchy.

Similarly, mutual submission and love apply not only to husbands and wives but to other relationships and to the whole church. Paul wrote to the Galatians, "You, my brothers and sisters, were called to be free. But do not use your freedom to indulge the sinful nature; rather, serve one another humbly in love" (5:13). And further, he wrote, "Make my joy complete by being like-minded, having the same love, being one in spirit and of one mind. Do nothing out of selfish ambition or vain conceit. Rather, in humility value others above yourselves, not looking to your own interests but each of you to the interests of the others" (Phil. 2:2-4).[7]

A group of adults had gathered downtown in the basement of an historic church building for an evening of Bible study on mutual submission. Jointly leading the meeting were New Testament scholar, Berkeley Mickelsen, and his wife, English professor, Alvera. Their content was rich, insights illuminating, and interaction spirited.

To at least one man who attended, however, it seemed too good to be true. He raised his hand with a question. "What you're saying is all well and good. But let's be honest. Get real! Let's say you need to make a decision and the two of you disagree. When all else fails, and someone *has* to have the last word, who's *really* in charge?"

A chuckle rippled through the embarrassed crowd. But Berkeley was not intimidated. Looking fondly at his wife he asked, "Would you like to answer that, Alvera?"

She looked back up at Berkeley with a twinkle in her eye. Now chuckling with those who had gathered that evening, Alvera responded, "No, Berkeley, I think you'd better handle that one."

"Well, to tell you the truth," Berkeley began, "Alvera and I value each other so much, that in the thirty-four years of our marriage, there has *never* been a time when someone has had to have the last word."

The Mickelsens went on to illustrate multiple approaches to coming to agreement without one having to force his or her will on the other. For example, Alvera explained, "I have to get down on my knees and ask God to help me be willing to do what Berkeley wants, if that's the right thing. And Berkeley has to get down on his knees and ask God to help him be willing to do what I want if that's the right thing. Then we both get down on our knees and ask God to show us His will, because that *is* the right thing!"

Who's responsible to God?

At times the church itself has taught women "lies" based on faulty Bible interpretation.[8] Some recent teachings for men have also emphasized wrong attitudes toward wives. One often-heard, but unbiblical, idea holds that a husband is priest of the home and relays God's will to the rest of the family. This position is sometimes pushed to extremes. For example, some of these teachers say: "The man is the spiritual leader of the home; and if he's not leading, the woman had better not try to take his place."

Is it true that God always works through the husband, as priest of his family? No. Sometimes God revealed His plan to the husband first—as He did to Abraham concerning the birth of Isaac (Gen. 17:16) and to Zechariah about John the Baptist (Luke 1:13).

Other times, however, God instructed the woman first, as He did the mother of Samson (Judg. 13:3) and the mother of Jesus (Luke 1:26). Paul addressed his teachings to both Christian men and women and even to *slaves* in 1 Corinthians 7, indicating that each person is directly responsible before God for their own choices. Whether married or single, "keeping God's commands is what counts" (v. 19).

Some have taught that if the man (as husband or father) tells members of his family to sin, because of their lower place in the chain-of-command, they should be obedient to him. Some think that the man bears the spiritual responsibility, not the wife and children under his authority. But is that what Scripture teaches? Who's responsible to God? In the matter of obeying God, one spouse cannot blame the other. Each person must give direct account to God for his or her own actions. In the story of Ananias and Sapphira (Acts 5:1-11), God held each of them responsible for lying and punished them equally.

Why is the chain-of-command theory (that the wife is responsible to her husband, the husband is responsible to Christ, and Christ is responsible to God) so popular? Some men like it because it reinforces their power. Some women also like the emphasis on men's authority because they think it frees them from sharing responsibility. The Bible teaches that God holds both husbands and wives accountable to Him. Though they tried to shift the blame, both Adam and Eve were held to be guilty and were driven from the Garden.

So who is responsible to God? Scripture teaches that our only Priest is Jesus Christ, who shed His blood for our sins. In Christ, all believers function as priests, regardless of gender (1 Pet. 2:9; Rev. 1:6). Sometimes a wife prays for the family. Other times the husband leads worship. God can reveal His plans to either partner, and they share His leading with the other. Then they pray together for further direction. This displays the unity and mutuality God intended in the home. Thus, it is always appropriate for a wife to be a spiritual leader in the home and it is absolutely essential if her husband is not a believer. God's will is to use her to "sanctify" and "save" her husband (1 Cor. 7:14-16). Clearly, wives are priests in their own right.

What about divorce?

The "one-flesh" pattern means both partners are to be faithful to their marriage vows. Genesis teaches spouses to "leave" their parents, "cleave" to each other, and become "one flesh." And what God joins together in marriage, no one is to separate through divorce. Marriage is a commitment that is to be ended only by death of a spouse.

The effects of sin threaten to tarnish this ideal as well. In Old Testament times patriarchy brought in a difference of status between husband and wife. If the wife were unfaithful, the husband considered that his property rights had been violated. She could be put to death (Deut. 22:22). Since the woman had become a subordinate instead of an equal, divorce became unequal too. A man could divorce his wife very easily (Deut. 24:1-4), but a wife could not divorce her husband.

Jesus said that Moses had permitted divorce because people's hearts were hard (Matt. 19:3-9). The careless practice of divorce was not in keeping with the one-flesh ideal. Jesus narrowed the legitimate cause to "sexual immorality." He saw marriage as so permanent, that remarriage of divorced persons was wrong because the first marriage still stood (Matt 5:32; 19:9; Mark 10:11-12; Luke 16:18). The apostle Paul softens the grounds for separation and/or divorce: "But if the unbeliever leaves, let it be so. The brother or sister is not bound in such circumstances; God has called us to live in peace" (1 Cor. 7:15). But he also emphasizes that marriage is a life-long covenant: "A woman is bound to her husband as long as he lives. But if her husband dies, she is free to marry anyone she wishes, but he must belong to the Lord" (1 Cor. 7:39). Although divorce is not God's will, many people experience its pain. God is gracious to all

His children and can bring good even out of such a situation (Rom. 3:23-24; 8:28).

Paul freed the unmarried and widows from society's pressure to marry (1 Cor. 7:8). Marital status does not qualify one for ministry. The Bible is unclear whether certain of the disciples were married or not. But Paul admonished married couples to stay together if possible.

"What if my spouse is not a believer?" one may ask. "Since I'm 'unequally yoked' (2 Cor. 6:14, KJV), shouldn't I seek a divorce?" Paul explained that if an unbelieving spouse is willing to stay in a marriage, the believing spouse's faith will have a positive spiritual impact on him or her. Their children will also be blessed. But if the unbelieving spouse chooses to leave the union, "the brother or sister is not bound" (1 Cor. 7:15). Paul's final word was for each person to "live as a believer in whatever situation the Lord has assigned" (v. 17).

Peter also taught that unbelieving husbands could be won over by the submissive behavior, purity, and reverence of their believing wives (1 Pet. 3:1-6). He went on to warn husbands that their prayers will be hindered if they do not treat their wives with respect and consideration (v. 7).[9]

How should husbands and wives relate in the church?

The mutual submission of Ephesians 5:21 is the believer's standard both in the home and in the church. Paul gave instructions for Christian living to every believer (Ephesians 4:17-5:20). Then he proceeded to describe how Spirit-filled Christians would treat each other if they were married to each other (5:21-33).

Paul wanted every Christian to excel in the gifts of the Spirit "that build up the church" (1 Cor. 14:12). As seen in Chapter 7, the New Testament theological texts make it clear that the Holy Spirit gifts individuals as He pleases. Who gets what gift is His choice. But whoever receives a gift is responsible before God to use it in the Lord's service.

What if a wife's gifts in certain areas surpass her husband's? Should she limit her leadership so as not to threaten him? Look at Paul's all-time favorite female role model, Priscilla. There is no evidence that she was asked to limit her ministry for the sake of Aquila's. Instead, Paul taught, "If one part [of the Body] is honored, every part rejoices with it" (1 Cor. 12:26). It follows then that a husband married to a woman in ministry should be her most enthusiastic admirer. Paul also taught, "[Love] does not envy ... it is not self-seeking" (1 Cor. 13:4-5). A loving husband who celebrates God's gifts to his wife frees her to be all she can be for Jesus.

Conclusion

Sin ruins God's ideals of equality and mutuality for marriage partners. But repentance and belief in Christ enables believers to live out Bible principles today. Although Jesus was worthy to be called "Master" and "Lord," He humbled himself and used His power to serve others. He died so that men and women could be released from sin and also from traditional cultural expectations that encourage sin. As redeemed persons, husbands and wives will not seek to exert control or to be in charge. Instead one will seek to serve the other and together they will guide their children. Each will understand that he or she is accountable to God for their actions. As such, they will do everything possible to build each other up and sustain their partnership unto death.

CONCEPTS AND SCRIPTURES CONSIDERED IN CHAPTER 11

COUNSEL FOR MARRIED COUPLES

Once biblical truth is understood, men and women can correctly apply those truths to their everyday lives.

- God intended for a man and woman to be joined as equal partners in marriage, each submitting to the other rather than striving for control.
- Though both wives and husbands have strayed from God's ideal, the Bible teaches Christians that their mutual submission is based on their dedication to Christ.
- Each person—whether married or not—is responsible to God for their choices.
- Christ taught that marriage should be for life, but He offers grace and redemption when people call on Him.
- Men or women who have unbelieving spouses may be the means of bringing them to faith.
- God bestows gifts on husbands and wives—so each must use their gifts to honor Him and extend His kingdom.

1 Corinthians 7:1-16, 39

Matthew 5:32, 19:3-9; Mark 10:1-12; Luke 16:18

Ephesians 5:21-33

1 Timothy 3:2-3

1 Timothy 5:14

1 Peter 2:9; Revelation 1:6

Acts 5:1-11

1 Peter 3:1-6

CHAPTER 12

AUTHORITY, POWER, AND LEADERSHIP

A SIGNIFICANT ISSUE IN THE WOMEN'S question involves authority, power, and leadership. A cluster of questions surrounds these topics, such as: Where does authority come from—is it given, earned, or seized? What's the difference between power and authority? What about women, do they have authority and power? Is it proper for women to lead? Finally, what does biblically-based leadership look like?

In this book, the answer to every question has come from the Bible. Scripture itself has been the starting point. And other sources of general information such as history, culture, and language have assisted in interpreting Scripture. In this chapter, sociology[1] will help shed light. Since the church is a community, it tends to mirror patterns of behavior common to other social groups. Authority, power, and leadership are all elements of social systems. Using Scripture and sociology to facilitate, this chapter examines the biblical view of authority, power, and leadership and how it affects women in the church.

Beginning with definitions of the terms helps a person to understand the issues.

Definitions

Authority.[2] Authority refers to the *influence* of certain persons over others. It is the right or power to enforce rules or to give orders.

Authority can be given by a group or earned by an individual. Thus, in reality, authority is a relationship in which influence is voluntarily conferred on the leader by those who choose to cooperate with him or her. For example, society may grant authority to the persons it endorses. And a person with the ability to gain the respect of other people and influence what they do is recognized by that group as one who has authority. One kind of authority, called "charisma," is "the quality imputed to persons ... because of their presumed connection with 'ultimate' powers."[3] That is, a group recognizes the authority of these persons because it believes they are inspired by the supernatural.[4] Persons with *charisma* are "transformational leaders," that is, they are able to bring about change.[5]

"Legal-rational authority" is granted by the social group to those who meet certain criteria the society values; and "traditional authority" is given to those of a certain social class.[6] But many times a person with "charismatic authority" has none of the social criteria, yet rises to a position of great authority on the basis of inspiration alone. Patriarchal societies, for example, give very few women any official authority. Yet, in spite of this, charismatic women have become effective leaders in patriarchal societies. The sociological concept of "charismatic authority" has its origin in the gifts of divine grace mentioned in 1 Corinthians 12 and 14.[7]

Joan of Arc (1412-31), for example, was the daughter of a peasant during the Hundred Years' War. A pious child, she experienced supernatural visitations that she described as a voice accompanied by a blaze of light, which revealed to Joan her mission to save France. After careful examination by theologians, she was permitted to lead a military expedition to Orleans. The troops followed her because they perceived she was connected to supernatural powers. Clad in a suit of white armor and bearing a banner with Christian symbols, she worked wonders and freed the city from the English siege. At the coronation of Charles VII, the rightful heir to the French throne, Joan was at his side. Her victory at Orleans and this crowning of their king virtually saved France.[8]

Power.[9] Power refers to the capacity to *control* the behavior of others.[10] Whereas a man or woman in a police uniform has the *authority* to stop traffic, a train crossing an intersection has the *power* to do so. Power may come from ability, skill, physical strength, or force. When a person uses power to force people (coerce them) to do things against their will, his or her power is considered illegitimate. It is the followers' acknowledgment and acceptance of someone's power that makes it legitimate. Legitimate power is the equivalent of authority.

Leadership.[11] Leadership refers to the ability to *guide, direct, or influence* people. It is the means to accomplish tasks with people. Whereas, people with power may direct by force, one is not considered a leader unless others follow of their own will. Thus, leaders are men or women who have authority (that is, legitimate power) and use it effectively.

The Biblical View (of Authority, Power, and Leadership)

The Bible identifies God as "the Almighty," which means that He has *all power* in heaven and on earth.[12] Consequently, God also has the *absolute capacity to control* all human behavior;[13] yet He limits His use of power. God gives people "free will," that is, the freedom to choose. As a loving God, He wants a relationship with His people. Thus, He desires that people choose to follow Him out of love and not by force. From cover to cover, the Bible demonstrates how much self-direction God permits His people. He wants people to choose wisely and well, for such choices will improve their quality of life and bring God great delight.

God *lovingly* leads those who choose to follow Him. And those who grant to Him ultimate authority, He will sovereignly guide. People who choose evil and break the heart of God may suffer consequences that redirect them to consider their choices again. For those who change their thinking and choose right the next time,

God will make up for their mistakes and "in all things" work for their good (Rom. 8:28). Both men and women are responsible to obey God—consider Adam and Eve, Ananias and Sapphira. After death, however, the choosing is over. God will justly judge all people. In the end, His power will be used. Then the penalties and rewards will last forever.

Where do power and authority come from according to the Bible? The ultimate source of legitimate power is God. He is able to set up and pull down rulers (Luke 1:51-53; 1 Cor. 15:24). He controls who is put in power (John 19:11). Therefore, God expects His followers to be subject to leaders (Romans 13:1-7) and to pray for them (1 Tim. 2:1-2)—even those who are unjust. For such righteous behavior will prove His people's goodness, will imitate Christ's example (1 Peter 2:13-3:14), and will be blessed by God. Furthermore, God promises to honor such obedience by delivering those who wait for Him. On the other hand, we should never obey commands against God's will. The apostles put it this way: "We must obey God rather than human beings" (Acts 5:29). God is the ultimate source of authority, for it is He who dispenses the abilities, skills, strengths, and gifts that result in the capacity to influence others (1 Cor. 12:4, 7, 11, 18, 24, 28). God is the Giver of spiritual gifts and of every good gift (James 1:17).

What about women, biblically speaking—is it proper for them to lead? Let God answer that question. Scripture records that God placed women in power. God chose to equip women with the capacity to influence people. God entrusted them with responsibility and held them accountable for how they used their authority. God empowered women with supernatural gifts that qualified them to minister in the church. And God chose women to speak to His people on His behalf.[14] Women bring certain strengths to leadership,[15] just as do men. Both are needed in interdependent ministry for leadership to be the most effective overall.[16]

"Don't be afraid to empower women," says the pastor of the world's largest church. David Yonggi Cho advises churches to let women become spiritual leaders. "If you ever train the women, and delegate your ministry to them, they will become tremendous messengers for the Lord."[17] Most leaders at Cho's Full Gospel Church in Seoul, Korea, are women. In 2000, the congregation numbered 700,000. The church was divided into 50,000 cell groups and about 47,000 of the cell leaders were women. Also, 400 of the church's 600 associate pastors are women. "In ministry they are equal with men," Cho told church leaders at a conference in Italy. "They are licensed. They are ordained. They become [deacons] and elders."[18]

After collapsing from exhaustion in 1964, trying to shepherd his then 3,000 members, Cho decided to adopt the cell church principle. His male leaders refused to implement the plan, so the pastor invited the female leaders to do it. They were eager to be trained. The church grew from 3,000 to 18,000 in the next five years, involving many more lay leaders in ministry. Cho concluded, "It is the will of God to have a growing church."[19] In the case of Pastor Cho's church, it was *women* God used to grow it.

Both scriptural precedents and modern examples show that God includes women among those He calls to minister and lead in the Church.

Biblical Models of Leadership

The greatest model of biblical leadership is God himself. God's will, based on His example, is to lead lovingly, use authority prudently, and never abuse one's power.

A most accessible and yet profound study on Christian leadership, entitled *People, Tasks, and Goals,* was written by Billie Davis. It teaches leadership theory with biblical applications. Each chapter presents one Bible character as an exemplary leader.[20] Here are three additional over-arching models of biblical leadership.

The King as God Wanted Him to Be. In the Old Testament the human leader with the greatest social power was the king. In Israel's early history God had functioned as the nation's only ruler, but His people wanted to be like the other nations around them who had kings. Knowing where it would lead them, when the people asked for a king, God told Samuel to "warn them solemnly and let them know what the king who [would] reign over them [would] do" (1 Sam. 8:9). Sustaining a monarchy would cost God's people dearly: taxes so high that life would be hard, a military draft of the finest young men, and servants so many that their children would be required to work for the king (1 Sam. 8:10-22).[21]

Moreover, the power entrusted to a king is more than many men can handle. Lord Acton is famous for the saying, "Power tends to corrupt and absolute power corrupts absolutely." Power can tempt a man or a woman to think that they are above the law and entitled to do whatever they want to do. The lust for power can lead them to feel threatened. Even people who start out good (like Israel's first king, Saul) can behave in evil ways when power goes to their head.

God permitted His people's exercise of free will and gave them a king. But God's desire was for their kings to behave like Him—not using their power selfishly, but using it selflessly on behalf of people who had no power of their own (Prov. 16:10-13; 20:26). The king was to be a protector of widows and orphans, a defender of the poor and powerless, and an advocate for the alien. God is the Helper of the helpless, and He desires all leaders—men and women—to be the same (Prov. 17:5; see also 23:10-11). Many are the negative examples of evil rulers, both Jewish and pagan, who mistreated God's people. God's Old Testament preachers, the prophets, speak harsh words against the kings who did not show compassion or care for the needy (Jer. 22; Ezek. 22:6-7). The greater the advantages granted to a leader, the greater level of accountability is required of the leader to resist exploiting them for himself or herself.[22]

A Shepherd Like God. But just as God had warned, the leadership of many of the kings was evil. Jeremiah pronounces God's judgment against the wicked kings (Jer. 22:1-30), describes them as bad shepherds (Jer. 23:1-2), and then promises that God himself will shepherd His own people, will place over them good shepherds, and will raise up as king a Good Shepherd like himself (Jer. 23:3-6).

This biblical image changes the metaphor of leadership from rulership to servanthood. Shepherding (as a leader) involves tending to the needs of God's people: caring for them, gathering them together, guiding them to pasture, protecting them, keeping them from fear and harm. These nurturing activities are often associated with women's roles. The bad shepherds were destroying and scattering the sheep of God's pasture, driving them away and not caring for them. But the Good Shepherd will reign wisely, do what is just and right, and God's people will live in safety.

Jeremiah 3:15 describes the servant-leadership of shepherds after God's own heart—whether they be men or women. (Both in ancient and modern times, women have raised and cared for sheep.) This biblical leadership model is *founded in calling* ("I will give you shepherds"), *expressed in character* ("after my heart"), and *confirmed in competency* ("who will lead you with knowledge and understanding").[23]

Jesus, in John 10:1-16, describes himself as the Good Shepherd. He enters the sheepfold by the gate and becomes a door for the flock. The sheep listen to and know His voice; He calls them by name and leads them out. He goes ahead of them and they follow Him. He lays down His life for the sheep. He doesn't flee when He sees the wolf coming, but He cares for the sheep. The Good Shepherd is a model of servant-leadership: a mediator, a companion, a guide, a defender to the death, and a friend.

The Life and Teachings of Jesus. How did Jesus use power? During Jesus' forty-day fast in the wilderness, Satan had tempted

Him to use His power to meet His own needs but Jesus refused.[24] Using His power selfishly, for His own comfort or convenience, would have been a misuse of the power God had entrusted to Him.

Not only as the Good Shepherd, but also in all of His life and ministry, Jesus taught that the essence of leadership, authority, and power is *service* not dominance. Jesus corrected James and John's confusion about these things. They were focused on the honor and position of leadership. Jesus turned their attention to its cost and commitment. The one who wants to be greatest must become servant of all. Jesus warned His disciples not to take their cues from the world where the powerful dominate the weak. Instead, they were to follow Christ's example, who came not to be served but to serve.

> Jesus called them together and said, "You know that those who are regarded as rulers of the Gentiles lord it over them, and their high officials exercise authority over them. Not so with you. Instead, whoever wants to become great among you must be your servant, and whoever wants to be first must be slave of all. For even the Son of Man did not come to be served, but to serve, and to give his life as a ransom for many" (Mark 10:42-45; see also Luke 22:24-27).

The greater the sphere of one's influence, the more people to whom that leader is a servant. The greatest of leaders is servant to all (Mark 9:35; 10:44).

At His Last Supper with His followers, Jesus demonstrated servant-leadership. He took the water basin and the towel and washed their feet (John 3:4-16). Jesus explained that He had done this humble act of service as an example for His followers. True leadership leads by example—"serving and *empowering* others for service rather than exercising power over them."[25] Whether in the Church or in society, today's followers—both God's women and God's men—must live like Jesus, who defined leadership in terms of humility and service.

Three Lies About Leadership[26]

At the root of the three lies about leadership is a commonly held, but false, belief about power: that the total amount of power in a social system is a *fixed quantity.* That error asserts that power can never increase or decrease, but that it always remains constant. It says that power is like a pie; no matter how you slice it, the pie is still the same size.

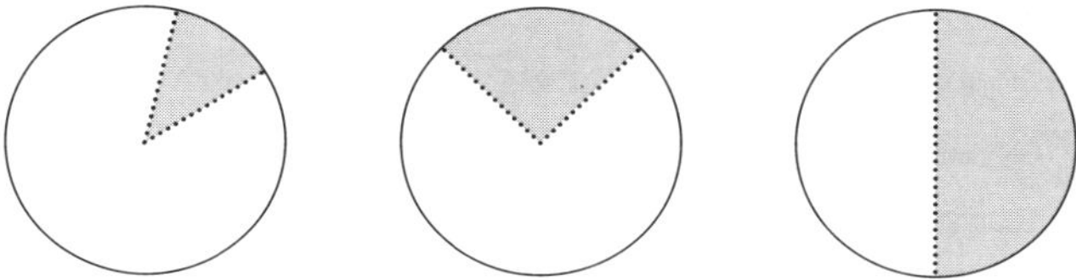

But this view of power is not accurate. The amount of power in a social system, an institution, or a church can increase or decrease. Christian leaders should grow every possible means of accomplishing things for Christ with people. No Christian leader should be threatened by any other leader—not by men, not by women. Followers of Christ should empower others. Because when everyone's power grows, the pie grows too!

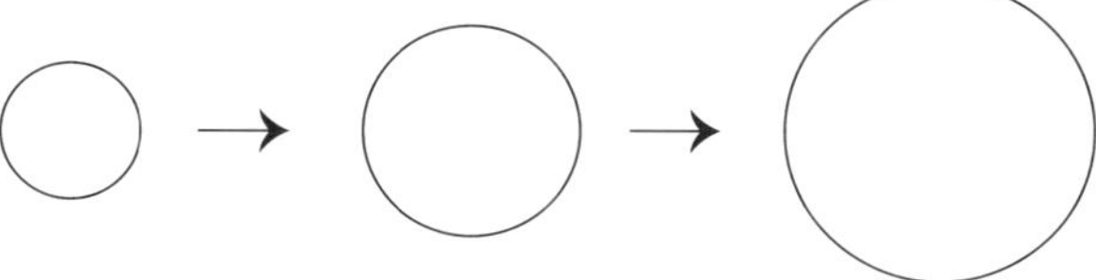

This "fixed quantity error" leads to three lies about leadership.

Lie Number 1: Leadership is the struggle for power. This lie asserts that leadership is the context of *conflict* in which the relative power of leaders and followers is constantly at stake. This lie is lived out in the lives of leaders who are selfish or insecure and thus feel threatened by others.

Lie Number 2: Leadership is one-sided. A second lie resulting from the "fixed quantity" view of power is that leadership is unilateral. It is an all or nothing view which says: A person either leads or is led; he is either powerful or powerless; she either controls or is controlled.

Lie Number 3: Leadership is a matter of coercion.[27] Based on the kind of "conflict theory" behind lie number 1, this lie asserts that leaders are only obeyed out of fear of punishment or hope of reward. Those whose leadership style includes manipulation, coercion, or intimidation are living out this lie.

Though all three of the above perspectives on leadership (as well as their starting premise, the "fixed quantity error") are not true, they can work. Those who lead in light of them may find success, but it is limited. Because this is not God's way. What then is the truth about leadership?

The Truth About Leadership

First, leadership should not be viewed as a struggle for personal power, but an opportunity to empower others. Instead of competing to seize power for one's self, a Christian should cooperate in partnering with others. Anyone who is not an opponent should be considered a partner (Mark 9:38-40). The combining of talents often results in synergy[28] and greater gains for God.

Secondly, healthy leadership is not unilateral but mutual. Instead of hoarding ministry leadership for the powerful elite, leaders who follow Christ should involve as many as possible in getting the good news of Jesus out to the world. There should be a give and take in every leadership relationship. Every member brings something to the team. Leaders must learn to value and empower others, building relationships of mutuality.

Thirdly, biblical leadership is not about the use of force but about freely sharing one's gifts. Coercion is the opposite of God's model of leadership. Leaders who follow Jesus must not use illegitimate power. God's way is "Not by ability, *not by force*, but by His Spirit" (Zech. 4:6, NLT, emphasis added]. There is much more to the leadership equation than extrinsic motivation—people invest themselves for motives other than punishment or reward. Leaders who empower others do not focus on punishing and rewarding but on learning to love and value others and on developing them according to God's will. Ideally, Jesus' followers contribute their best efforts with a pure motive of obedience to Christ.

> The paradox of empowerment is that the more you empower someone else ... the more powerful you become. As you empower another person, you both become more powerful. As you transfer power from your reserves to another, both reserves grow.
>
> By doing someone a favor, sharing knowledge, or delegating authority, you do not lose anything. You can still do what you could before, plus you can expect improved input from your new partner. ... Everybody wins.[29]

Social power is not a fixed quantity but a commodity that we can increase—for ourselves, for each other, and for the cause of Christ. Every time another person—male or female—is empowered in ministry, the influence of Christ's kingdom is enlarged.

It might be helpful to rethink authority, power, and leadership with new paradigms.

Shared versus Solo Leadership. The same kind of mutuality that God desires in the home between husband and wife is integral to His design for the Church as well. Chapter 7 addressed the spiritual gifts passages (1 Cor. 12-14, Rom. 12:3-8, and Eph. 4:4-16). In addition to demonstrating that there are no gender restrictions to spiritual gifts, these passages also present theological insights into how the Church is to involve all these gifted persons.

Every member of the Body has an important and necessary contribution to make. Since God placed the parts in the body of Christ as He wanted them to be (1 Cor. 12:17), no one should consider themselves or anyone else unnecessary (vv. 15-26). Interdependence is essential! We are one Body, "and each member belongs to all the others" (Rom. 12:5).

Thus an important part of a Christian leader's role is to

acknowledge, encourage, and involve all the members of the Body and their gifts in the work of the Lord. And that also means *sharing leadership*—empowering others to exercise *their* gifts and fulfill *their* callings. Even what some call the "offices of the Church" (Eph. 4:11) are really people gifted to equip *others* for ministry. Apostles, prophets, evangelists, and pastor-teachers are not to hoard leadership for themselves! No—first these leaders equip God's people (Eph. 4:12), and then they empower them to lead in the area of *their* strengths. The result of this biblical approach is that the Church will grow in unity, orthodoxy, maturity, and edification in love (vv. 12-16). Empowerment involves matching *authority* with accountability.

Women and men who desire to pattern their church leadership after New Testament leadership will be inclusive, drawing together the contributions of all members and their gifts (1Cor. 14:26). They will be responsive to God's speaking to the church through members other than the pastor or primary leader (for example Agabus, Acts 11:27-30; 21:10-15). Such messages are not accepted uncritically. But if they are judged to be in line with Scripture and inspired by the Lord, they bear just as much weight as the words of a sermon delivered by a staff member. And those who desire to pattern their leadership after the New Testament model will practice mutuality and shared leadership. (When, in Acts 15, the first church council met in Jerusalem to decide whether or not circumcision should be required of Gentiles, input from all sides was considered: the opinion of "the believers who belonged to the party of the Pharisees," the testimonies of Peter, Barnabas and Paul, and the exposition of Scripture by James.)

Edmund L. Tedeschi, senior pastor of Summit Church, St. Paul, Minnesota, illustrates how his Board of Deacons uses the principle of mutual submission to come to consensus. "Summit's board does *not* operate democratically, by majority rule," he explains.

"Political power can be too easily abused. And just because a view gains more votes, doesn't mean it's right."

"We respect the input of each member of the board so much, that if even a minority is uncomfortable with a decision, we may hold off making it. We'll pray some more, continue discussion, and gather more facts." And what have been the results of this approach? "Often, when we return to the matter again," Pastor Ed relates, "the majority has shifted its perspective to that of the minority. But in *every* case, the final decision is superior to the one that would have been made if we had pushed for a decision or had gone with the majority! Perhaps the many were sensing their own will, and the few were sensing God's. If we had forced the issue and let the majority decide, we might have missed the will of God."

Mutual submission is a biblical principle for both the Christian home and church—a relational ideal from God. Its practice goes more smoothly in situations in which all parties are sincerely motivated to reverence Christ in all things. Where no party has a personal agenda, but each is surrendered to the other and to the Lord, God's guidance through consensus and mutual submission is unhindered. Unfortunately, sin's effects may influence even Christ's followers to resist *God's* will at times. Just as majority rule can be abused, so also a coercive minority can thwart God's intent.

In such cases, much more is required of the leader committed to mutuality than of those who lead by autocracy.[30] Mutuality does not abdicate leadership in the face of disagreement, surrendering God's best for peace at any cost. Leaders committed to following the biblical principle of mutual submission need even greater strength, wisdom, and a dependence on the Holy Spirit. They must discern the true source of the various views (God's Spirit, the enemy's, or a human spirit). They need insight to know *God's* will, wisdom to know *how* to lead in that direction, and God's *strength* to follow through. Leaders are called to teach God's principles and bring correction when needed. To move people on to *God's* agenda, a spiritual leader must not only be clear on God's agenda, but also know how to help God's people discover it together and then direct them in fulfilling it.

Thus, sharing leadership is not always the simplest solution, but it is the best solution. It is best because it is biblical and it is blessed in that it is practical. Shared leadership, mutuality, empowerment, and cooperation result in *synergy*: much more than the sum of its parts—more leadership, authority, and power for each believer involved and more for the cause of Christ.

Circles versus Ladders. Leadership is considered by many to be a ladder of power to climb. Rung by rung the leader ascends to higher rank, greater status, and increased benefits. Such a hierarchical view of leadership has been around since antiquity. This is a selfish view of leadership, which focuses on what the leader gets out of leadership—power, privilege, and "perks." Biblical leadership, however, is based not on rank and status but on humility and service. The ground is level at the foot of the cross. Even leaders, whether male or female, are the servants of those they lead.

Instead of seeing power, authority, and leadership vertically, start seeing it spatially. That is, instead of leadership as a hierarchy of power, see it as spheres of authority. Instead of rungs of a ladder, links in a chain of command, or levels on an organizational chart, see leadership as *circles of influence*, some concentric, some overlapping, and all in Christ. Ladders and linear models have limited potential for connections, but circles abound in opportunities for networking.

Service versus Control. Instead of thinking of leadership in the Church as a mechanism of control, start understanding it as a means of serving others. After all, that's what the New Testament word for ministry really means.[31] Ministry, if it is about power at all, is about power to be used on behalf of others, not for the sake of the leader. Jesus laid down His life for the Church; the role of the king was to defend the powerless, and the role of a minister is to serve others. The leader is a steward, using whatever influence God gives selflessly, instead of selfishly.

There are equal opportunities in the Church for all who will serve: men and women, rich and poor, old and young, educated and illiterate. But it is not that some serve and others rule based on their social position. There is a clear difference between servanthood and servitude.

> Servitude is a forced social status, imposed on a person, depriving that person of the freedom to choose.
>
> Servanthood, on the other hand, is voluntary, a free choice to be of service to others. Human dignity is undermined in servitude; it is enhanced in servanthood. Jesus condemned servitude; he encouraged servanthood.[32]

Women, for example, are welcomed to serve in the Church—not because they are of any inferior status, but because they have made a choice to invest themselves in the lives of others for the cause of Christ.

Biblical leadership is a relationship of influence in service to Christ while serving others. To rephrase the late United States President John F. Kennedy, a Christian leader should "ask not what your people can do for you, but what you can do for your people."

Conclusion

Every Christian leader must examine how he or she exercises authority. The biblical view of power is "the ability to influence the behavior of others without violating free moral choice."[33] This is what it means to lovingly lead.

Just because a person is religious, however, does not guarantee their proper use of power. There are basically two ways to use one's power: selfishly or selflessly. Both have shaped world history.

> When the selfish use of power has been exercised, the world has been thrown into chaos, as with the Spanish Inquisition, the rise of Adolf Hilter, and [the former] South African apartheid. When power has been wielded selflessly, the course of history has been altered by such people as William Wilberforce, Mahatma Gandhi and Martin Luther King, Jr.[34]

These two uses of power originate with Satan and with Jesus. Christ's awesome demonstration of absolute authority through suffering and death is meant to demolish our carnal concept of power. And God's wisdom in choosing those marginalized by society to proclaim His most important message is meant to radically transform our image of leadership in ministry. Indeed, as Paul says, both the message (of the Cross) and its God-appointed messengers (often those who are low and despised in the world) are a stumbling block and foolishness to those who are perishing. Yet, we who are being saved can see in God's choice of message and messengers both the wisdom and power of God (1 Cor. 1:18)!

CONCEPTS CONSIDERED IN CHAPTER 12

WHAT DOES BIBLICALLY-BASED LEADERSHIP LOOK LIKE?

The Old Testament offers models and principles of biblical leadership.

- The truth about leadership involves following the **example of God**—who, though He has all power chooses to limit its use, respecting the individual and granting free will.

- From the role of an **ideal king**, it can be observed that God's desire was for those with position to behave like Him—not using their power selfishly, but using it selflessly on behalf of people who had no power of their own.

  In fact, the **purpose of power** is not for leaders to enjoy greater benefits for themselves, but that they may have the capacity to enforce justice for the needy.

  The greater the advantages granted to a leader, the greater level of accountability required of the leader to resist exploiting them for themselves.

- The model of the **shepherd** emphasizes humble servanthood.

The New Testament offers the greatest model for biblical leadership.

- The truth about leadership involves following the example of **Jesus**—who refused to use His power for himself.
- He modeled servant-leadership and personified the **Good Shepherd.**

Sociology concurs with the biblical model.

- Power is not a fixed quantity.
- It can actually grow if competition is replaced with cooperation and empowerment.

Consider new paradigms for leadership.

- Shared versus Solo Leadership.
- Circles versus Ladders.
- Service versus Control.

CHAPTER 13

GOD'S WOMEN NOW

HOW DOES THE PRESENT STATE OF AFFAIRS in the Church square with the biblical theological position? Do biblical precedents still apply? Is that which was normative for the Early Church also normative for us today?

Both men and women, as "new creations," are called first of all to the ministry of reconciliation as "Christ's ambassadors, as though God were making His appeal through us" (2 Cor. 5:14-21). Every Christian is to be used by God to win souls, make disciples, and build up the body of Christ. We believe that it is God's will for our day that the Church be blessed by its prophesying daughters.

Forming a Personal Theology

The forming of one's personal theology concerning the role of women in the church, home, and society usually takes place over a period of time. Equally devout Christians sometimes find themselves having differing viewpoints, depending on what they have been taught, their study, or life experiences as they have walked with the Lord. Believing that the Bible is the ultimate source of truth, the authors of this book have suggested guidelines to help readers in their task of interpreting and applying relevant passages. We have tried to explain useful terms, provide clear illustrations, and give brief background information to help understand each text in its context. We invite you on the journey of forming your personal theology of God's women.

Accurate theology begins with Scripture. Three defining moments of Scripture reveal God's overall plan for the interdependence of women and men. At Creation God first revealed His ideals for men and women. Christ modeled God's ideals in His life and teachings. And on the Day of Pentecost the Holy Spirit equipped the Church to live up to God's ideals.

(1) Creation. One's starting point is so important. Beginning in Genesis, God showed His ideals as He created the first man and first woman in His own image. He made them equal partners in ruling and subduing the earth. Though the Fall into sin marred God's creation ideals, throughout the Old Testament God, in His patience and mercy, continued to direct people back from their sinful ways toward His will. And He chose and anointed both men and women to lead them.

(2) Christ. The historical context of the New Testament helps readers understand the amazing contrast Jesus' treatment of women made to that of His contemporaries. The egalitarian style and content of His teaching included both women and men. His ministry reached out to all; He was no respecter of persons—that is, He did not value one person more than another. He called both men and women to become His disciples and to proclaim His truth "to the ends of the earth" (Acts 1:8).

(3) Pentecost. On the Day of Pentecost the Holy Spirit empowered both male and female disciples for ministry. Traditionally in Judaism Pentecost was celebrated only by Jewish males. But New Testament Pentecost was the birthday of the Church. And the Spirit that was first outpoured on that day became the impetus for the spreading of the good news to all parts of the world by God's men and God's women.

These defining moments of Scripture regarding men and women establish which passages in the New Testament are theological (that is, of a normative nature). The historical passages describe the ministry and leadership women contributed to the New

Testament Church and demonstrate that the Church lived out its theology of women. And the corrective passages help to clarify God's intent regarding New Testament Church problems in which women were involved. As followers of Christ we affirm the authority of Scripture in shaping theology and practice both then and now.[1]

Accurate theology brings Scripture to bear on life experience. Just as there are defining moments in Scripture, there are also defining moments in one's life that influence the development of a personal theology. What has been learned from various teachers, experienced personally, and studied from the Bible is often challenged by everyday happenings. Suddenly a position one has held for some time has to be reexamined through a fresh study of Scripture and changed.[2] Bobby Clinton, professor at Fuller Theological Seminary, testifies to this very thing happening in his own life.[3] He describes such defining moments in his personal journey of forming a theology on women in the Church as "paradigm shifts."

A *paradigm* is a framework of concepts through which a person views the world and interprets events around them. One's framework of values and perspectives is shaped and conditioned by one's culture. When experiences reexamined in the light of Scripture challenge a person to change the framework through which they view the world, a *paradigm shift* has occurred.[4] Such a change may take place in a short time, as in Paul's experience on the road to Damascus and the three days following (Acts 9:1-19). Or in other cases, the shift can be a process that takes place over a longer period of time, as in Peter's acceptance of the Gentile believers (Acts 10:9-35; 11:1-18; 15:7-11; Gal. 2:11-16).

The story of Clinton's pilgrimage involved several defining moments that resulted in a paradigm shift in his personal theology. Clinton grew up in a part of American culture where he saw only men in the roles of preacher or senior church leaders and women in what he considered lesser roles of teaching children or doing missions work. He had never heard a woman preach or seen one serve as pastor of a church, so he assumed that was the way things should be.[5] Over a long period of time, however, God brought people, their stories, and events into his life that challenged his assumptions. Such personal narratives are vital tools of persuasion. Clinton calls these experiences "critical incidents" that shaped his thinking over a period of twenty-three years.

He recalls the first time he heard a woman preach with spiritual authority. Then his studying and writing on spiritual gifts led him to conclude that all the gifts were for both men and women. Further studies led to an understanding of a "starting-point-plus-process" model by which God changes people and practices over time from a "non-ideal starting point toward some ideal."[6] (In fact, this is the process referred to in Chapter 4, wherein God worked within the limits of Israel's culture to show them His ideals and to reveal himself to them.) Books on gender issues, gifted female students in his classes, and more serious study of biblical passages further convinced Clinton to make a paradigm shift. He came to "receive leadership for women as being biblically valid," and further, to believe that they *must* lead. He concluded that the body of Christ is missing something without women's "interdependent contribution to leadership."[7]

Either Men or Women May Lead

A biblical theology regarding men and women, affirming that either may lead, has significant implications for the present day. God is still calling both women and men to ministry and to the extending of His kingdom. How can one pray, "Lord, send out workers into Your harvest field" (see Matt. 9:38), and yet hold the position that half the workers God calls should be sent away?[8]

Interdependence is God's plan. Jesus modeled the mutual cooperation, assistance, and interaction He expected of the men and women who followed Him. He included women as disciples in the middle of a culture that often discriminated against them. Women supported Jesus and the Twelve "out of their own means" (Luke 8:3) and sat under His daily teaching. Religious leaders of the day taught that it was disgraceful for a man even to speak to a woman in public. But Christ treated women as equal to men and commissioned them to carry the Resurrection message. By so doing, He challenged His followers to trust the witness of faithful women. Since Calvary, "all believers are equally redeemed and therefore equally eligible to serve."[9] Demonstrating a new unity, men and women in Christ "are being built together to become a dwelling in which God lives by his Spirit" (Eph. 2:22; compare John 17:20-23).

God has designed the Church in such a way that its members are not intended to exist or survive without each other. Every member of the body of Christ is needed; every gift of the Spirit is to be valued. The Holy Spirit empowered men and women alike. And those the apostle Paul commended by name for "struggling together" in the ministry with him were both male and female "co-workers" (Rom. 16; Phil. 4:2-3).

Barbara Becker, in *Becoming Colleagues: Women and Men Serving Together in Faith* (2000), has defined nine criteria for such inter dependent male-female leadership teams in mission and church-related settings. She studied twenty-three actual teams and consulted numerous focus groups. She concluded that when the criteria are met,[10] the teams become more effective and their ministry together becomes more mutually satisfying. Becker also wrote, *Leading Women: How Church Women Can Avoid Leadership Traps and Negotiate the Gender Maze* (1996).[11]

Cultural or Organizational, Not Theological Barriers. The source of the limitations that women often experience in ministry and leadership are rooted in cultural and organizational restrictions, not biblical theology. Yet these restrictions have not limited God.

For example, Jewish tradition granted certain privileges to the firstborn, the wealthy, and those with religious or civil status. Yet as early as Genesis 4, God showed that He does not always align himself with the obviously privileged ones. He chose Abel and Seth over their elder brother Cain. God calls whom He will and extends His grace to enable them. He told Rebekah that the older of her twins would serve the younger, in spite of traditional cultural expectations (Gen. 25:23). Paul explained that God chose Jacob even before his birth, before he had done anything good or bad, because of "God's purpose … not by works but by him who calls" (Rom. 9:11-12).[12] The parable of the workers in the vineyard (Matt. 20:1-6) teaches that it is entirely God's prerogative to choose whomever He will whenever He wills. God's calling transcends traditional expectations and cultural barriers. He is faithful to call workers; it remains for the body of Christ to evaluate, endorse,[13] encourage, equip, and empower the called.

Though various cultures and traditions have hindered the full expression of their gifted women, church history records the spiritual exploits of female stalwarts in ministry: Boniface's nuns in the eighth century, early Methodist women of the eighteenth century,[14] and female missionaries of the nineteenth century.[15]

Clinton, in studying the contemporary church, has come to believe "that women or men can exercise leadership in any positional role if gifted and called" by God. The Christian Reformed Church, for example, moved from having no women in church authority, to allowing women to serve as deacons (1984), to permitting, in 1990, "churches to use their discretion in utilizing the gifts of women members in all offices of the church."[16] Clinton says, "I see the problem of having women in leadership positions in churches or parachurches is cultural or organizational (a matter of change dynamics) not theological."[17] There are denominations that restrict the ministry positions women may hold, but even in some of these, as women "exercise their gifts, they change attitudes" and doors open. Local congregations who choose to recognize women's gifts rather than upholding their denomination's version of traditionalism often receive ministry that changes lives.[18]

Women can be effective in a variety of spiritual roles traditionally reserved for men. Let us "recognize and celebrate the essential and varied ministry gifts of women, as seen both in the Scriptures and in history."[19]

> The instances of women filling leadership roles in the Bible should be taken as a divinely approved pattern, not as exceptions to divine decrees. Even a limited number of women with scripturally commended leadership roles should affirm that God does indeed call women to spiritual leadership.[20]

Response to Difficult Passages

No matter where the discussion about the role of God's women begins, it seems to find its way to 1 Corinthians 14:34-35 and 1 Timothy 2:11-12. One of the reasons the book you are reading was written is the conviction that men and women need to have clear answers to sincere questions about these passages. Every person should be able to explain concisely *why* they believe *what* they believe God's Word is saying through these texts in their contexts. The key to interpreting both of the texts is to examine what they meant to their original readers and then how they apply today. Chapters 9 and 10 have dealt with several possible interpretations of these passages based on the historical context and the kinds of specific problems Paul was writing to correct. But what, in the final analysis, is the meaning and application of these passages for all time?

No one should disrupt the worship service (1 Cor. 14:34-35). Insights from context clarify that Paul was not referring to absolute silence for women but probably to curbing the kind of disruptive questioning or chatter that was causing disorder in the church. A major portion of the chapter (vv. 26-39) focuses on orderliness in worship. Three times in that section Paul silenced specific groups one by one: tongues speakers who had no interpreter, prophets who may have been dominating the service, and women who were disrupting the service. These three commands addressed specific problems in the first-century church in Corinth. They are not meant to be taken out of context and applied universally to prohibit public tongues, prophecy, or participation of women for all time. (If, however, a church has any of these specific problems upsetting its worship services today [uninterpreted tongues, dominating prophets, or disruptive women] the same correctives should be applied.) Paul was not against these things—he wanted everyone to speak in tongues (12:5a), desired that they prophesy (12:5b), and welcomed women's appropriate participation in the service (11:5). He also wanted women to learn (14:35a), but in a way that would not disturb the service, because "everything [is to] be done in a fitting and orderly way" (14:40). No one should disrupt the worship service.

People, whether male or female, must learn right doctrine before they're allowed to teach others (1 Tim. 2:11-12). Here again, the historical context of the first-century Ephesian church helps one interpret the text. Heresy had plagued that church. The Pastoral Epistles are full of references to this issue, of names of false teachers, and of ways Timothy is instructed to deal with them. Other concentric circles of context this passage must be set in are: the overall teaching of the Bible on women, Paul's commendations of his female co-workers, and his high regard for a specific female teacher in Ephesus (Priscilla). The false teaching had involved women, and it had to be stopped! Paul was forbidding specific false teaching and correcting its errors of doctrine and practice in the Ephesian congregation, not prohibiting female teachers for all time. He wanted women to be taught right doctrine—a revolutionary concept for his day. Then they could teach others, whether women or men.

Dealing with Differences

The essence of Christian community is the love that believers have for each other (1 Cor. 12). Although the body of Christ is characterized by its diversity, it is to be known for its unity. But that's not easy! Even New Testament leaders, like Paul and Barnabas, show how differences of opinion can threaten unity (Acts 15:36-40). Jesus prayed that the future generations of His followers "be one." Their unity is to be a testimony to the world (John 17:20-23). Their love for each is the proof that they are Christ's disciples (John 13:35). How, then, are Christians to deal with differences among brothers and sisters in Christ? Like Jesus—with *grace and truth* (John 1:14, 17). Our conversations are to be seasoned with grace (Col. 4:6) while "speaking the truth in love" (Eph. 4:15, see also 1 Cor. 8:1). Just as important as speaking the truth, is being gracious—using wisdom and gentleness (Matt. 10:16).

Jesus demonstrated His dependence on God through ceaseless prayer and surrender to His Father. In following Christ's example, men and women must prayerfully and humbly address those to whom they speak, even if their Christian character may be questioned because of their differences in belief. Believers must rely on the Holy Spirit to lead them in deciding when, where, and how they are to speak and what they are to say.

Show respect. The key to avoiding or solving gender conflicts is not women's submission to men but to God. Paul commands us to "submit to one another out of reverence *for Christ*" (Eph. 5:21, emphasis added). As both men and women submit to Him, they will be able to work together to know and do His will. Even though some of their secular leaders were tyrants, the early Christians were to treat them with respect (Rom. 13:1-7; 1 Tim. 2:1-2; 1 Peter 2:13-3:14). Clearly, submission "as unto the Lord" (for example, Eph. 5:22; 6:1, 5, 7; Col. 3:18, 20, 23) excludes submitting to anything that would displease the Lord. But, in the case of people who have not earned or do not deserve respect, the respect Christ's followers show is based, not on the virtue of the person to whom they're showing respect, but out of obedience to Christ.

One Bible character not mentioned yet in this book is Esther. She lived in a male-dominated culture, where a king could banish his queen for disobeying his command to expose herself to his drunken male guests. After doing just that, this king ordered hundreds of virgin girls to be brought in for him to exploit, while in the process of choosing a new queen. In this difficult situation, Esther—a godly Jewish woman—showed respect to this ungodly king. And she had the courage and inner strength to obey God and risk her own personal safety in order to save the Jewish people. She did not keep silent (Esther 1-9), and she did not lose her faith. Esther's respect for the king is not a sign of weakness but of her great strength and obedience to God.[21] As difficult as it may be, differences of religion, race, and age, as well as gender must be approached with respect for others.

Don't be dogmatic. A person may be convinced of his or her views but must still present them with grace, not dogmatism.[22] After people have studied, in effect they have "done their homework," then they must ask God to help them share their position in the right spirit. (Even the volume and tone of voice conveys meaning.) Finding areas of agreement and building a relationship must be accomplished first. Then one person can more easily communicate truth in a way that someone else can receive it and be open, ultimately, to changing their mind about an issue.

Missionary Cheryl Barton has faced differences among missionaries on the field. Such disputes "go to the heart of what kind of churches are being planted and what kind of theology is being exported."[23] She believes in egalitarianism, but missionaries from other ecclesiastical cultures do not. At the same time, in many non-Western countries, women have such pressing concerns of survival that they are not interested in teaching or leading in the church. Barton has adopted a non-dogmatic attitude saying: "We must be careful not to force our culture upon other cultures. If we do, we run the risk of losing the privilege to be heard. ... We must consistently share our 'light,' but allow the people with whom we're working time to accept."[24]

Gary Corwin, editor of *Evangelical Missions Quarterly*, says finding a middle ground on the issue of women's roles is not possible without a change of heart from both sides:

> Yes, there are important biblical, hermeneutical, cultural, and historical issues ... which must be addressed and resolved if any kind of permanent peace is ever to exist over these matters. But ... there must first be repentance and forgiveness between the sexes before we can fruitfully address the underlying issues.[25]

Humility, repentance, and forgiveness are essential antidotes for dogmatism.

Let love rule. Jesus said, "A new command I give you: Love one another. As I have loved you, so you must love one another. By this everyone will know that you are my disciples, if you love one another" (John 13:34-35). It's often hard to *feel* love toward someone whose position on an issue is the opposite of your own. Yet relationships should not be based on feelings, but on a conscious *choice* to relate with a Christ-like spirit.

Even if a person feels wounded by the attitudes or behavior of another, it is the responsibility of Christ-followers to guard their own hearts (Prov. 4:23). Jesus taught, "Love your enemies and pray for those who persecute you, that you may be children of your Father in heaven. ... If you love those who love you, what reward will you get? ... And if you greet only your own people, what are you doing more than others? Do not even pagans do that?" (Matt. 5:44-47). If Jesus required such a response toward non-believing enemies, how much more does He demand a loving attitude toward disagreeing believers. "Make every effort to live in peace with everyone ... . See to it ... that no bitter root grows up to cause trouble and defile many" (Heb. 12:14-15). The apostle Paul encouraged, "rather *be* wronged" than wrong another brother or sister (1 Cor. 6:7). Animosity and bitterness toward brothers and sisters do not belong in the family of God.

Withdrawal is another common human response in dealing with differences, but Christ calls His followers to a higher road. Too often, when a person finds out what his or her spouse is really like, they head for the divorce court. Differences with supervisors on the job may lead to the worker's withdrawal from productive interaction. Even church members who disagree with their pastor often just leave and find another church. The higher road is to continue loving and trying to stay in relationship with those who disagree. If rejection persists, even after love and patience have been applied, God may either give a person even more grace to persevere, or lead them to other ministry opportunities where their calling and gifts can be used. But God's will is for a person to "make every effort to keep the unity of the Spirit through the bond of peace" (Eph. 4:3; see also Psa. 133:1).

The previous chapters of this book have addressed many of the theological questions—some at length. But, as Alvera Mickelsen explains, "The issue of egalitarianism is far more emotional than theological. ... The prejudices and emotional threats ... must be dealt with on emotional levels, demonstrating the gentleness and strength of Jesus our Lord."[26] It is not a debate between those who support obedience to Scripture and those who don't—both sides espouse a high view of Scripture. The real issue is that each person must fulfill his or her calling as God, in His wisdom, grace, and mercy, has revealed it.

Enter doors that are open. God does not call every person to the ordained or full-time ministry, though He definitely does call some and uses them there. Ordination simply acknowledges God's prior "setting apart" of a person for ministry. In some cases, it is an artificial ritual because it can be given or withheld arbitrarily by organizations to enable or bar people from position or privilege. The Bible lists some spiritual requirements for church offices but leaves most, if not all, ministry and leadership functions open to any believer, male or female.[27] Scripture gives no gender or credential requirement for those who serve communion, baptize in water, lead in prayer or worship, testify, prophesy, teach, or preach.[28] If God ordains that a person serve in a particular role, there will be a part of the body of Christ that will come to acknowledge that gift and anointing. Scripture promises that a person's gift will make room for them (Prov. 18:16).

A girl in Thailand by the name of Piyarot was carried around for twenty years on a grass mat, unable to sit or stand, much less walk. They called her "the girl who has no purpose for living." One day her family brought her to a tent meeting where she heard about Jesus and the evangelist prayed for her healing. That day she walked for the first time in her life. Later, she went to Bible school and eventually back to her village to start a church. People came to hear her message. They said, "We know what she was! We have never known a god who can do what her God has done and we want to hear about Him." No mission board or national church would have chosen Piyarot to be trained as a pastor or church planter, but God did. He saved and healed her that He might reveal His purpose for her life.[29]

women and men. Be willing for God to open new doors through you—for you may be the one whom He uses to go where no one has gone before.

We have traced divine ideals for God's women through the span of the Scriptures from Genesis to Revelation. God's intent was egalitarianism from the beginning. Sin's result has been hierarchy since the Fall. Christ's sacrificial death brought redemption and opened the way back towards God's ideal. Pentecost provided the Spirit's empowerment to equip women and men to serve as equals. And that is where we are today. Though challenges continue, the fulfillment of the promise is in process. And you are helping to bring it to pass. But one day, when we see Christ and are like Him, we will be restored back to His full image again. The curse will be cancelled; all discrimination removed; and absolute egalitarianism perfected.

CREATION	FALL	REDEMPTION	PENTECOST	PERFECTION
Genesis 1-2	Genesis 3	Genesis 12 until Christ's coming	Acts 2 until Christ's return	Revelation 21
Egalitarianism—God's intent	Hierarchy—Sin's result	Tension—God's plan unfolding	Promise—Fulfillment in process	Egalitarianism—Glorified like Him

Contemporary Role Models

God's women are serving the Church today as educators, secretaries, evangelists, social workers, church planters, counselors, missionaries, pastors, musicians, office workers, teachers, deacons, as well as in a host of other positions. In addition, many work admirably as wives and mothers or in secular positions. Stereotypic roles for women are gradually being replaced with allowing an individual's unique gifts to be used in whatever way she is called, not just in the church kitchen or nursery.[34] Every woman has a place and need not fear God's rejection when she offers Him her service. Joy comes from knowing God's will and doing it!

A 2004 conference for women in ministry carried the theme

and description, "For such a time as this ... Called, Connected, Contemporary ... to support, connect, and strengthen women of God and the infinitely creative callings they embrace in the 21st century." The female plenary speakers included a chaplain, two missionaries, an evangelist, a preacher-educator, and a pastor who also serves as a presbyter in her district. Among the workshop presenters were women involved in ministry on the Internet, writers, a youth pastor, a director at the denominational level, a leader in the corporate world, a broadcaster, and many others.

Various vocations and ministries of women who have come from non-typical backgrounds have often been featured in Christian publications. A female political lobbyist, a single parent, a police woman, a doctor, a prison chaplain, an interior decorator, and dozens of others demonstrate how one can do the work of God's kingdom without being an employee of a church. Just being a positive woman in a negative world can be a strong testimony to God's grace and power.

God speaks through the Bible, prayer, other believers, and circumstances (events and experiences) to guide those who diligently seek His will. God may be guiding even before a person is consciously aware of His purpose for them. He can use seemingly disjointed pieces of life's puzzle, and bring them all together to reveal the beautiful picture of His plan.

One woman describes her journey by relating how God began to work in her heart when she was a young girl, even before she accepted Christ as her Savior. She heard television appeals for the starving children of the "killing fields" of Cambodia. The faces of the children and the name of the country became etched on her mind at that time.

As a teenager, her high school organized a program to receive Cambodian refugee youth who had fled for their lives by escaping to neighboring countries. They had become dislocated people, refugees with no place to call home. Upon the refugees' arrival in the United States, the American students began to tease them because they looked and sounded so different. Yet the faces from the television program years earlier triggered a response in the girl. She befriended the students, even taught them how to skip school and hang out at the fast food restaurant. By her own admission she was moving on the fringes of a relationship with the Lord. So when her peers began to harass her for befriending the refugees, she severed her relationships with her new Cambodian friends.

God patiently introduced this young woman to Cambodia a third time while she was a Bible college student struggling to understand God's will. She had determined to study there only one year and then move on to her own agenda. (Having observed that missions students did not know how to dress cool or match their socks, she had no interest in becoming one.) Gradually she sensed, however, that she was becoming spiritually obese. Every day she fed on spiritual lessons in classes and chapel, yet she had no outflow of ministry. No sooner had she asked God for an opportunity to volunteer somewhere, than a classmate asked her to help with a youth group consisting of Southeast Asians. God gave her another chance!

This time she built relationships with the families and observed animal sacrifices, witchcraft, idols, shrines, and animistic practices in their homes. She became so burdened for these people that she even went back to her high school to invite her former Cambodian friends to Christ. As she searched the Bible, she found passages on animal sacrifices that have to be offered again and again, because they have no power to remove sin (Heb. 9:11-10:18), and on the destiny of those who make and worship idols (Psa. 97:7). She cried, "Who is going to tell them about the sacrifice of Jesus? Who will tell them about the living God?" Immediately she knew that God wanted her to go to Cambodia herself, but Khmer Rouge Communism and civil war prevented entry to the country at that time.

Since she could not go to their country, she felt led to continue working with the Cambodians in her own city and to plant a church among them. To better understand their culture and their hearts, she moved in with a family of nine members living in a one-bedroom house. She listened to their stories and slowly learned their language as they taught her to speak, read, and write Cambodian. She practiced her conversation with others in the neighborhood and eventually moved into an apartment among thirty families. She shared the gospel and discipled believers there for six years.

Finally the day came for which God had been preparing her. The government of Cambodia invited her denomination to send personnel for compassion ministries. Because she was already equipped with knowledge of the language and culture, she soon received the church's blessing and support and left for an assignment in Cambodia. The call to ministry God had placed in her heart years earlier became a reality.

Whether you are single or married, young or older, male or female, God has a purpose for your life and a ministry for you. Some ministries will be private, even one-on-one; some will be more public. Whatever His plan for you, no experience of your life will be wasted. With "singleness of heart and action" (Jer. 32:39), pursue God's plan. He will guide your steps, redeem your mistakes, and work in your circumstances for your good and the fulfillment of His purposes (Rom. 8:28-30). Let us strive to know Christ and make Him known!

Conclusion

If a woman is called by God to serve Him in ministry, what is she to do? And what can we do to help her? [35]

What's a woman to do? Obey God!—it's just that simple. In the same way as any man who is called of God, she is responsible to be faithful to fulfill her calling. She has no other choice. If she is a disciple, disobedience is not an option.

And what can we do to help her? Here are seven proactive steps to facilitate a woman's quest to confirm her calling.

Establish the legitimacy of her calling from the Word. This book has been devoted to that purpose. It is the prayer of its authors that its readers will be able to use this material as well as this approach to demonstrate to her, as well as to others, the biblical basis of her calling.

Affirm her calling from any official statements that exist within her denomination or yours. In the denomination of the authors, for example, there is a position paper on women in ministry[36] and a section in the bylaws[37] that sanctions that ministry.

Inspire the pursuit of her calling with models from the past. Several sources previously mentioned are treasure chests of biographies of women in ministry: *Guardians of the Great Commission.*[38] *American Protestant Women in World Mission,*[39] *"You Have Stept out of Your Place": A History of Women and Religion in America,*[40] *No Time for Silence: Evangelical Women at the Turn of the Century,*[41] and *American Women in Mission.*[42] The stories of women in these volumes are sure to inspire her!

Facilitate the fulfillment of her calling with mentors from the present. If you know of women role models, try to connect her with them.[43] If you are in a position of leadership, use female ministers in positions of visibility. If you are not in leadership, ask your leaders to do this.

Articulate your personal endorsement of her calling by encouragement and example. Nothing is quite as affirming as a true friend who believes in you. Using supportive remarks, including women as positive examples in conversation, and eliminating sexist remarks and jokes will be meaningful to her and a positive example to others.

Contribute to the realization of her calling with opportunities to serve. One of the greatest affirmations of one's call is an invitation to minister. If you are in a position of leadership, be intentional to schedule women into your ministry calendar on a regular basis. If you are not in leadership, ask your leaders to do this.

Pray that the Lord will raise up workers, and be careful not to send away those whom God calls. The harvest is great, the (female) laborers are few, and the positions for them are even fewer. Why not be a change agent to reverse that trend?

CONCEPTS CONSIDERED IN CHAPTER 13

GOD'S WOMEN TODAY

What should the reader do with what he or she has learned?

- Form your personal theology on the topic by starting with Scripture and re-examining life experiences in light of it.
- Recognize that either women or men may lead because interdependence is God's plan and barriers against women's leadership are either cultural or organizational, but not theological.
- Prepare a personal response to the difficult passages, 1 Corinthians 14:34-35 and 1 Timothy 2:11-12, and be able to articulate their timeless truths.
    - No one should disrupt the worship service.
    - People, whether male or female, must learn right doctrine before they're allowed to teach others.
- Recognize that others, even within the Church, may hold a different view, and determine to relate to them in a Christ-like manner.
    - Show respect.
    - Don't be dogmatic.
    - Let love rule.
    - Enter doors that are open.
    - Let God open new doors through you.
- Look for contemporary role models that will encourage you to be all you can be for God.
- Commit yourself and encourage others, whether male or female, to serve God fully as He desires.

AFTERWORD

The call of God is very precious to both of us co-authors (Deborah and Barbara). And we are blessed to be in an ecclesiastical organization that credentials women for ministry. (We are both ordained to preach.) We have been honored to have served in ministry both when we were single and now that we are married. (One of us is married to a minister and one of us is married to a lay person.) Between the two of us we have had the joy of serving the Lord full-time in missions ministry, in Christian higher education ministry, in pastoral ministry, and at the national level of our denominational fellowship for a combined total of sixty-two years. We are inspired by the heritage of women who have served in our church and appreciative of the many men and women who have supported our callings to serve Christ.

Anyone called to follow Jesus experiences resistance, sometimes even from within the Church. One additional source of resistance for a woman in ministry can be differences of opinion on God's women. There have been Christian leaders whom we love and esteem (some of whom we've worked with closely), who have held a different view on women's roles. Opposition to the idea of women in ministry can feel like invalidation of the *woman* who is in ministry. So we've intentionally endeavored to guard our hearts against discouragement or negativity. If the enemy of our souls could make us bitter, we could render our own ministries worthless. Thus, it has been our goal—both at the same time—to respect our colleagues in ministry and to be faithful and obedient to our Lord.

Over the years that I (Deborah) have practiced this attitude and approach, I have witnessed God's wonderful faithfulness. To my knowledge I have never lost a relationship due to a difference of view in this area. By doing my best for Jesus while honoring the person who has disagreed, we have maintained genuine friendships. I have always been willing to share information with those who have honestly sought for it, but I have never forced the issue with those whose minds were made up in the opposite direction.

I am not sure that my life has changed their view, but other circumstances like Clinton's "critical incidents" and defining moments have challenged their assumptions. Sometimes it has been the sovereign work of the Spirit through a life-changing supernatural experience. Often it has been a close friend or female family member of theirs who has been called to ministry. Knowing the character of their loved one and trusting the conviction of her calling from God, some of these friends have become angered by other people's opposition to a woman's calling. When such experiences have sent my colleagues back to Scripture for more study, some of them have asked me for help or asked if I would encourage their loved ones. It has been a pleasant surprise to be able to offer assistance in pointing them to the biblical support for their loved one's calling.

I know of men of great stature, who've even put in print a position of opposition, who later came to a different conclusion. How I respect a person, man or women, who has the honesty and humility to change! As a disciple of Jesus Christ, I am personally committed to life-long repentance—I want to keep changing to become ever more like Jesus all my life long.

I think we make it easier for people to change when we are not dogmatic in presenting our position. My mother has often told me, "A person convinced against their will is of the same opinion still." We may think we've won an argument, when we've actually lost the war. Even in this book, our sincere desire has been to present truth and let it speak for itself. The tone of our voice may decide our case.

We don't want anything to distract our readers from the good work God can do with truth.

Our prayers go with you, reader, as you develop your personal theology of God's women. May you live it out with confidence, imitating Christ's example. Freely follow the call to ministry, if you have one, and heartily support all who do, both women and men. And most of all, we pray that Jesus

> will be more and more at home in your hearts, living within you as you trust in him. May your roots go down deep into the soil of God's marvelous love; and may you be able to feel and understand, as all God's children should, how long, how wide, how deep, and how high his love really is; and to experience this love for yourselves, though it is so great that you will never see the end of it, or fully know or understand it. And so at last you will be filled up with God himself (Eph. 3:17-21, LB).

NOTES

CHAPTER ONE

[1] Suppression: being put or kept down by authority or force.

[2] Subordination: being controlled by someone else's authority; being made subject or subservient, treated as of less value or importance; placed in a lower class, rank, or position.

[3] Klaus Fiedler, *The Story of Faith Missions* (Oxford: Regnum, 1994), 304-306.

CHAPTER TWO

[1] George Wood, "Exploring Why We Think the Way We Do About Women in Ministry," *Enrichment* 6, no. 2: 9-14.

[2] Berkeley and Alvera Mickelsen, *Studies on Biblical Equality* (Minneapolis, MN: Christians for Biblical Equality, n.d.), 6-7.

[3] Genre: a category of literature based on form, style, or subject matter.

[4] On interpreting the various kinds of writing, see chapters 3-13: Gordon D. Fee and Douglas Stuart, *How to Read the Bible for All Its Worth*, 2nd ed. (Grand Rapids, MI: Zondervan, 1993).

[5] Fee and Stuart, 26.

[6] Historical particularity: relevance limited to a specific time and place. See Fee and Stuart, 13-27.

[7] B. and A. Mickelsen, 7-11.

[8] New Testament quotations are from *Today's New International Version* (TNIV), unless otherwise noted.

[9] Golden Rule: Jesus' command found in Matt. 7:12, considered a concise summary of the Christian code for interpersonal behavior.

[10] See also Heb. 8:13, where God calls the Old Covenant obsolete and 9:13-15, which explains that Christ is the mediator of the New Covenant.

[11] See Chapter 6 under "His Ministry Practice" and "His Specific Attitude Toward Women—Jesus included women among those who proclaimed the gospel."

[12] Patricia Gundry, "Why We're Here," in *Women, Authority, and the Bible*, ed. Alvera Mickelsen (Downers Grove, IL: InterVarsity, 1986), 12.

CHAPTER THREE

[1] This untrue version of the story comes from "Paradise Lost," in Robert M. Hutchins, ed., *Great Books of the Western World*, vol. 32, *English Minor Poems*, by John Milton (Chicago, IL: Encyclopedia Brittanica, 1952), 93-333.

[2] Old Testament quotations are taken from the NIV unless otherwise noted.

[3] The Hebrew word *adam* can be translated different ways, depending on the context. Because this word refers to "male and female," it is understood to mean humankind. In Gen. 2:1, the same word with a definite article is understood to mean "man" and in 2:2, the man "Adam."

[4] Yahweh: The Old Testament identifies the Almighty Creator God as Yahweh, sometimes pronounced Jehovah, or expressed as "the LORD."

[5] For example, contrary to what might be expected (based on most English translations) the following scriptures use the word *anthropos* (human being, person) not *aner* (male person, man) for Christ. The location of italics marks a literal translation.

The centurion at the Cross said, "Surely this *person* is the Son of God!" (Mark 15:39).

When Pilate presented Jesus, he said, "Here is the *human being!*" (John 19:5).

Paul describes Adam's sin and Christ's overcoming it as God's grace "through the one *person*, Jesus Christ!" (Rom. 5:15, 17).

"For there is one God and one mediator between God and human beings, Christ Jesus, *himself human*" (1 Tim. 2:5 TNIV).

All of the "Son of Man" references are literally "Son of Humanity."

[6] Mutuality: the state of being directed by each toward the other, having the same feelings one

for the other, marked by intimacy and sharing something in common.

[7] Allen M. Harman,"'*ezer*" (#6468), vol. 3, *New International Dictionary of Old Testament Theology and Exegesis*, ed. Willem A. VanGemeren (Grand Rapids, MI: Zondervan, 1997), 378-379. The noun form meaning,"help, support, succor" occurs twenty times.

[8] Stanley Grenz and Denise Kjesbo, *Women in the Church: A Biblical Theology of Women in Ministry* (Downers Grove, IL: InterVarsity, 1995), 164. Of twenty occurrences of *ezer* (helper) in the Old Testament, seventeen refer to God and three to a military ally—both "helpers" superior in power and strength. No single English word expresses the meaning of *ezer kenegdo*, literally "a power or strength equal to him."

[9] Harman, 378-379.

[10] The Hebrew word used for "made" in reference to Eve is the word usually translated "built" *(banah)*. Also, God took part of the *sela*, man's side (NIV footnote), not a rib. She doesn't belong to him, but has her own identity as a result of God's building. The word *sela* is never translated as rib in the sense of part of the body.

[11] Hebrew words *ish* and *ishah* (Gen. 2:23) can be literally translated "man" and "female-man or womb-man."

[12] Hierarchy: the ranking or classifying of people so that each level is subordinate to the one above it.

[13] Gen. 3:4-5 "'You (pl.) will not surely die,'" the serpent said to the woman. 'For God knows that when you (pl.) eat of it your eyes will be opened, and you (pl.) will be like God, knowing good and evil.'"

[14] Berkeley and Alvera Mickelsen, *Studies on Biblical Equality* (Minneapolis, MN: Christians for Biblical Equality, n.d.), 13.

[15] Verse 16 is often misunderstood to be God's command for the husband to rule over the wife. But the Hebrew grammar of this verse is not a command, but a statement. The verse is predictive, not prescriptive.

[16] The original Greek does not use the word "man" in either clause in this verse. It simply reads "the likeness of the earthly, … the likeness of the heavenly."

[17] The gifts of the Spirit are given to male and female alike according to Acts 2:17-18; 1 Corinthians 12:4-11, 18, 27-28; and Ephesians 4:4-16. (See Chapter 7 under these passage references.)

[18] Body of Christ: word picture used by Paul for the Church in such passages as 1 Corinthians 12:12-27; Romans 12:4; and Ephesians 5:30.

CHAPTER FOUR

[1] "As Creator and Lord, Yahweh embraces and transcends both sexes." Phyllis Trible, "Depatriarchalizing in Biblical Interpretation," *Journal of the American Academy of Religion* 41, no. 1: 34.

[2] Trible, 32: "These activities belonged to the mother, not to the father, in ancient Israel."

[3] See also Psalm 71:6: "You brought me forth from my mother's womb."

[4] Virginia R. Mollenkott, *Women, Men, & the Bible* (Nashville, TN: Abingdon, 1977), 56-57. See also Isaiah 49:15, comparing the Lord to a woman who cannot forget her nursing child, and Psalm 131:1-2.

[5] Deborah Menken (Gill), "Gynecomorphisms in the New Testament" (Honors Thesis, Assemblies of God Graduate School, 1979).

[6] N. B. C. Love, *John Stewart: Missionary to the Wyandots* (New York, NY: Missionary Society of the Methodist Episcopal Church, n.d.), 4-11.

[7] Gary B. McGee, "Miracles and Missions Revisited," *International Bulletin of Missionary Research* 25 (Oct. 2001): 146-156.

[8] Patriarchy: social organization marked by the supremacy of the father in the clan or family and legal dependence of wives and children; control by men of the largest share of power.

[9] J. Robert Clinton, *Gender and Leadership: My Personal Pilgrimage* (Altadena, CA: Barnabas

Publishers, 1995), 2-3. He calls this "starting-point-plus-process," whereby "God begins where people are and progressively reveals himself and applicable truth to move them toward supracultural ideals."

[10] Egalitarianism: the view that all people are equal.

[11] Berkeley and Alvera Mickelsen, *Studies on Biblical Equality* (Minneapolis, MN: Christians for Biblical Equality, n.d.), 15-16.

[12] Deborah Menken Gill, "The Female Prophets: Gender and Leadership in the Biblical Tradition" (Ph.D. Dissertation, Fuller Theological Seminary, 1991), 28.

[13] Gill, 31. Deborah is a "mother in Israel" (Judg. 5:7), chosen by God, standing as a female counterpart to the patriarchs.

[14] Miriam and Deborah were two of the five persons identified as prophets prior to the monarchy. The others were Abraham, Aaron, and Moses. Women played prominent roles in leadership of the religion of Yahweh in this early period. Gill, 15.

[15] Gill, 40-41.

[16] Miriam, Exod. 15:20; Deborah, Judg. 4:4; Huldah, 2 Kings 22:14; Noadiah, Neh. 6:14; the wife of Isaiah, Isa. 8:3; Elizabeth, Luke 1:41-45; Mary, Luke 1:46-55; Anna, Luke 1:36-38; Jezebel, Rev. 2:20 (a false prophet); and Philip's four daughters, Acts 21:9.

[17] Gilbert Bilezikian, *Beyond Sex Roles: A Guide for the Study of Female Roles in the Bible* (Grand Rapids, MI: Baker, 1985), 69.

[18] Bilezikian, 73-78.

[19] Gretchen Gaebelein Hull, *Equal to Serve: Women and Men in the Church and Home* (Old Tappan, NJ: Fleming H. Revell, 1987), 113.

[20] Accommodate: to make room for, allow for, to adapt oneself or work within.

CHAPTER FIVE

[1] Much of the writing of this period that prohibits women's roles in the public sphere permits them in the private.

In the interest of gaining a broader perspective on gender in the social context in which Christianity flowered, several other social conventions must be acknowledged. In addition to this "public-private gender system," are a second and a third gender-based ideology.

Second is the ancient Greco-Roman "honor-shame system," which associated honor with the male and shame with the female. Virtues of courage, justice, and self-mastery were considered to be masculine. Chastity, silence, and obedience were thought to be virtues of women. Women exhibiting "masculine" virtues were considered "shameless." Too public a role for a woman caused her chastity to be questioned.

A third gender-based ideology is the "Greek theory of the self, in which the lower part of the self was characterized as female, sexual, and dangerous."

Karen Jo Torjesen, *When Women Were Priests: Women's Leadership in the Early Church ...* (San Francisco, CA: HarperCollins, 1993), vii-ix, 5-7, 53-82, 115-121.

[2] Torjesen, 9.

[3] Bernadette Brooten has found 19 inscriptions in ancient synagogues that show women held offices/titles as "ruler of the synagogue," elder, priest, and "mother of the synagogue." *Women Leaders of the Ancient Synagogue* (Chico, CA: Scholars Press, 1982), 11. Ross Kraemer has added to the list six other epitaphs of women elders. *Maenads, Martyrs, Matrons, Monastics* (Minneapolis, MN: Fortress, 1988), 219.

[4] See Cunningham and Hamilton, *Why Not Women? A Biblical Study of Women in Missions, Ministry, and Leadership* (Seattle, WA: YWAM, 2000), 71-92.

[5] Pagans: People who do not follow the God of the Old Testament. Robert H. Gundry lists mythology, state religion, emperor worship, mystery religions, superstition and syncretism, gnosticism, and various philosophies as the elements of Greco-Roman paganism. *A Survey of the New Testament*, rev. ed. (Grand Rapids, MI: Zondervan, 1981), 33-37.

[6] Robert M. Hutchins, ed., *Great Books of the Western World*, vol. 7, *Plato: The Republic* (Chicago,

IL: Encyclopedia Brittanica, 1952), V.455: 359.

[7] Hutchins, vol. 9, *Aristotle: Politics,* trans. Benjamin Jowett, I.1254b.3-15: 448.

[8] Don C. Barker, *Papyri from the Rise of Christianity in Egypt* (Ancient History Documentary Research Centre, Macquarie University, Sydney, Australia); available from www.anchist.mq.edu.au/doccentre/PCEhomepage.html; Internet.

[9] See Cunningham and Hamilton, chapter 8, 101-109.

[10] Institutionalization: the process, over time, of a movement's becoming more formal, structured, rigid, and hierarchical.

[11] Secularization: the process toward accommodating to non-religious norms.

[12] Intertestamental Period: the 400 "silent years" between the writing of Malachi and the coming of John the Baptist, the four centuries before the birth of Christ.

[13] Hellenization: the attempt to "Greek-ize," that is, to influence people to adopt Greek ways.

[14] Torah: the first five books of the Hebrew Bible, the Pentateuch—Genesis through Deuteronomy.

[15] Apocrypha: books excluded from the Jewish and Protestant canons of the Old Testament, but included in the Greek and Latin versions. The Roman Catholic Bible contains the Old Testament Apocrypha.

[16] Pseudepigrapha: writings falsely claiming they were authored by important religious figures.

[17] Talmud: Jewish oral traditions put into writing.

[18] The Law (capital "L") is the same as Torah: the first five books of the Hebrew Bible, the Pentateuch—Genesis through Deuteronomy.

[19] Subjective: based more on opinion than on fact.

[20] A Palestinian Talmud came out in the fourth to fifth century AD and a Babylonian Talmud (three times longer) in the fifth to sixth century AD. Gundry, 46.

[21] I. Epstein, ed., *The Babylonian Talmud: Seder Tohoroth,* vol. 1, *Niddah,* trans. Israel W. Slotki (London: Soncino Press, 1948), 1-509.

[22] Leonard Swidler, *Biblical Affirmations of Woman* (Philadelphia, PA: Westminster, 1979), 156.

[23] Ibid., 155.

[24] Rabbinic Judaism lasted from about AD 70 to AD 600. Modern Judaism is figured from AD 600 to the present. Today Reform Jews dialogue about the place of women, but Orthodox Jews still restrict women severely in religious activities.

[25] Bruce M. Metzger and Roland E. Murphy, eds. *The New Oxford Annotated Apocrypha, New Revised Standard Version,* NRSV (New York: Oxford University Press, 1991), 121.

[26] Ibid., 115.

[27] Ibid., 121.

[28] James A. Charlesworth, *The Old Testament Pseudepigrapha,* vol. 2 (Garden City, NY: Doubleday, 1985), 258.

[29] Ibid., 287.

[30] James A. Charlesworth, *The Old Testament Pseudepigrapha,* vol. 1 (Garden City, NY: Doubleday, 1983), 784.

[31] Philo, *Philo Supplement I: Questions and Answers on Genesis,* trans. Ralph Marcus (Cambridge, MA: Loeb Classical Library, Harvard University Press, 1953), I.33: 20.

[32] Philo, *On the Special Laws* in *Philo,* vol. VII, trans. F. H. Colson (Cambridge, MA: Loeb Classical Library, Harvard University Press, 1937), I.200-201: 215 .

[33] Josephus, "Flavius Josephus Against Apion," in *Josephus: Complete Works,* trans. William Whiston (Grand Rapids, MI: Kregel, 1960), 2.25: 632.

[34] Edgar Hennecke and Wilhelm Schneemelcher, eds. *New Testament Apocrypha,* vol. 1 (Philadelphia: Westminster, 1963), 381.

[35] Henrietta Szold, "Beruriah," in *The Jewish Encyclopedia,* 1948 ed.

[36] Brooten, *Women Leaders of the Ancient Synagogue.*

[37] A. Roberts and J. Donaldson, eds., *The Ante-Nicene Fathers,* vol. 4, *Tertullian, On the Apparel of*

Women (Grand Rapids, MI: Eerdmans, 1972 Rep. [1885]), I.1: 14.

[38] Quoted in Swidler, 348-350.

[39] Hutchins, vol. 19, *Thomas Aquinas: I, The Summa Theologica,* vol. I, Q. 92, Art. 2: 489.

[40] Emma T. Healy, *Woman According to Saint Bonaventure* (New York: Georgian, 1956), i-ii.

[41] Evangelicalism: the Protestant Christian wing that teaches that each individual deserves to hear the good news of Jesus (evangel) and to be given the option of choosing for themselves to follow Him. In their theology, this is the only way to become a Christian. This voluntary decision to follow Christ is called becoming born again.

[42] Quoted in Ilona Rashkow, *Upon the Dark Places* (Sheffield, England: Almond Press, 1990), 91.

[43] Helmut T. Lehmann, ed., *Luther's Works,* vol. 54, *Table Talk,* ed. and trans. Theodore Tappert (Philadelphia: Fortress, 1967), 8.

[44] Quoted in Rashkow, 91.

[45] Ibid.

[46] C. I. Scofield, *Scofield Reference Bible* (New York: Oxford University Press, 1917), notes on Gen. 3:14 and Zech. 5:6.

[47] Letha Scanzoni and Susan Setta, "Women in Evangelical, Holiness, and Pentecostal Traditions," in *Women & Religion in America,* vol. 3, ed. Rosemary Ruether and Rosemary Keller (San Francisco, CA: Harper & Row, 1986), 233.

[48] Janette Hassey, *No Time for Silence: Evangelical Women in Public Ministry Around the Turn of the Century* (Grand Rapids, MI: Academie Books/Zondervan, 1986). Ph.D. Dissertation, University of Chicago, Divinity School.

[49] See "Precedent Movements and Women's Roles, Pre-1914," in Barbara Cavaness, "Factors Influencing the Decrease in the Number of Single Women in Assemblies of God World Missions," (Ph.D. Diss., Fuller Theological Seminary, 2002), 15-64.

CHAPTER SIX

[1] Leonard Swidler, *Biblical Affirmations of Woman* (Philadelphia, PA: Westminster, 1979), 154. Rabbi Eliezer: "'Rather should the words of the Torah be burned than entrusted to a woman. ...Whoever teaches his daughter the Torah is like one who teaches her obscenity' (Mishnah Sotah 3, 4)."

[2] Blood taboo: Jews considered women to be unclean during their menstrual cycle and after giving birth. Anyone who touched them would also become unclean.

[3] Gretchen Gaebelein Hull, *Equal to Serve: Women and Men in the Church and Home* (Tappan, NJ: Fleming H. Revell, 1987), 115.

[4] See Chapter 4 under "Nature of God Relative to Gender."

[5] In the first century, in both Greek and Hebrew, mixed groups were addressed as males. Based upon their cultural values, this is the way these two languages constructed their grammar. But Jesus, in spite of the grammatical convention, demonstrated a different model when teaching.

[6] In "Appendix IX. Jesus' Rhetoric in the Cultural Milieu," of *Gynecomorphisms in the New Testament,* Gill lists 45 examples of Jesus' use of complementary or coupled discourse instead of collective masculine address in the Gospels.

[7] David M. Scholer, *The Role and Status of Women in the New Testament,* cassette tape series available from The Sanders Christian Foundation, Gordon-Conwell Theological Seminary, P. O. Box 2094, S. Hamilton, MA 01982-0094.

[8] Actually, the passage in Deuteronomy 24:1–4 (on which the debate is based) is not condoning divorce but recognizes that divorce existed in Israel and lays down a complicated rule that a man cannot remarry his first wife after divorce. It gives formalized procedures for the divorces that already existed.

[9] From a concordance study of this and similar statements, we see that Jesus made this kind of faith-affirming statement only to marginalized people, those rejected by society.

[10] Although this passage is not found in all ancient manuscripts, it is an accurate description of

Jesus' attitude and actions.

[11] Why didn't Jesus have female apostles?

It is flawed logic to argue from silence—basing the argument on the lack of evidence—but since the question is a legitimate one, here is its response.

First, the logic of this question implies that since Jesus did not have any women apostles we should not have women ministers today. A similar application of this argument is that since Jesus did not have one Gentile apostle, we must not accept the ministry of Gentiles today either. We can easily see the absurdity of enforcing such a prescription. The fact is that both the gender and ethnicity of Jesus' followers were restricted by the cultural setting. It would have been impossible for Jesus to invite a Gentile or a woman into his intimate group. Neither, for example, could have entered the Temple's inner courts.

Second, the makeup of Jesus' initial, intimate group is not necessarily the normative model for Christian ministry. Who the apostles were did not determine how ministry came to function in the Early Church. The apostles were not the structure of the church. Church government developed on other terms.

Third, there were many Gentiles and women in Christian leadership subsequent to the initial twelve apostles. In these many other positions, women served alongside men.

More pertinent than the absence of women among the Twelve is the fact that Jesus *did* include women in his larger group of disciples.

For more information see Richard and Catherine Kroeger, "Why Were There No Women Apostles?" *Equity*, 1982:10–12. (Republished by Christians for Biblical Equality, Minneapolis, MN, in pamphlet form.)

[12] And after Jesus, the Early Church recognized at least one female as an apostle, that is, Junia (Rom. 16:7). See Chapter 8 under "Romans 16:1-7, 12-13, 15."

[13] The women were not believed very readily. Given the social milieu, it is not surprising that the male disciples thought their testimony was an idle tale. (See Chapter 12 under "Conclusion.")

CHAPTER SEVEN

[1] S. Scott Bartchy, "Power, Submission, and Sexual Identity Among the Early Christians," in *Essays on New Testament Christianity*, ed. C. Robert Wetzel (n.p.: Standard Publishing, 1978). This discussion takes Bartchy's categories as a starting point and expands the list of verses in each.

[2] Day of the Lord: those special times of God's moving with justice and judgment on a large scale (Isa. 2-4, Joel 1-4, Zeph. 1).

[3] "Phoebe Palmer, an influential proponent of holiness theology, found equal rights for female preachers in the 'promise of the Father' (Acts 1:4, KJV)." Gary B. McGee, *The People of the Spirit: The Assemblies of God* (Springfield, MO: Gospel Publishing, 2004), 27-29. McGee tells the stories of more than thirty women who impacted the denomination.

[4] Reciprocal: shared, felt, or shown by both sides; mutually corresponding.

[5] Figurative: emblematic; representing by a figure, resemblance, symbol, or analogy.

[6] *Webster's New Twentieth Century Dictionary*, Unabridged 2d ed. (1979), s.v. "head, *n.*," definition number 15.

[7] Walter Bauer. *A Greek-English Lexicon of the New Testament and Other Early Christian Literature.* Trans. and adapted by William F. Arndt and F. Wilbur Gingrich, 3rd ed., revised and edited by Frederick W. Danker (Chicago, IL: University of Chicago Press, 2000), s.v. "*kephale.*"

[8] Henry George Liddell and Robert Scott, *A Greek-English Lexicon*, rev. Henry Stuart Jones and Roderick McKenzie (Oxford: Clarendon Press, 1968), s.v. "*kephale.*"

[9] Hamilton devotes a chapter, "The Question of Headship," to this passage, including a summary of the debate in chapter 12. Loren Cunningham and David J. Hamilton, *Why Not Women? A Biblical Study of Women in Missions, Ministry, and Leadership* (Seattle, WA: YWAM, 2000), 159-175.

[10] Christology: the branch of theology concerned with the study of the nature, character, and actions of Jesus Christ.

[11] Subordinationism: the theological doctrine that the first person of the Holy Trinity is superior to the second, and the second to the third.

[12] Arian: a follower of the ancient Greek Christian theologian, Arius, who argued that Jesus Christ was the highest created being, but was not divine.

[13] The following three articles are representative of the position the authors of this book have found to be most convincing. Berkeley Mickelsen and Alvera Mickelsen,"What Does *Kephale* Mean in the New Testament?" in *Women, Authority and the Bible,* ed. Alvera Mickelsen (Downers Grove, IL: InterVarsity, 1986), 97-110. Philip Barton Payne,"Response," in Ibid., 118-132. Catherine Clark Kroeger,"Appendix III: The Classical Concept of'Head' as 'Source,'" in *Equal to Serve: Women and Men in the Church and Home,* Gretchen Gaebelein Hull (Old Tappan, NJ: Fleming H. Revell, 1987), 267–283.

[14] Payne, 124-125, discusses examples of *kephale* meaning"source of life" from first and second century Greek writings.

[15] Payne, 126-127. He adds that"1 Cor. 8:6 states,'all things came from God' and 11:12 of this very passage says, 'all this comes from God.'" See also Philippians 2:5-11 concerning the Incarnation.

[16] Note, for example, the fifty-one pages Keener devotes to its discussion (28-1/2 pages of text and 22-1/2 of footnotes). Craig S. Keener, *Paul, Women & Wives: Marriage and Women's Ministry in the Letters of Paul* (Peabody, MA: Hendrickson Publishers, 1992), 19-69.

[17] Paul did not use any chain of command to deliver his instructions to the Corinthian women in chapter 7. He addressed both genders directly.

[18] Spiritualize: to give a spiritual meaning to or understand in a religious or supernatural sense rather than a literal sense.

[19] David Scholer,"Male Headship: God's Intention or Man's Invention?" *Watchword* 12, no. 1 (Feb/Mar 1988): 7.

[20] Note that in close proximity to all three gifts passages is an emphasis on love (1 Cor. 13:1-13, Rom. 12:9-12, and Eph. 4:15).

[21] Don and Katie Fortune, *Discovering Your God-given Gifts* (Grand Rapids, MI: Chosen Books, 1987), 16.

[22] It may be more accurate to count the equipping gifts as four since the Greek text seems to identify"pastor-teachers" as one spiritual gift to the Church.

[23] Orthodoxy: accurate or right teaching, conforming to established doctrine.

[24] J. Robert Clinton, *Gender and Leadership: My Pilgrimage* (Altadena, CA: Barnabas Publishers, 1995), 12, 20.

[25] Maria Woodworth, *Life and Experience of Maria B. Woodworth* (Dayton, OH: United Brethren, 1885), 18.

[26] Maria Woodworth-Etter, *Signs and Wonders God Wrought in the Ministry for Forty Years,* rep. ed. (Bartlesville, OK: Oak Tree, 1916), 28.

[27] Woodworth, 38.

[28] Ibid., 41.

[29] Ibid., 54.

[30] Wayne Warner,"Maria Woodworth-Etter and the Early Pentecostal Movement," *Heritage* 6 (Winter 1986-1987): 13. See also Warner's *The Woman Evangelist: The Life and Times of Charismatic Evangelist Maria B. Woodworth-Etter* (Metuchen, NJ: Scarecrow Press, 1986).

[31] Woodworth-Etter, 30-31.

[32] Magna Carta: the great charter of 1215 (England) was a fundamental guarantee of rights and privileges.

[33] Judaize: to adopt the customs, beliefs, or character of a Jew; to make Jewish. This refers to those who wanted to make Christian Gentile believers adopt Jewish customs. The Apostle

Paul wrote the Epistle to the Galatians to argue against the Judaizers who had tried to rob these young believers of their freedom in Christ.

[34]Some scripture versions, such as the *New American Standard Bible* (NASB), place words supplied by translators in italics. "Wives *be subject* to your own husbands, in the Lord." Thus the NASB makes it clear, even to the English reader, that the verb is not present in the original Greek text.

[35] Both pagans and Jews expressed the view that having a wife was a troublesome obligation, but necessary for producing legitimate heirs. They looked for love elsewhere.

[36] "To him who loves us and has freed us from our sins by his blood, and has made us to be a kingdom and priests to serve his God and Father—to him be glory and power for ever and ever! Amen" (Rev. 1:5b-6).

CHAPTER EIGHT

[1] See also Chapter 9 under "Insights from the Book Itself, Internal Consistency of the Letter."

[2] Karen Jo Torjesen, *When Women Were Priests: Women's Leadership in the Early Church...* (San Francisco, CA: Harper Collins, 1993), 16.

[3] Though Phoebe was a female, it is neither lexically nor historically accurate to alter her title to a grammatically feminine form. In Greek there is a vast difference in status and function between a *female deacon* and a *deaconess*—they are not one and the same. In this case, to feminize the title is to dramatically diminish Phoebe's ministerial role. See Berkeley and Alvera Mickelsen, "Does Male Dominance Tarnish Our Translations?" *Christianity Today*, 22 (5 October 1979): 23-29.

[4] Furthermore, to be faithful to the New Testament pattern, women who serve on deacon boards in churches today should be called deacons and not deaconesses.

[5] The term also could have financial connotations—perhaps she was a wealthy benefactor of the church as well. It is very possible, therefore, that she hosted and led a house church in her home.

[6] See also Chapter 9 under "Insights from the Time and Place, Geography."

[7] Henry Chadwick, "Rufinus and the Tura Papyrus of Origen's Commentary on Romans," *Journal of Theological Studies*, 10 (April 1959): 41–42.

[8] Adolf Harnack, "Probabilia ueber die Adresse und den Verfasser des Hebraerbriefs" (Hypothesis Concerning the Destination and Author of the Letter to the Hebrews), *Zeitschrift fuer die neutestamentliche Wissenschaft* (*Journal of New Testament Knowledge*), 1 (1900): 16-41.

Ruth Hoppin also supports Priscilla's authorship with extensive research. Ruth Hoppin, *Priscilla's Letter: Finding the Author of the Epistle to the Hebrews* (Fort Bragg, CA: Lost Coast Press, 1997).

[9] David M. Scholer, "Paul's Women Coworkers in Ministry," *Theology, News and Notes* 42 (March 1995): 20-22.

[10] Papyri: manuscripts written on scrolls made of papyrus plant stem material.

[11] Edwin Judge, Ancient History Documentary Research Centre, Macquarie University, North Ryde 2109, Sydney, New South Wales, AUSTRALIA.

[12] Cunningham and Hamilton, 145.

[13] Scholer, "Paul's Coworkers," 22.

[14] Among them are the *Amplified Bible*, the *Contemporary English Version*, *God's Word*, JB, *Living Bible* (LB), *The Message*, Moffatt, NASB, NEB, NIV, Phillips, RSV, and *Today's English Version* (TEV).

[15] It is possible, though less clear, that 1 Timothy 5:2 should also be included in this list. "[Treat] older women [women elders] as mothers, and younger women as sisters, with absolute purity."

[16] In fact, *none* of the ancient manuscripts specify that these are qualifications for male officers. There is absolutely *no* manuscript evidence to believe that this was even an issue to the Early Church.

[17] See NASB, NIV, JB, NEB, *Phillips*, and LB.

[18] The Greek word *gynaikas*, can be translated either as "women" or "wives."

[19] See Chapter 5 under "Evangelical Revival Movements." Another book documents women's vast contributions as missionaries in the nineteenth and early twentieth centuries. R. Pierce Beaver, *American Protestant Women in World Mission*, rev. ed. (Grand Rapids, MI: Eerdmans, 1980); (first published as *All Loves Excelling*, 1968).

[20] Since the beginning of its early twentieth-century revival, women in Pentecostal circles have been recognized as called and gifted by God for ministry. The Assemblies of God, for example, has a rich history of stalwart women ministers.

[21] Recent evidence documenting women's extensive participation in ministry in the Early Church as well as lexical and background studies have caused scholars to challenge the basis of their interpretations of several New Testament passages.

For example, exciting recent discoveries document women's leadership as deacons and elders in the Early Church immediately following the New Testament period. Greg Horsley's extensive studies of papyri (of ancient church documents) and ancient inscriptions (including tombstone epitaphs) have recovered the names and evidence for five female elders, one official female teacher, and nine female deacons of the Early Church. A summary of these sources appears in "Early Evidence of Women Officers in the Church," *Priscilla Papers*, 1 (Fall 1987): 3–4.

[22] See note 21 above.

[23] Researchers at the Ancient History Documentary Research Centre (note 8 above) have discovered that there is a far higher proportion of women's names mentioned in the New Testament than in other Greco-Roman literature. It is also interesting to note that a great number of these are upper class names.

CHAPTER NINE

[1] "In the Greek of the New Testament, women are shown to be church leaders, teachers, elders, and deacons. Evidence from the papyri and inscriptions reveals women in these positions at the time of the New Testament and in successive centuries." Ann Nyland, "Papyri, Women, and Word Meaning in the New Testament," *Priscilla Papers*, 17, no. 4 (Fall 2003): 8-9.

[2] See Chapter 8 under "Romans 16:1-7, 12-13, 15."

[3] See Chapter 7, note 33.

[4] Nyland, 3-9; Karen Jo Torjesen, *When Women Were Priests: Women's Leadership in the Early Church …* (San Francisco, CA: Harper Collins, 1993), 16.

[5] See Chapter 7, under 1 Corinthians 12-14.

[6] Ibid.

[7] See Richard and Catherine Clark Kroeger, "Pandemonium and Silence at Corinth," *The Reformed Journal*, 28 (June 1978): 6–10.

[8] Lexical: insights from the exact Greek words.

[9] The dictionary form (first person, singular, present, indicative, active) of both verbs *lego* and *laleo* are used for purposes of this discussion. Such is not, however, the grammatical form of the verb as it appears in the text. Interpretation Number 4 discusses the grammatical form and its significance.

[10] This was Helen B. Montgomery's view in her New Testament translation and footnote on these verses. It was later taken up by Catherine Bushnell, and most recently by some Roman Catholic scholars.

[11] Robin Scroggs, "Paul and the Eschatological Woman," *Journal of the American Academy of Religion*, 40 (1972): 283-303.

[12] Text criticism: insights from the ancient manuscripts.

[13] Lexicology: the study of words, their use, meaning, and vocabulary relationships.

[14] *Laleo* is the dictionary form of the verb (first person, singular, present, indicative, active). In this verse, and the one following it, it appears as *lalein* (present, active, infinitive).

[15] Bernadette Brooten, *Women Leaders of the Ancient Synagogue* (Chico, CA: Scholars Press, 1982). This book is the result of her Ph.D. dissertation, Harvard University.

[16] Monologue: a long, uninterrupted speech by one person.

[17] Conrad Gempf, *Jesus Asked* (Grand Rapids, MI: Zondervan, 2003).

[18] Even a master teacher like Jesus, who knew all the answers and wanted to motivate His learners, chose not to answer every question at the time it was asked.

Students who have ever been in a class where one classmate hijacked the discussion, and the class was dismissed without settling the important issues, appreciate a teacher with skill in handling tangents (questions not relevant to the subject under consideration).

CHAPTER TEN

[1] What Chapter 2 identifies as a "Category 2" text.

[2] What Chapter 2 identifies as "Category 1."

[3] What Chapter 2 identifies as "Category 3."

[4] J. Robert Clinton, *Gender and Leadership: My Personal Pilgrimage* (Altadena, CA: Barnabas Publishers, 1995), 43.

[5] "Errors of interpretation happen when a person makes up his or her mind on a subject and then selects only certain passages to support that view. Using this method, the Bible can be misused to try to 'prove' human ideas." (See Chapter 2 under "Mistakes to Avoid").

[6] Also known as Prisca in some translations of the New Testament.

[7] Since Priscilla, Aquila, and Paul were tentmakers, he stayed with them and they worked together.

[8] Chapter 8 under "Romans 16:1-7, 12-13, 15" summarizes the glowing New Testament record regarding Priscilla.

[9] In this discussion the order of the couple's names reflects the New Testament's ordering of their names. Though first-century convention was to list the husband first, both Luke and Paul generally list Priscilla's name first. Chapter 8 under "Romans 16:1-7, 12-13, 15" explains why.

[10] Karen Jo Torjesen, *When Women Were Priests: Women's Leadership in the Early Church …* (San Francisco, CA: Harper Collins, 1993), 16.

[11] This was at the end of the second and beginning of the third of Paul's missionary journeys.

[12] These are three epistles from the apostle Paul to younger pastors.

[13] The theme of the whole letter can be identified as "Putting Things Right in Ephesus." Sandwiched between an Introduction (1:1-20) and a Conclusion (6:11-21), the epistle has two main sections: "I. Setting the Church in Order: General Principles for Grounding the Troubled Church in Ephesus" (2:1-3:13); and "II. Setting Timothy Straight: Specific Counsel for Establishing Young Timothy in Leadership" (3:14-6:10). The theme of the paragraph can be identified as "On Women's Dress and Lifestyle." Deborah M. Gill, "The Pastorals," in *Full Life Bible Commentary to the New Testament*, ed. French L. Arrington & Roger Stronstad (Grand Rapids, MI: Zondervan, 1999), 1225-1226.

[14] The Roman province where Ephesus is located was called, in the first century, Asia Minor. New Testament writers shortened the name to Asia. Scholars also refer to the area (the western part of the Asian peninsula) as Anatolia.

[15] The background information which follows is drawn from the introduction of Gill's commentary on "The Pastorals," 1220-1221. See also Richard and Catherine Clark Kroeger, *I Suffer Not a Woman* (Grand Rapids, MI: Baker, 1992), 47–55; and Loren Cunningham and David J. Hamilton, *Why Not Women? A Biblical Study of Women in Missions, Ministry, and Leadership* (Seattle, WA: YWAM, 2000), 205-206.

[16] Syncretism: the combining of different forms of religious belief or practice.

[17] Catherine C. Kroeger, Mary Evans, and Elaine Storkey, *Study Bible for Women: The New Testament,* (NRSV) (Grand Rapids, MI: Baker, 1995), 439. See also R. and C. Kroeger, *I Suffer Not a Woman*, 59-76, 110-133, 145-152, 213-222.

[18] Dualism: a theory that considers reality to consist of two basic elements, matter and spirit.
[19] *Epitrepo* is the dictionary form of the verb (first person, singular, present, indicative, active) and also the form in which it appears in this sentence in 1 Timothy 2:12.
[20] Nuance: shades of meaning.
[21] Paul offered high praise for many women in religious leadership (compare Phil. 4:2–3 and Rom. 16:1–7,12,13, and15), and left Priscilla as leader of the Ephesian congregation when he moved on.
[22] *Authenteo* is the dictionary form of the verb (first person, singular, present, indicative, active). In this verse it appears as *authentein* (present, active, infinitive).
[23] A word that occurs only once is called a *hapaxlegomenon.*
[24] Classicist: somebody who studies ancient Greek and Latin.
[25] R. and C. Kroeger, *I Suffer Not,* Chapter 7: "That Strange Greek Verb *Authentein,*" 87-98.
[26] It can be a severe word, often having negative connotations of abuse, violence, and even murder. In some ancient texts and traditions the term was associated with sex hostility, promiscuity, reversal of gender roles, and even a mingling of sex and murder. Ibid., 93-98.
[27] See the discussion of the Amazons and other ancient religions of female dominance practiced in Ephesus. Ibid., 93, and 193-196.
[28] Ibid., 93.
[29] S. Scott Bartchy, "Power, Submission, and Sexual Identity Among the Early Christians," *Essays on New Testament Christianity,* ed. C. Robert Wetzel (n.p.: Standard Publishing, 1978), 71-72.
[30] Syntax: the grammatical relationships between words in a sentence.
[31] Or, "I do not allow a woman to teach or represent herself as the originator of man."
[32] R. and C. Kroeger, *I Suffer Not,* 99-104.
[33] The Greek root *authenteo,* shares etymology (origin and history) with the English word to "author," that is originate. Ibid., 99-104.
[34] Ibid., 102.
[35] Infinitive: a form of a verb with no reference to a particular person or subject, usually translated "to [do something]."

The two infinitives in this verse are *didaskein*—"to teach" and *authentein*—"to originate, to represent oneself as originator, etc."

[36] Negatives: words that change the meaning of a statement to its opposite.

Among the meanings of the two used used here (*ouk* [negative particle] and *oude* [negative conjunction]) are "no, not, neither" and "nor, and not, not even," respectively.

[37] See R. and C. Kroeger, *I Suffer Not,* 189-191.
[38] Indirect discourse: quoting a statement indirectly, beginning with the word "that."

Infinitives of indirect discourse are negated with negatives based on *ouk* (instead of *me*). Herbert Weir Smyth, *Greek Grammar* (Cambridge, MA: Harvard University, 1963), 449 [paragraph 2020].

[39] R. and C. Kroeger, *I Suffer Not,* 103.
[40] The Gnostics taught that salvation came through enlightenment.
[41] Gnostic writings are full of this phrase. This is their reason no woman can be saved, unless she "exchange the works of femaleness."
[42] Cunningham and Hamilton, 205.
[43] Ibid., 215.
[44] Ibid., 217.
[45] Aida Besancon Spencer, *Beyond the Curse: Women Called to Ministry* (Nashville, TN: Thomas Nelson, 1985), 74.
[46] Cunningham and Hamilton, 217-218.
[47] R. and C. Kroeger, *I Suffer Not,* 68.
[48] Cunningham and Hamilton, 218-219.

[49] Hamilton suggests, "Paul held Adam more accountable for his sin because he ... decided to disobey God. However, Eve's sin was the fruit, not of knowing disobedience but of deception." Ibid., 216.

Hamilton even claims, "Eve didn't become deceived because of some inherent weakness in women. God said that everything He created was good, including the first woman. No. If Eve was deceived, it was because Adam didn't teach her well." Ibid., 223.

[50] Ibid., 224.

[51] Ibid., 219.

Hamilton speculates, "If [Adam] had done a good job as a teacher, Eve would have known exactly what God had and hadn't said to Adam. The very fact that Adam silently 'stood by her side during the whole sorry episode' places the blame squarely on his shoulders for not faithfully passing on the Word of the Lord. No wonder God first addressed Adam when their transgression came to light." ... The story of Adam and Eve shows how important it is to faithfully teach others so that no one falls into deception. ... Paul's one command in this chapter was: The woman must learn." Ibid., 223.

[52] Ibid., 218.

[53] Faith: When capitalized, "Faith" refers to the body of Christian doctrine.

CHAPTER ELEVEN

[1] Sin's results include also, at times, the exploitation of men by women.

[2] Joachim Jeremias, "Appendix: The Social Position of Women," *Jerusalem in the Time of Jesus*, trans. F.H. and C.H. Cave (Philadelphia, PA: Fortress, 1969), 359-376.

[3] Ibid.

[4] S. Scott Bartchy, "Issues of Power and A Theology of the Family," (presentation for the Consultation on a Theology of the Family, Fuller Seminary, November 1984), 3.15 (in authors' files).

[5] See Chapter 7 under "1 Corinthians 7:4-5, 7."

[6] David M. Scholer, "Male Headship: God's Intention or Man's Invention?" *Watchword* 12 (Feb/Mar 1988): 3-4, 7.

[7] See also Col. 3:18-4:1; Rom. 12:9-10, 16; 13:1-10; John 15:12-17.

[8] J. Lee Grady, *Ten Lies the Church Tells Women: How the Bible Has Been Misused to Keep Women in Spiritual Bondage* (Lake Mary, FL: Creation House, 2000). These are the lies Grady discusses: "(1) God created women as inferior beings, destined to serve their husbands. (2) Women are not equipped to assume leadership roles in the church. (3) Women must not teach or preach to men in a church setting. (4) A woman should view her husband as the 'priest of the home.' (5) A man needs to 'cover' a woman in her ministry activities. (6) Women who exhibit strong leadership qualities pose a serious danger to the church. (7) Women are more easily deceived than men. (8) Women can't be fulfilled or spiritually effective without a husband and children. (9) Women shouldn't work outside the home. (10) Women must obediently submit to their husbands in all situations."

[9] "In what way are women 'weaker' than men? They live longer; are less subject to most diseases; have more endurance. But they are weaker in upper body strength. Is this what Peter was talking about? Probably not. More likely he was recognizing that in his day (as in ours) women have less power economically, socially, and politically but that husbands and wives are 'joint heirs of the grace of God,' and unless husbands *honor* their wives, their prayers will be hindered." Berkeley and Alvera Mickelsen, *Studies on Biblical Equality* (Minneapolis, MN: Christians for Biblical Equality, n.d.), 25.

CHAPTER TWELVE

[1] Sociology: the study of human societies and the behavior of individuals and groups within them.

[2] An academic introduction to the sociology of authority is: Robert L. Peabody, "Authority," in *International Encyclopedia of the Social Sciences (IESS)*, 1968 ed.

[3] Edward Shils, "Charisma," in *IESS*, 1968 ed.

[4] Ibid. Shils describes these charismatic leaders as "prone to experience direct contact with transcendent powers."

[5] Ibid. "The charismatic person is a creator of a new order as well as the breaker of routine order."

This technical (that is, social-scientific) meaning is not to be confused with the popular definition of "charismatic" as one having enthusiasm or special magnetic charm due to natural gifts.

[6] "Rational authority" is granted on the basis of people's technical knowledge, "legal authority" on the office they hold, and "traditional authority" on the cultural basis of their "right to rule" (usually passed down by heredity).

[7] Rudolf Sohm (1892-1923) was the first to use the term "charisma" sociologically. Max Weber formulated the concept most thoroughly in his writings on organizational theory. Shils, "Charisma."

[8] J. Quicherat, "Joan of Arc, St." in *Oxford Dictionary of the Christian Church*, 1978 rep.

[9] An academic introduction to the sociology of power is: Robert A. Dahl, "Power," in *IESS*, 1968 ed.

[10] The most famous technical definition of power is that of the 19th century sociologist, Max Weber. He defined power as "the chance of a [person] or a number of [persons] to realize their own will in a social action even against the resistance of others who are participating in the action." Max Weber, *Economy and Society*, vol. 2 (Berkley, CA: University of California Press, 1978), 926.

[11] Arnold S. Tannenbaum, "Leadership: II. Sociological Aspects," in *IESS*, 1968 ed.

[12] The theological term for "all powerful" is omnipotent.

[13] This concept is called sovereignty. Sovereign: having supreme authority or power.

[14] Deborah Menken Gill, "The Female Prophets: Gender and Leadership in the Biblical Tradition" (Ph.D. Dissertation, Fuller Theological Seminary, 1991), xiii, 267.

[15] Janet L. Kobobel, *But Can She Type?—Overcoming Stereotypes in the Workplace* (Downers Grove, IL: InterVarsity, 1986); Sally Helgesen, *The Female Advantage: Women's Ways of Leadership* (New York: Doubleday, 1995); and Sally Helgesen, *The Web of Inclusion* (New York: Currency/Doubleday, 1995).

[16] J. Robert Clinton, *Gender and Leadership: My Personal Pilgrimage* (Altadena, CA: Barnabas Publishers, 1995), 12-13, 19-23.

[17] "Pastor of World's Largest Church Endorses Ministry by Women," Religious News Service, July 12, 2000.

[18] Ibid.

[19] Ibid.

[20] Billie Davis, *People, Tasks, and Goals: Studies in Christian Leadership*, 2nd ed. (Irving, TX: ICI University, 1997), 279. She explains what leaders are like and how they relate to other people, what leaders do and how they guide others in the work, and how leaders establish objectives and work with people to achieve the goals of the church. Examples used are Joseph, Moses, Barnabas, David, Joshua, Nehemiah, Esther, Peter, and Paul. Davis writes: "A Christian leader is a person who stimulates and develops the capacities of others and guides them in the attainment of Christian goals." Such leaders relate with empathy to people, accomplish tasks with competence, and approach goals with a sense of mission and God's guidance.

[21] The Blackabys bring good insights to this passage regarding the poor judgment concerning leadership, of separating the spiritual from the secular. Henry and Richard Blackaby. *Spiritual Leadership: Moving People on to God's Agenda* (Nashville, TN: Broadman & Holman, 2001), 11-13.

[22] King Lemuel's mother taught him, for example, that though a king had unrestricted access to

wine, he should not indulge himself and get drunk. Because, a king who did so could compromise his ability to defend the rights of the poor and needy (Prov. 31:4-9).

[23] Robert E. Cooley, Presentation on Leadership at the meeting of the Commission to Study General Council Schools, Springfield, Missouri, 18-19 December 2003.

Cooley also summarized biblical leadership with these three principles: (1) God's leaders are called not made; (2) biblical leadership is mutual, it is shared; and (3) character is more important than skill.

[24] Though He had the supernatural capacity to turn stones to bread, He refused to exploit God's divine power to meet His everyday physical needs. Though He had the confidence that God could preserve His life if He fell from the heights of the Temple, Jesus refused to throw himself down. He would not flaunt this power in order to impress people and increase His popularity. If Jesus would only bow in worship to Him, Satan promised to give Him all the kingdoms of the world. But Jesus rejected a strategy that would abolish self-sacrifice. Jesus knew that suffering and death on the cross were necessary parts of God's plan for His life. So, He submitted himself (instead of resisting) God's will. And this He did at great personal cost.

[25] Berkeley and Alvera Mickelsen, *Studies on Biblical Equality*, (Minneapolis, MN: Christians for Biblical Equality, n.d.), 44.

[26] Tannenbaum, "Leadership."

[27] Coercion: the use of force to make people do things against their will.

[28] Synergy: the working together of two or more things, people, or organizations, producing a result that is greater than the sum of their individual influence or capabilities.

[29] Daniel Lee Menken, "On Power," in *Faith, Hope, and the Corporation: Sharpening Your Business Philosophy and Business Ethics* (St. Paul, MN: Phrontisterion, 1988), 124-145.

[30] Autocracy: the unlimited political power of a single ruler. Autocrat: a ruler who holds unlimited power and is answerable to no other person.

[31] The Greek term, *diakonia*, means ministry *or* service. The two concepts are translations of the same Greek word.

[32] Caleb Rosado, "The Stewardship of Power," *Health and Development* 11, no. 1 (1991): 23.

[33] Ibid., 21.

[34] Ibid., 20-21.

CHAPTER THIRTEEN

In discussing gender and spiritual authority, Rebecca Groothuis says, "If our case is true, it is biblical; if it is not biblical, it is not worth defending. ... [F]aith, not gender, qualifies believers in Christ to discern God's will, understand God's Word, and teach biblical truth" "Your Daughters Will Prophesy: Which Way Evangelical Egalitarianism—A Prism Forum," *Prism* 7, no. 4 (2000): 18.

[2] John R. Kohlenberger describes his journey: "From Male Superiority to Mutual Submission," *Christian Management Report* 24, no. 2: 15-16.

[3] J. Robert Clinton, *Gender and Leadership: My Personal Pilgrimage* (Altadena, CA: Barnabas Publishers, 1995).

[4] Clinton defines *paradigms* as "conceptual frameworks through which we view and interpret the reality around us." A *paradigm shift*, then, is "a change in perspective which allows one to see the same data in a different way and hence get different conclusions from it" (Ibid., 6).

[5] How different was the experience of George Wood, as can be seen from reading the Foreword.

Don and Pat Argue shared about women ministers in their family backgrounds in a monthly newsletter from the president to pastors. "Women in Ministry," *Northwest Arguemeants (c.2001): 2.* "Both of our families came into Pentecost during the early days. We both have mothers and aunts who ministered, preached, and even pastored churches before marriage. From this connection we have counted over two dozen women, some now retired or in heaven, who have served in full-time pastoral ministry. In a practical way, growing up with these women preachers around us was a positive example."

[6] Ibid., 2. Clinton describes various starting points ranging from "unacceptable," to "sub-ideal but acceptable," to "more favorable" (showing some progress toward the ideal).

[7] Ibid., 5-9.

Paradigm shifts take place through new ideas, new experiences, new choices one makes, or a combination of two or three of these ways.

[8] *The Role of Women in Ministry as Described in Holy Scripture* (Springfield, MO: Gospel Publishing, 1990), 13.

[9] Gretchen Gaebelein Hull, *Equal to Serve: Women and Men in the Church and Home* (Old Tappan, NJ: Fleming H. Revell, 1987), 73.

[10] Carol E. Becker, *Becoming Colleagues: Women and Men Serving Together in Faith* (San Francisco, CA: Jossey-Bass, 2000), 310-313. The criteria are reflecting and taking action, learning, believing, naming, including, communicating, working together, influencing, and modeling teamwork.

[11] Carol E. Becker, *Leading Women: How Church Women Can Avoid Leadership Traps and Negotiate the Gender Maze* (Nashville, TN: Abingdon, 1996).See also Donna Schaper, *Common Sense About Men & Women in the Ministry* (Washington, DC: Alban Institute, 1990).

[12] God also chose Ephraim over Manasseh, David over his elder brothers, Solomon over Adonijah, and the tribe of Judah over the tribes of Reuben, Simeon, or Levi.

[13] "Of course, it is biblical for all to come under the authorities instituted by God. We do not suggest that every woman or man who declares a calling should be automatically placed in some position of authority. In the local congregation pastors who want to free women in their giftedness to be elders, deacons, etc. and find resistance from the body may find that gentle, consistent teaching over time is the only way to effect change." Don and Pat Argue, 3.

[14] Ruth A.Tucker and Robert Liefeld, *Daughters of the Church* (Grand Rapids, MI: Zondervan Academie Books, 1987), 135-137, 239-242.

[15] R. Pierce Beaver, *American Protestant Women in World Mission* (Grand Rapids, MI: Eerdmans, 1980).

[16] "Your Daughters Will Prophesy," 16.

One must understand, however, that what is allowed on paper and what is put into practice by a group may be two different things. For examples of mixed messages, see Barbara L. Cavaness,"Factors Influencing the Decrease in the Number of Single Women in Assemblies of God World Missions" (Ph.D. Diss., Fuller Theological Seminary, 2000), 191-256.

[17] Clinton, 1.

[18] "Your Daughters Will Prophesy," 15.

[19] Gary Corwin,"Women in Mission," *Evangelical Missions Quarterly* (October 1997): 401. (The fact that the spiritual leadership of women seems to have been more the exception than the rule may be due in part to male recorders of church history.)

[20] *Role*, 6.

[21] Billie Davis, *People, Tasks, and Goals: Studies in Christian* Leadership, 2nd ed. (Irving, TX: ICI University, 1997). See discussion of Esther's leadership qualities, pages 185-188.

[22] Dogmatism: positiveness in asserting one's view, especially to the point of arrogance or unwarranted certainty.

[23] Stan Guthrie,"A Woman's Place in Missions," *Evangelical Missions Quarterly* (July 2000): 360.

[24] Ibid., 363.

[25] Corwin, 400.

[26] "Your Daughters Will Prophesy," 18.

[27] The Assemblies of God position paper on the role of women says,"We do not find sufficient evidence in *kephale* to deny leadership roles to women. ... After examining the various trans-

lations and interpretations of biblical passages relating to the role of women in the first-century church, and desiring to apply biblical principles to contemporary church practice, we conclude that we cannot find convincing evidence that the ministry of women is restricted according to some sacred or immutable principle." *Role*, 12.

[28] Though Scripture does not give such requirements, organizations often do. Clinton, 12-13: "For most male dominated organizations males can occupy any position for which they are gifted or experienced or manage to achieve. Females, on the other hand, have often been limited." He defines a spectrum of six basic views of persons/organizations concerning women in ministry: from "tight position" (against), to interdependent ministry.

[29] Barbara Cavaness, "A Higher Purpose," *Pentecostal Evangel*, 4 July 1993: 12.

[30] Clinton, 10.

[31] Ibid., 11, 21: "*Spiritual authority* is the right to lead that is conferred upon a leader by followers because of a perception of spirituality based on giftedness, deep experiences and knowledge of God, and a modeling of the Christian life which demonstrates godliness. ... Neither men nor women should lead due to positional power alone; there must be spiritual authority. If a man or woman has true spiritual authority, they will lead and people will follow."

[32] Carolyn Tennant, "Rediscovering the Pioneer Spirit," *Enrichment* 6, no. 2 (Spring 2001): 46-50.

[33] Cavaness, "Factors," Chapter 3: Female Forerunners and Pentecostal Leaders, 15-64.

[34] Ruth Haley Barton, *Equal to the Task: Men and Women in Partnership* (Downers Grove, IL: InterVarsity, 1998), 80-97. See the excellent chapter, "Beyond Stereotypes to Partnership."

[35] Portions previously published in *Enrichment*: Deborah Menken Gill, "Called by God—What's a Woman to Do, and What Can We Do to Help Her?" *Enrichment* 2, no. 2 (Spring 1997): 32-35.

[36] *Role*.

[37] "Eligibility of women (for ministry)," *General Council of the Assemblies of God Bylaws*, Article VII., Section 2.k (Springfield, MO: Gospel Publishing, 1990).

[38] Tucker and Liefeld.

[39] Beaver.

[40] Susan Hill Lindley, *"You Have Stept out of Your Place": A History of Women and Religion in America* (Louisville, KY: Westminster John Knox Press, 1996).

[41] Janette Hassey, *No Time for Silence: Evangelical Women in Public Ministry Around the Turn of the Century* (Zondervan: Grand Rapids, 1986).

[42] Dana Robert, *American Women in Mission: A Social History of Their Thought and Practice* (Macon, GA: Mercer University, 1996).

[43] Isaac Olivarez, "Women Who Answer God's Call Provide Valuable Local Ministries," *Pentecostal Evangel*, 11 January 2004: 6-7. See also Barbara Cavaness, "God Calling: Women in Assemblies of God Missions," *Pneuma* 16, no. 1 (Spring 1994): 49-62.

Glossary

Accommodate: to make room for, allow for, to adapt oneself or work within.
Accountability: an obligation or willingness to accept responsibility or to account for one's actions.
Apocrypha: books excluded from the Jewish and Protestant canons of the Old Testament, but included in the Greek and Latin versions. The Roman Catholic Bible contains the Old Testament Apocrypha.
Arian: a follower of the ancient Greek Christian theologian, Arius, who argued that Jesus Christ was the highest created being, but was not divine.
Authority: referring to the influence of certain persons over others. It is the right or power to enforce rules or to give orders.
Autocracy: the unlimited political power of a single ruler. (Autocrat: a ruler who holds unlimited power and is answerable to no other person.)
Blood taboo: Jews considered women to be unclean during their menstrual cycle and after giving birth. Anyone who touched them would also become unclean.
Body of Christ: word picture used by Paul for the Church in such passages as 1 Corinthians 12:12-27; Romans 12:4; and Ephesians 5:30.
Christology: the branch of theology concerned with the study of the nature, character, and actions of Jesus Christ.
Classicist: somebody who studies ancient Greek and Latin.
Coercion: the use of force to make people do things against their will.
Day of the Lord: those special times of God's moving with justice and judgment on a large scale (Isa. 2-4, Joel 1-4, Zeph. 1).
Dogmatism: positiveness in asserting one's view, especially to the point of arrogance or unwarranted certainty.
Dualism: a theory that considers reality to consist of two basic elements, matter and spirit.
Egalitarianism: the view that all people are equal.
Evangelicalism: the Protestant Christian wing that teaches that each individual deserves to hear the good news of Jesus (evangel) and to be given the option of choosing for themselves to follow Him. In their theology, this is the only way to become a Christian. This voluntary decision to follow Christ is called becoming born again.
Faith: when capitalized, refers to the body of Christian doctrine.
Figurative: emblematic; representing by a figure, resemblance, symbol, or analogy.
Genre: a category of literature based on form, style, or subject matter.
Gnostics: those who teach that salvation comes through enlightenment.
Golden Rule: Jesus' command found in Matt. 7:12.
Hapaxlegomenon: a word that occurs only once.
Haustafel: a domestic code.
Hellenization: the attempt to "Greek-ize," that is, to influence people to adopt Greek ways.
Hierarchy: the ranking or classifying of people so that each level is subordinate to the one above it.
Historical Particularity: relevance limited to a specific time and place.
Indirect discourse: quoting a statement indirectly, beginning with the word "that."
Infinitive: a form of a verb with no reference to a particular person or subject, usually translated "to [do something]."
Institutionalization: the process, over time, of a movement's becoming more formal, structured, rigid, and hierarchical.
Intertestamental Period: the 400 "silent years" between the writing of Malachi and the coming of John the Baptist.

Judaize: to adopt the customs, beliefs, or character of a Jew; to make Jewish. This refers to those who wanted to make Christian Gentile believers adopt Jewish customs.
The Law (capital "L"): the same as Torah.
Leadership: the ability to guide, direct, or influence people.
Lexical: insights from the exact Greek words.
Lexicology: the study of words, their use, meaning, and vocabulary relationships.
Magna Carta: the great charter of 1215 (England), was a fundamental guarantee of rights and privileges.
Modern Judaism: from A.D. 600 to the present. It exhibits more tolerance about the place of women in society.
Monologue: a long, uninterrupted speech by one person.
Mutuality: the state of being directed by each toward the other, having the same feelings one for the other, marked by intimacy and sharing something in common.
Negatives: words that change the meaning of a statement to its opposite.
Nuance: shades of meaning.
Omnipotent: the theological term for "all powerful."
Orthodoxy: accurate or right teaching, conforming to established doctrine.
Pagans: people who do not follow the God of the Old Testament.
Papyri: manuscripts written on scrolls made of papyrus plant stem material.
Paradigms: conceptual frameworks through which we view and interpret reality around us.
Paradigm shift: a change in perspective that allows one to see the same data in a different way and hence draw different conclusions.
Pastoral Epistles: the three epistles from the Apostle Paul to younger pastors, including 1, 2 Timothy and Titus.
Patriarchy: social organization marked by the supremacy of the father in the clan or family and legal dependence of wives and children; control by men of the largest share of power.
Polygamy: having more than one wife.
Power: the capacity to control the behavior of others.
Prerogative: an exclusive or special right, power, or privilege.
Primary sources: the original ancient documents and records.
Pseudepigrapha: writings falsely claiming they were authored by important religious figures.
Rabbinic Judaism: from about A.D. 70 to A.D. 600. It severely restricted women in religious activities.
Reciprocal: shared, felt, or shown by both sides; mutually corresponding.
Reformation: a 16th century religious movement marked ultimately by rejection or modification of some Roman Catholic doctrine and practice and establishment of the Protestant churches.
Renaissance: the transitional movement in Europe between medieval and modern times beginning in the 14th century in Italy, lasting into the 17th century, and marked by a humanistic revival of classical influence expressed in a flowering of the arts and literature and by the beginnings of modern science.
Secularization: the process toward accommodating to non-religious norms.
Sociology: the study of human societies and the behavior of individuals and groups within them.
Sovereign: having supreme authority or power.
Spiritual authority: the right to lead that is conferred upon a leader by followers as a result of a perception of spirituality based on giftedness, deep experiences and knowledge of God, and a modeling of the Christian life which demonstrates godliness.
Spiritualize: giving a spiritual meaning to or understand in a religious or supernatural sense rather than a literal sense.
Subjective: based more on opinion than on fact.

Subordination: being controlled by someone else's authority; being made subject or subservient, treated as of less value or importance; placed in a lower class, rank, or position.
Subordinationism: the theological doctrine that the first person of the Holy Trinity is superior to the second, and the second to the third.
Suppression: being put or kept down by authority or force.
Syncretism: the combining of different forms of religious belief or practice.
Synergy: the working together of two or more things, people, or organizations, producing a result that is greater than the sum of their individual influence or capabilities.
Syntax: the grammatical relationships between words in a sentence.
Talmud: Jewish oral traditions put into writing.
Text criticism: insights from the ancient manuscripts..
Torah: the first five books of the Hebrew Bible, the Pentateuch—Genesis through Deuteronomy.
Yahweh: The Old Testament identifies the Almighty Creator God as Yahweh, sometimes pronounced Jehovah, or expressed as "the LORD."

Bibliography

Argue, Don and Pat. "Women in Ministry." *Northwest Arguemeants* (c. 2001):1-4.

Barker, Don C. *Papyri from the Rise of Christianity in Egypt*. Ancient History Documentary Research Centre, Macquarie University, Sydney, Australia; available from www.anchist.mq.edu.au/doccentre/PCEhomepage.html; internet.

Bartchy, S. Scott. "Issues of Power and a Theology of the Family." Presentation for the Consultation on a Theology of the Family, Fuller Seminary, November, 1984.

_________. "Power, Submission, and Sexual Identity Among the Early Christians." In *Essays on New Testament Christianity*, ed. C. Robert Wetzel. n.p.: Standard Publishing, 1978.

Barton, Ruth Haley. *Equal to the Task: Men and Women in Partnership*. Downers Grove, IL: InterVarsity, 1998.

Bauer, Walter. *A Greek-English Lexicon of the New Testament and Other Early Christian Literature*. Trans. and adapted by William F. Arndt and F. Wilbur Gingrich, 3rd ed. Rev. and ed. Frederick W. Danker. Chicago, IL: University of Chicago, 2000. S. v. "*kephale*."

Beaver, R. Pierce. *American Protestant Women in World Mission*. Rev. ed. Grand Rapids, MI: Eerdmans, 1980.

Becker, Carol E. *Becoming Colleagues: Women and Men Serving Together in Faith*. San Francisco, CA: Jossey-Bass, 2000.

_________. *Leading Women: How Church Women Can Avoid Leadership Traps and Negotiate the Gender Maze*. Nashville, TN: Abingdon, 1996.

Bilezikian, Gilbert. *Beyond Sex Roles: A Guide for the Study of Female Roles in the Bible*. Grand Rapids, MI: Baker, 1985.

Blackaby, Henry and Richard. *Spiritual Leadership: Moving People on to God's Agenda*. Nashville, TN: Broadman & Holman, 2001.

Brooten, Bernadette. *Women Leaders of the Ancient Synagogue*. Chico, CA: Scholars Press, 1982.

Cavaness, Barbara L. "A Higher Purpose." *Pentecostal Evangel*, 4 July 1993: 12.

_________. "Factors Influencing the Decrease in the Number of Single Women in Assemblies of God World Missions." Ph.D. Dissertation, Fuller Theological Seminary, 2002.

_________. "God Calling: Women in Assemblies of God Missions." *Pneuma* 16, no. 1 (Spring 1994): 49-62.

Chadwick, Henry. "Rufinus and the Tura Papyrus of Origen's Commentary on Romans." *Journal of Theological Studies* 10 (April 1959): 10-42.

Charlesworth, James A. *The Old Testament Pseudepigrapha*. Vol. 1. Garden City, NY: Doubleday, 1983.

_________. *The Old Testament Pseudepigrapha*. Vol. 2. Garden City, NY: Doubleday, 1985.

Clinton, J. Robert. *Gender and Leadership: My Personal Pilgrimage*. Altadena, CA: Barnabas Publishers, 1995.

Cooley, Robert E. Presentation on Leadership at the meeting of the Commission to Study General Council Schools, Springfield, Missouri, 18-19 December 2003.

Corwin, Gary. "Women in Mission." *Evangelical Missions Quarterly* 33, no. 4 (October 1997): 400-401.

Cunningham, Loren, and David Hamilton. *Why Not Women? A Biblical Study of Women in Missions, Ministry, and Leadership*. Seattle, WA: YWAM, 2000.

Dahl, Robert A. "Power." In *International Encyclopedia of the Social Sciences (IESS)*, 1968 ed.

Dana, Robert. *American Women in Mission: A Social History of Their Thought and Practice*. Macon, GA: Mercer University, 1996.

Davis, Billie. *People, Tasks, and Goals: Studies in Christian Leadership*. 2nd ed. Irving, TX: ICI University, 1997.

"Eligibility of women (for ministry)." In *General Council of the Assemblies of God Bylaws*. Article VII., Section 2.-k. Springfield, MO: Gospel Publishing, 1990.

Epstein, I., ed. *The Babylonian Talmud: Seder Tohoroth*. Vol. 1. *Niddah*, trans. Israel W. Slotki. London: Soncino Press, 1948.

Fee, Gordon D., and Douglas Stuart. *How to Read the Bible for All Its Worth*. 2nd ed. Grand Rapids, MI: Zondervan, 1993.

Fiedler, Klaus. *The Story of Faith Missions*. Oxford: Regnum, 1994.

Fortune, Don and Katie. *Discovering Your God-given Gifts*. Grand Rapids, MI: Chosen Books, 1987.

Gempf, Conrad. *Jesus Asked*. Grand Rapids, MI: Zondervan, 2003.

Gill, Deborah M. "Called by God—What's a Woman to Do, and What Can We Do to Help Her?" *Enrichment* 2, no. 2 (Spring 1997): 32-35.

_________. "The Female Prophets: Gender and Leadership in the Biblical Tradition." Ph.D. Dissertation, Fuller Theological Seminary, 1991.

_________. "The Pastorals." In *Full Life Bible Commentary to the New Testament*, ed. French L. Arrington & Roger Stronstad. Grand Rapids, MI: Zondervan, 1999.

Grady, J. Lee. *Ten Lies the Church Tells Women: How the Bible Has Been Misused to Keep Women in Spiritual Bondage*. Lake Mary, FL: Creation House, 2000.

Grenz, Stanley, and Denise Kjesbo. *Women in the Church: A Biblical Theology of Women in Ministry*. Downers Grove, IL: InterVarsity, 1995.

Groothuis, Rebecca. "Your Daughters Will Prophesy: Which Way Evangelical Egalitarianism—A Prism Forum." *Prism* 7, no. 4 (2000): 13-18.

Gundry, Patricia. "Why We're Here." In *Women, Authority, and the Bible*, ed. Alvera Mickelsen. Downers Grove, IL: InterVarsity, 1986.

Gundry, Robert H. *A Survey of the New Testament*. Rev. ed. Grand Rapids, MI: Zondervan, 1981.

Guthrie, Stan. "A Woman's Place in Missions." *Evangelical Missions Quarterly* 36, no. 3 (July 2000): 356-364.

Harman, Allen M. "'ezer" (6468). Vol. 3. *New International Dictionary of Old Testament Theology and Exegesis*, ed. Willem A. VanGemeren. Grand Rapids, MI: Zondervan, 1997.

Harnack, Adolf. "Probabilia uber die Adresse und den Verfasser des Hebraerbriefs." *Zeitschrift fur die neutestamentliche Wissenschaft* 1 (1900): 16-41.

Hassey, Janette. *No Time for Silence: Evangelical Women in Public Ministry Around the Turn of the Century*. Grand Rapids, MI: Academie Books/Zondervan, 1986.

Healy, Emma T. *Women According to Saint Bonaventure*. New York: Georgian, 1956.

Helgesen, Sally. *The Female Advantage: Women's Ways of Leadership*. New York: Doubleday, 1995.

_________. *The Web of Inclusion*. New York: Currency/Doubleday, 1995.

Hennecke, Edgar, and Wilhelm Schneemelcher, eds. *New Testament Apocrypha*. Vol. 1. Philadelphia: Westminster, 1963.

Hoppin, Ruth. *Priscilla's Letter: Finding the Author of the Epistle to the Hebrews*. Fort Bragg, CA: Lost Coast Press, 1997.

Horsley, Greg. "Early Evidence of Women Officers in the Church." *Priscilla Papers* 1 (Fall 1987): 3-4.

Hull, Gretchen Gaebelein. *Equal to Serve: Women and Men in the Church and Home*. Old Tappan, NJ: Fleming H. Revell, 1987.

Hutchins, Robert M., ed. *Great Books of the Western World*. Vol. 7, *Plato: The Republic*. Chicago, IL: Encyclopedia Brittanica, 1952.

_________. ed. *Great Books of the Western World*. Vol. 9, *Aristotle: Politics*, trans. Benjamin Jowett. Chicago, IL: Encyclopedia Brittanica, 1952.

_________. ed. *Great Books of the Western World*. Vol. 19, *Thomas Aquinas: I, The Summa Theologica*. Vol. I. Chicago, IL: Encyclopedia Brittanica, 1952.

_________. ed. *Great Books of the Western World*. Vol. 32, *English Minor Poems*, by John Milton. Chicago, IL: Encyclopedia Brittanica, 1952.

Jeremias, Joachim. "Appendix: The Social Position of Women." *Jerusalem in the Time of Jesus*, trans. F.H. and C.H. Cave. Philadelphia, PA: Fortress, 1969.

Josephus. "Flavius Josephus Against Apion." In *Josephus: Complete Works*, trans. William Whiston. Grand Rapids, MI: Kregel, 1960.

Judge, Edwin. Ancient History Documentary Research Centre, Macquarie University, North Ryde 2109, Sydney, New South Wales, AUSTRALIA.

Keener, Craig S. *Paul, Women & Wives: Marriage and Women's Ministry in the Letters of Paul*. Peabody, MA: Hendrickson Publishers, 1992.

Kobobel, Janet L. *But Can She Type?—Overcoming Stereotypes in the Workplace*. Downers Grove, IL: InterVarsity, 1986.

Kohlenberger, John R. "From Male Superiority to Mutual Submission." *Christian Management Report* 24, no. 2: 15-16.

Kraemer, Ross. *Maenads, Martyrs, Matrons, Monastics*. Minneapolis, MN: Fortress, 1988.

Kroeger, Catherine C., Mary Evans, and Elaine Storkey. *Study Bible for Women: The New Testament*, NRSV. Grand Rapids, MI: Baker, 1995.

Kroeger, Catherine Clark. "Appendix III: The Classical Concept of 'Head' as 'Source,'" in *Equal to Serve: Women and Men in the Church and Home*, by Gretchen Gaebelein Hull. Old Tappan, NJ: Fleming H. Revell, 1987.

Kroeger, Richard Clark, and Catherine Clark Kroeger. *I Suffer Not a Woman: Rethinking 1 Timothy 2:11-15 in Light of Ancient Evidence*. Grand Rapids, MI: Baker, 1992.

_________. "Pandemonium and Silence at Corinth." *The Reformed Journal* 28 (June 1978): 6–10.

_________. "Why Were There No Women Apostles?" *Equity*, 1982.

Lehmann, Helmut T., ed. *Luther's Works*. Vol. 54. *Table Talk*, ed. and trans. Theodore Tappert. Philadelphia: Fortress, 1967.

Liddell, George Henry and Robert Scott. *A Greek-English Lexicon*, Rev. Henry Stuart Jones and Roderick McKenzie. Oxford: Clarendon, 1968. S.v. "*kephale.*"

Lindley, Susan Hill. *"You Have Stept out of Your Place": A History of Women and Religion in America*. Louisville, KY: Westminster John Knox Press, 1996.

Love, N. B. C. *John Stewart: Missionary to the Wyandots*. New York, NY: Missionary Society of the Methodist Episcopal Church, n.d..

McGee, Gary B. "Miracles and Missions Revisited." *International Bulletin of Missionary Research* 25 (October 2001): 146-156.

_________. *The People of the Spirit: The Assemblies of God*. Springfield, MO: Gospel Publishing, 2004.

Menken, Daniel Lee. "On Power." In *Faith, Hope, and the Corporation: Sharpening Your Business Philosophy and Business Ethics*. St. Paul, MN: Phrontisterion, 1988.

Menken (Gill), Deborah. "Gynecomorphisms in the New Testament." Honors Thesis, Assemblies of God Graduate School, 1979.

Metzger, Bruce M, and Roland E. Murphy, eds. *The New Oxford Annotated Apocrypha, New Revised Standard Version*, NRSV. New York: Oxford University Press, 1991.

Mickelsen, Berkeley and Alvera. "Does Male Dominance Tarnish Our Translations?" *Christianity Today*, 22 (5 October 1979): 23-29.

_________. *Studies on Biblical Equality*. Minneapolis, MN: Christians for Biblical Equality, n.d..

_________. "What Does *Kephale* Mean in the New Testament?" In *Women, Authority & the Bible*, ed. Alvera Mickelsen. Downers Grove, IL: InterVarsity, 1986.

Mollenkott, Virginia R. *Women, Men, & the Bible*. Nashville, TN: Abingdon, 1977.

Nyland, Ann. "Papyri, Women, and Word Meaning in the New Testament." *Priscilla Papers* 17, no. 4 (Fall 2003): 8-9.

Olivarez, Isaac. "Women Who Answer God's Call Provide Valuable Local Ministries." *Pentecostal Evangel* 11 January 2004: 6-7.

"Pastor of World's Largest Church Endorses Ministry by Women," *Religious News Service*, 12 July 2000.

Payne, Philip Barton. "Response." In *Women, Authority & the Bible*, ed. Alvera Mickelsen. Downers Grove, IL: InterVarsity, 1986.

Peabody, Robert L. "Authority." In *International Encyclopedia of the Social Sciences (IESS)*, 1968 ed.

Philo. "On the Special Laws." In *Philo*. Vol. VII, trans. F. H. Colson. Cambridge, MA: Loeb Classical Library, Harvard University Press, 1937.

_________. *Philo Supplement I: Questions and Answers on Genesis*, trans. Ralph Marcus. Cambridge, MA: Loeb Classical Library, Harvard University Press, 1953.

Quicherat, J. "Joan of Arc, St." In *Oxford Dictionary of the Christian Church*, 1978 rep.

Rashkow, Ilona. *Upon the Dark Places*. Sheffield, England: Almond Press, 1990.

Roberts, A., and J. Donaldson, eds. *The Ante-Nicene Fathers*. Vol. 4, *Tertullian, On the Apparel of Women*. Grand Rapids, MI: Eerdmans, 1972.

The Role of Women in Ministry as Described in Holy Scripture. Springfield, MO: Gospel Publishing, 1990.

Rosado, Caleb. "The Stewardship of Power." *Health and Development* 11, no. 1 (1991): 20-23.

Scanzoni, Letha, and Susan Setta. "Women in Evangelical, Holiness, and Pentecostal Traditions." In *Women & Religion in America*. Vol. 3, ed. Rosemary Ruether and Rosemary Keller. San Francisco, CA: Harper & Row, 1986.

Schaper, Donna. *Common Sense About Men & Women in the Ministry*. Washington, DC: Alban Institute, 1990.

Scholer, David M."Male Headship: God's Intention or Man's Invention?" *Watchword* 12, no. 1 (Feb/Mar 1988): 3-4, 7.

_________."Paul's Women Coworkers in Ministry." *Theology, News and Notes* 42, no. 1 (March 1995): 20-22.

_________. *The Role and Status of Women in the New Testament*. Cassette tape series available from The Sanders Christian Foundation, Gordon-Conwell Theological Seminary, P. O. Box 2094, S. Hamilton, MA 01982-0094.

Scofield, C. I. *Scofield Reference Bible*. New York: Oxford University Press, 1917.

Scroggs, Robin."Paul and the Eschatological Woman." *Journal of the American Academy of Religion* 40 (1972): 283-303.

Shils, Edward."Charisma." In *International Encyclopedia of the Social Sciences (IESS)*, 1968 ed.

Smyth, Herbert Weir. *Greek Grammar*. Cambridge, MA: Harvard University, 1963.

Spencer, Aida Besancon. *Beyond the Curse: Women Called to Ministry*. Nashville, TN: Thomas Nelson, 1985.

Swidler, Leonard. *Biblical Affirmations of Woman*. Philadelphia, PA: Westminster, 1979.

Szold, Henrietta."Beruriah," in *The Jewish Encyclopedia*, 1948 ed.

Tannenbaum, Arnold S."Leadership: II. Sociological Aspects." In *International Encyclopedia of the Social Sciences (IESS)*, 1968 ed.

Tennant, Carolyn."Rediscovering the Pioneer Spirit." *Enrichment* 6, no. 2 (Spring 2001): 46-50.

Torjesen, Karen Jo. *When Women Were Priests: Women's Leadership in the Early Church and the Scandal of their Subordination in the Rise of Christianity*. San Francisco, CA: Harper Collins, 1993.

Trible, Phyllis."Depatriarchalizing in Biblical Interpretation." *Journal of the American Academy of Religion* 41, no. 1 (March 1973): 30-48.

Tucker, Ruth A., and Robert Liefeld. *Daughters of the Church*. Grand Rapids, MI: Zondervan Academie Books, 1987.

Warner, Wayne."Maria Woodworth-Etter and the Early Pentecostal Movement." *Heritage* 6 (Winter 1986-1987): 11-14.

_________. *The Woman Evangelist: The Life and Times of Charismatic Evangelist Maria B. Woodworth-Etter*. Metuchen, NJ: Scarecrow Press, 1986.

Weber, Max. *Economy and Society*. Vol. 2. Berkley, CA: University of California Press, 1978.

Webster's New Twentieth Century Dictionary, Unabridged 2nd ed. (1979). S.v."head."

Wood, George."Exploring Why We Think the Way We Do About Women in Ministry." *Enrichment* 6, no. 2 (Spring 2001): 8-14.

Woodworth, Maria. *Life and Experience of Maria B. Woodworth*. Dayton, OH: United Brethren, 1885.

Woodworth-Etter, Maria. *Signs and Wonders God Wrought in the Ministry for Forty Years*. Rep. ed. Bartlesville, OK: Oak Tree, 1916.